The Romance of Crossing Borders

The Romance
of Crossing Borders

Studying and Volunteering Abroad

Edited by

Neriko Musha Doerr

and

Hannah Davis Taïeb

berghahn

NEW YORK • OXFORD

www.berghahnbooks.com

Published in 2017 by

Berghahn Books

www.berghahnbooks.com

© 2017 Neriko Musha Doerr and Hannah Davis Taïeb

Library of Congress Cataloging-in-Publication Data

Names: Doerr, Neriko Musha, 1967- editor. | Davis Taïeb, Hannah, editor.
Title: The romance of crossing borders : studying and volunteering abroad /
    edited by Neriko Musha Doerr and Hannah Davis Taïeb.
Description: New York : Berghahn Books, 2017. | Includes index.
Identifiers: LCCN 2016053198 (print) | LCCN 2016058381 (ebook) | ISBN
    9781785333583 (hardback : alk. paper) | ISBN 9781785333590 (ebook)
Subjects: LCSH: Foreign study—Social aspects. | Volunteerism—Social
    aspects. | International education—Social aspects. | College students—
    Intellectual life. | Educational anthropology.
Classification: LCC LB2375 .R66 2017 (print) | LCC LB2375 (ebook) | DDC
    370.116/2—dc23
LC record available at https://lccn.loc.gov/2016053198

British Library Cataloguing in Publication Data

A catalogue record for this book is available from the British Library

978-1-78533-358-3 ISBN (hardback)
978-1-78533-359-0 ISBN (ebook)

For the McChesneys, my counselor, Priests, Strands, Davises, and Park-ers, my host families, and all my friends in Kapiti Coast, Aotearoa/New Zealand, my beloved study abroad destination.

—Neirko Musha Doerr

For my colleagues at the CIEE Paris center, for my fellow resident di-rectors throughout the world, and for my trusted US colleagues, with gratitude for all the wonderful conversations that inspired me to reflect on our practice.

—Hannah Davis Taïeb

Contents

**Part III. Serving with Passion: Romantic Images
of Self and Other in Volunteering Abroad**

Tables

Preface
The Romance of Study Abroad

Michael Woolf

There are broadly three concepts covered by the word "romance": romance as a courtship process, as an artistic sensibility, and as a kind of fanciful delusion. In all three, there are demonstrable connections with study abroad. The essays in this collection, explicitly or implicitly, explore these connections that, by way of introduction, I will categorize as "love at first sight/site," as "the exalted mood," and as "stereotypical myopia." In love at first sight/site, students engage in a relationship with location that is analogous to courtship. The exalted mood (William Wordsworth's term) is marked by heightened sensibility, emotional intensity, and a focus on the self, what Georg Wilhelm Friedrich Hegel called "absolute inwardness":[1] notions that for good and/or ill reverberate around student experience abroad. Stereotypical myopia relates to the state of semiawareness in which student preconceptions are not challenged or disrupted: a failure of educational responsibility.

The romance of study abroad is then a set of dynamics that may form and inform ways in which students engage with their host environments.

Love at First Sight/Site

Romance is a ritual that seems oddly archaic in these more utilitarian times. It was a process through which (when I was a lad) we aspired to move from attraction to seduction: a set of gestures aimed at ultimate intimacy. Important artifacts such as flowers and music were employed as visual and audio aids. For an earlier generation, by way of example, the songs of Frank Sinatra proved to be somewhat effective. This was particularly true of the Capitol Record years, from 1953 to 1961, when liquid tones melted hearts with lyrics in which the pain of unrequited love was tragically interesting and irresistibly attractive (or so we hoped). In this context a romantic is the sort of person for whom moon in June are logical collocations. They also keep florists in business.

This form of romance may, ostensibly, have tenuous connection with study abroad, but the process of attraction, romance, and seduction (with the co-related potential for rejection and abandonment) resonates metaphorically with the student experience in a number of ways. Martha Johnson argues that, in predeparture phases, student expectations parallel romantic expectations: "The anticipation and preparation are analogous to a long awaited first date, and in many cases a 'blind date' by the time the student departs" (2012: 33).

Study abroad is, at some level, an engagement with a dreamed landscape populated by iconic images: projections that are formed by a combination of curiosity, imagination, and passion, as Martha Johnson indicates: "the ability of the city to elicit a visceral and emotional response is a powerful but often also untapped element of the experience abroad" (2012: 32).

As in any relationship, the early days of engagement are marked by euphoria, unease, excitement, embarrassment, and all the cluster of feelings that frequently characterize rituals of romantic engagement. At some point the student may discover that they love Paris or hate Berlin, adore London but are oddly indifferent to Rome. The language of romance is embedded in the ways in which we relate to the discovery of place.

The Exalted Mood

The romantic is not, of course, solely about the curious business of falling in and out of love, in what the Greeks called "Eros." As Wordsworth demonstrates in "The Prelude" (1799–1805), something closer to spiritual love, or "Agape," is expressed through the exalted mood; encounters with ideas and landscape marked by heightened intensity:

> This spiritual Love acts not nor can exist
> Without Imagination, which, in truth,
> Is but another name for absolute power
> And clearest insight, amplitude of mind,
> And Reason in her most exalted mood.

Wordsworth engaged with natural and built environments (a field of daffodils and Westminster Bridge) with the kind of intensity that transformed the external world into internal epiphany. Place is more than geography and history; it has the power to transform consciousness. Tim Blanning argues that in the Romantic imagination, "the inner self was everything: if the light did not shine brightly from within, nothing worthwhile could be achieved" (2010: 31).

The Romantics embedded movement in their philosophy both in a literal sense (engagement with place acts as a catalyst for heightened perception), and metaphorically in that an objective was to move from one level of consciousness to another higher form of intensity.[2] At the center of our endeavor is the notion of disturbance as an educational aspiration. The heart of the liberal educational ideal is the aspiration to create experiences that broaden, challenge, and disrupt students' assumptions. In a domestic context, the challenge of new ideas can achieve that purpose. In study abroad the process of disturbance is both physical and intellectual; opportunities to broaden and deepen student thought are enhanced by simultaneous engagement with the unfamiliar in both ideas and locations.

The paradox through which exposure to new external environments may enlighten and enrich the inner self was well understood by the Romantic poets, as demonstrated by Shelley in "Mont Blanc: Lines Written in the Vale of Chamouni":

> Thou art pervaded with that ceaseless motion,
> Thou art the path of that unresting sound—
> Dizzy Ravine! and when I gaze on thee
> I seem as in a trance sublime and strange
> To muse on my own separate fantasy,
> My own, my human mind . . .

The interplay of mind and space reflects, in rhetorical and idealized form, the kind of creative engagement that is aspirational for study abroad students.

The Romantics were essentially cosmopolitan in that they sought to expand their consciousness beyond the parochial. In a literal sense, many of them traveled widely and recognized that new locations (particularly the Hellenic and Mediterranean worlds) offered radical ways of understanding place as the interaction of sensibility, history, geography, and myth. Perception is redefined and transformed in the process. The redefinition of perception is a core value in study abroad.

A Hopeless Romantic

A far less desirable outcome is signaled by the idea of romance as a delusion and a form of distorted myopia. In this sense, a romantic view may endorse stereotypical constructs. By way of illustration, European locations are frequently presented through unchallenged assumptions about "authenticity." Those usually derive from romantic nostalgia for lost identities that were, in any case, mostly illusory.

The idea of authenticity derives from an idea of what constitutes the "real" Spain or Italy, or wherever. These notions are usually rooted in idealized images: Jerusalems of the imagination. Lamentations about the loss of the real England, for example, customarily derive from a version of a dreamed landscape shaped by Ealing comedies or films starring Hugh Grant, conservative (and Conservative) delusions about the good old days, and countless fantasies of pastoral community. They are, for the most part, based on romanticized images untouched and untarnished by time, or by current reality.

The notion of the real Spain is filtered through imperfect recollections of Hemingway's heroic landscapes, populated by noble and silent men, and mysterious dark-haired, temperamental women of outstanding, if menacing, beauty; but are the beaches of Benidorm really less authentic, less real, than the sawdust bars of Pamplona? British tourists drinking lager in the pubs by Levantine Beach look very real. What would an unreal Spain look like? Where is it? In short, notions of authenticity are usually expressions of romantic nostalgia for lost worlds that exist, if at all, in fictions, myths of nation and identity, thoughtless study abroad marketing, and, of course, tourist offices.

Study abroad is littered with romantic versions of national identity filtered through some combination of stereotype, manufactured tradition, iconic images, advertising, commerce, and myth. In reality the true Spaniard is as likely to be an accountant as a bullfighter and there are, anecdotally, more accountants than bullfighters in Madrid.

Conclusion: This Is a Fine Romance

It is apparent that there are many ways in which consideration of romance resonates with the endeavor of study abroad. It may offer a metaphor for understanding student engagement with new spaces; in the Romantic imagination, it represents a form of enriched and heightened sensibility that could profitably disturb and disrupt students' precon-ceptions; in an alternative sense, it should teach us what to avoid: the dissemination of unchallenged stereotypes.

Perhaps most significantly the Romantic Movement reminds us of the power that creative thought and imaginative introspection has to reshape ways in which we see the world. If our students learn what Michael Ferber identifies as a key element in the Romantic imagination, we will surely enrich their lives:

> The imagination was not a blank slate, not just the passive power to register, remember and compare perceptions or "images," but an active power to shape the perceptions themselves in fundamental ways. And everyone had it. (2010: xx)

In Blanning's view "the romantic revolution is not over yet" (2010: 186). The potential for profound alteration remains within all of us as we con-template, explore, and analyze the troubled spaces of our world.

Dr. Michael Woolf is the deputy president for strategic development at CAPA Global Education Network. Mike has had much of his career in an international context. Prior to working in mainstream international education, he taught American literature in the universities of Hull, Mid-dlesex, Padova, and Venice and worked as a researcher-writer for BBC radio. He has held leadership roles in international education for many years with FIE, CIEE, and Syracuse University. He has written widely on international education and cultural studies. He serves on a number of boards and was a member of the Board of Directors of the Forum on Education Abroad from 2006 to 2012.

Notes

1. Cited in Blanning 2010, 9.
2. From a cynical viewpoint it may be argued that the exclamation mark, a recurrent indication of multiple epiphanies in Romantic poetry, is a form of hyperbole that resonates with the kinds of inflated rhetoric familiar in study abroad. Beyond that somewhat superficial critique, there is also a more positive implication for our learning objectives.

References

Berlin, Isiah. 1999. *The Roots of Romanticism*. Princeton, NJ: Princeton Univer-sity Press.

Blanning, Tim. 2010. *The Romantic Revolution.* London: Weidenfeld and Nicolson.

Ferber, Michael. 2010. *Romanticism: A Very Short Introduction.* Oxford: Oxford University Press.

Galitz, Kathryn Calley. *Romanticism.* Department of European Paintings, Metropolitan Museum of Art, http://www.metmuseum.org/toah/hd/roma/hd_roma.htm, accessed 29 April 2015.

Johnson, Martha. 2012. "City as Relationship." In *The City as Text: Urban Environments as the Classroom in Education Abroad,* Occasional Paper 1, ed. A. Gristwood and M. Woolf, 32–35. London and Boston: CAPA International Education.

Shelley, Percy Bysshe. 1817. "Mont Blanc: Lines Written in the Vale of Chamouni." In *History or a Six Weeks Tour through a part of France, Switzerland, Germany and Holland.* London: Hookham, 177.

Wordsworth, William. 1888. "The Prelude, Book Fourteenth." In *The Complete Poetical Works.* London: Macmillan.

Acknowledgements

We are grateful to the students who participated in our studies and contributed to this volume, the study-abroad and volunteering-abroad professionals who welcomed us as we carried out these studies, colleagues who commented on our presentation based on these chapters at the Forum on Education Abroad conference in 2013, and our family and friends who helped us formulate the ideas and supported us while we engaged in this work. We would also like to thank the anonymous peer reviewers; we have tried to integrate into this volume our reactions to their helpful and stimulating comments. The text's deficiencies are wholly our responsibility.

PART I
Introduction

CHAPTER 1

Affect and Romance in Study and Volunteer Abroad

Introducing our Project

Neriko Musha Doerr and Hannah Davis Taïeb

Romance is at the heart of our travel fever. We romanticize landscapes, people, languages, and the very fact of moving across borders, of encountering and learning something new, of transforming ourselves as well as others. Study abroad and volunteering abroad are fueled by these passions, by this romance. And along with this romantic passion comes other emotions: fear of the unknown mixed with thrilling attraction to its temptations; longing for liberation; yearning to make a difference; guilt about one's privilege; moral righteousness; and hope for growth, transformation, and enlightenment.

What kind of affect helps students form deep, long-lasting relationships with people during their travels? What kind of affect thwarts or dehumanizes encounters? What kind of affect drives study abroad students to understand their sociocultural surroundings and participate in wider social activities? What kind of affect leads them to withdraw into transient observer or consumer positions? How do study and volunteering abroad programs generate, shape, or transform such affect? What drives the romanticization of border-crossing and the construction of the border itself? And how does affect tie in to larger social and economic structures around us, to neoliberal and globalist and other world transformations, to the subjectivities of our time? These are the questions that inspired us to put together this volume.

As a collaboration between researchers and study abroad practitioners with diverse expertise—cultural anthropology, geography, education, foreign language education, and psychoanalysis—this edited

volume seeks to explore the romantic passions and related affect of border crossing in the context of study abroad and volunteering abroad by
students from American colleges and universities.

The framework that we bring to this multidisciplinary volume is that
of *affect*. As we will discuss below, we use the notion of affect to focus not only on bodily response that cannot be signified (Buda 2015;
d'Hauteserre 2015), but on how affect is mobilized and managed and
how it shapes subjectivities—and how these processes are embedded in
broader economic and political processes, in relations of power.

Why examine study abroad and volunteering abroad in this way?
First of all, because of the intensity of the affective load that surrounds
study and volunteer abroad. Before travelling the destination is often
surrounded in the mind by a romantic aura, driving and heightening
the desire for change, for discovery. Once the student or volunteer arrives at the destination, other, equally strong emotions may come into
play: love, or shame, or guilt, anger or fear, exhilaration, deep disappointment. The strength and importance of these emotions is evident,
and is reflected in their use in marketing study abroad and volunteering
abroad programs, as well as in the many practices of predeparture and
on-site professionals intended to handle these emotions to enhance
outcomes defined as optimal, and in the writings of students and volunteers about their experience. Furthermore, in the literature written
by and for study abroad and volunteering abroad professionals, there
is growing interest in looking at emotions and affect and bringing this
aspect of student experience squarely into discussions in the field. Our
approach to affect, primarily anthropological but also emerging from
other fields, can contribute to these discussions, and is thus of interest
for international education and community service professionals.

This book is also geared for anthropologists, geographers, and
cultural studies scholars who study affect in globalist/globalizing processes, encounters with cultural Others, travel and tourism, education,
and humanitarian work. Our turning of the lens onto study and volunteer abroad contributes a new field of affect analysis that focuses on the
construction and sustenance of difference in globalist processes, border
crossings involving less apparent relations of power, a field of experiential
learning in which what constitutes "learning" is not clear, volunteer and
service work, and on intersections of affect and wider political economy.

We consider the field of study and volunteering abroad to be a rich,
understudied domain for understanding the emergence of the subjectivities of twenty-first-century selves. Study and volunteer abroad are

growing dramatically, but little serious attention has been paid to the analysis of these phenomena, to what they suggest about what young Americans in particular are becoming and are being encouraged to become. Thus this volume, at once geared to the scholar and to the professional.

Our professional motivation leads us to ask questions with proactive intervention and practical suggestions in mind. What kind of affect connects people instead of creating boundaries? How can we make sure our romantic desire and curiosity for the exotic do not make our relationship with the cultural other into voyeurism? How can we harness and redirect emotions in order to humanize the encounter? What kinds of mobilization and management of affect reduce relations of power and domination and instead reinforce egalitarian relations?

In what follows, we will first present a broader theoretical framework and an overview of our approach to affect. We will then go on to situate this volume's contributions in four fields whose interests touch upon the issue of affect and border crossing: affect in the national belonging and the global, affect in the encounter with the cultural Other in relations of power, affect in learning, and affect in helping others. After introducing the chapters in this volume, the chapter ends with a postscript that explains how this project began.

Affect: Theoretical Frameworks

There is no single theory of affect (Seigworth and Gregg 2010). For Brian Massumi, one of the influential scholars of affect writing today (cf. Massumi 1995, 2010), the distinction between emotion and affect is central, as they follow "different logics and pertain to different orders" (1995: 88). Massumi uses the word "emotion" to mean the quality of experience from that point on defined as personal; it is a "qualified intensity" to be inserted into the system of meaning. Affect, in contrast, is irreducibly bodily and autonomic: passion. Eric Shouse further clarifies Massumi's distinctions, writing that "[f]eelings are personal and biographical, emotions are social, and affects are prepersonal"; affect here is "a nonconscious experience of intensity" (Shouse 2005: 5). Julia Kristeva, as discussed by Karen Rodriguez in this volume, distinguishes the emotions, shared with other vertebrates, from the passions, which are human and involve reflexive consciousness (Kristeva 2011: 80, quoted in chapter 3).

Some (e.g., Besnier 1990) are wary of such distinctions, however, because they impose West-centered taxonomies of psychological process. They also warn about the assumption that affect can exist independent of and prior to ideology and to shared meanings (see Leys 2011 for discussions). For our part, though we do see Massumi's, Shouse's and Kristeva's distinctions as key for some purposes, in this work we do not focus on the distinction between feeling, emotion, passion, and affect. Thus, we avoid imposing researchers' interpretation of these processes. Instead, we use these terms synonymously, using the term *affect* interchangeably with feelings, or emotion, or sentiments, and focusing on the relationship of affect to broader social, economic, and political processes. In so doing, we follow the approach of Richard and Rudnyckyj (2009: 57) who use affect as a way to conceptualize "the relationship between structures and sentiments."

This also contrasts with earlier anthropological approaches to emotion as culturally mediated (Geertz 1973; Rosaldo 1984) that relied on a static and bounded notion of culture. Instead, we pay attention to wider political, economic, and social forces that shape "culture" as well as affect—passion, desire, romantic feelings, discomfort, fear, anxiety, etc. This approach allows us to link subjectivity and action, to explore in meaningful ways the connection between lived experience (including its visceral manifestations) and broader processes, "the shifting relationships between the state, market and society" (Richard and Rudnyckyj 2009: 57).

In particular, our volume examines the mobilization and management of affect, which then shapes actions and fosters particular subjectivities. For individuals choosing to study or volunteer abroad, the main affect connected to these activities is positive, at least initially: the emotions that drew them to participate. Therefore, our main focus is on romance and the other alluring feelings that draw people to study or volunteer abroad. However, other types of affect are also discussed.

What does it mean to talk about how affect is mobilized? A flight attendant may mobilize her empathy for passengers and her good humor to live up to her employers' promises of providing "sincere smiles" to customers (Hochschild 2003); a care-giver from the Philippines or Sri Lanka, separated from her own loved ones, may divert her affections and transform them into love for those she has been hired to nurture (Hochschild 2004). Letter writers in the Nukulaelae Atoll in the Pacific mobilize love or *alofa* to control the flow of gifts with their relatives living abroad (Besnier 1990); leaders of Mexican NGOs "build bridges of love" between local people and foreign volunteers, fostering solidarity that will lead to ongoing donations and structural assistance, all the while trying to avoid "emotional blackmail" (Richard and Rudnyckyj 2009: 67). Not only love and affection but fear can be analyzed in this way; for example, in the post-9/11 United States fear was mobilized to bind subjects together (Ahmed 2004; Massumi 2010).

In this volume, we ask: How is affect mobilized, through what discourses, by whom and to what ends? How is the affective experience of students and volunteers aroused by marketing materials, by orientation sessions, by on-site interventions (Rink, Taïeb et al.)? How is our romantic search to be helpful to others and make a difference shaped through media images and news reports in ways that move us across the globe (Jakubiak) and how does it intersect with other types of discourses such as modernism and anticolonialism (Li)? Are there paradoxes involved in study and volunteering abroad—practices that must emphasize difference to evoke romantic passion in potential "customers," but must overcome difference to some extent to be successful? How do these processes fit in with the larger economic and social context—what kind of desire, fear, guilt, and aspirations do current neoliberalist, globalist, and other world transformations inspire, and how do these direct our movements and actions?

Another way we look at affect is in terms of how it is managed. This management of affect can be part of a "technology" for governing individuals (Good 2004), as modes of governmentality shift from welfare states that sought to govern "through society" to advanced liberalism that seeks "to govern through the regulated and accountable choices of autonomous agents ... and ... through intensifying and acting upon their allegiance to particular 'communities'" (Rose 1996: 61). The shift toward neoliberalism has been shown to involve the production of subjectivities through the management of affect. For example, affect-laden spiritual development sessions known as ESQ, Emotional and Spiritual Quotient, were instituted in Indonesian corporations, mixing management techniques with Koranic verses, with employees and high-level managers, leaders, and participants sharing in tears that showed "an open heart" and that led to a renewal that would improve business practices (Richard and Rudnyckyj 2009). Those who established these practices shared in the affect and were moved themselves to new kinds of subjectivities. A second example can be seen in the work of Ana Ramos-Zayas, who shows how emotions like belonging or pride in one's desirability or commercial viability can be managed to enhance an individual's "Blackness" and overall worth in terms of race, sexuality, and gender in the current wider race politics (2009). In the example mentioned above concerning Mexican NGOs, the affect elicited for volunteers by hard work with local people and shared food is purposefully molded by local leaders into warmth that will lead to ongoing partnerships. The NGO local leaders conceive of this as a kind of therapy, working against the alienated emotions and "coldness" that they see as characteristic of human relations for their foreign volunteers, and fostering warmth, creating solidary subjectivities (Richard and Rudnyckyj 2009: 67).

It should be clear from these examples that the management of affect can occur in very different sites and with very different goals. In the field of study and volunteering abroad, we can ask: How is affect managed, by whom (students and volunteers themselves, local partners onsite, education abroad professionals, researchers)? To what ends? What discourses and political, economic, and social environments move students and volunteers to overcome certain affect, such as fear of the unknown, anxiety about novel experiences, and a sense of guilt about privilege in the face of social injustice? What neoliberalist and globalist restructuring of higher education and employment pushes us to think about what affect and what affect-management skills a successful employee should have? What kind of interpretative strategies are used to "read" students' affect in order to manage it?

In this volume, we see how curiosity about and desire for the romantic "dark continent" (Africa) or the "City of Love" (Paris) can be reframed and problematized by study abroad professionals and students, in contexts involving laughter, urban exploration, and study (Rink, Taïeb et al.). Other authors consider how students' themselves manage their affect—various degrees and contours of fascination about the destination—in ways that may highlight the sometimes contradictory goals of studying abroad (Doerr, Kumagai); or how the affect evoked by volunteering abroad—ranging from a sense of being useful and loved to guilt and doubt—are managed by participants as they evaluate their experience (Jakubiak, Li).

Affect also shapes our subjectivities and our own and others' actions. The notion of affect has a double aspect—it is a noun and also a transitive verb. This fits well with the idea that affect simultaneously is what one has and acts on others: a particular form of affect, such as the feeling of shame for example, shapes others' actions, while shaping oneself as a subject (Richard and Rudnyckyu 2009).

In this volume, our authors explore how passion for the language of the destination transforms subjectivities and shapes the borders of the self as well as the surrounding social terrain (Rodriguez). Romantic attachment to destinations makes the study abroad students observant as they hope to become like local people by copying their behavior and attire but also become critical and reflexive when romanticism turns into disappointment (Taïeb et al., Doerr). The desire to serve others generates for volunteers a sense of themselves as good and caring (Jakubiak) but also guilt as they come to view themselves as colonialist imposers of "Western values," depending on the type of project and context (Li).

While our main theoretical frames are thus analyses of affect as it is mobilized, is managed, and produces subjectivities and actions, our discussions intersect with four fields of research, to which we turn below.

The Global, the National, and Affect

Current study and volunteering abroad are often framed within the notion of the global. Researchers and administrators, as well as guidebooks and brochures, highlight the merit of these experiences as ways of gaining "global/intercultural competence" (Savicki 2008) and becoming "global citizens" (Lewin and Van Kirk 2009, see Chapter 2 of this volume for extensive discussion of these issues). The notion of the global is often uncritically viewed as positive (for exceptions to this see Doerr 2012, 2014; Grünzweig and Rinehart 2002; Johnson 2009; Woolf 2007, 2010; Zemach-Bersin 2009, 2011). The notion's reliance on pre-existing differences among people (see Doerr 2012, 2013) and how this relates to students' affect are rarely discussed. In this subsection, we review the notion of the global and discuss its relation to affect, starting with the research on nationalism/nationhood that serves as the unit of "difference" to be noticed, learned, and bridged.

The sense of belonging to a nation—patriotism, *Volkgeist*, etc.—has been a major topic of investigation in studies of nationalism. How does one come to feel attachment and belonging to fellow nationals in the bounded territory of the nation-state—people that one may never meet in one's lifetime? This question was at the heart of the now classic work on nationalism, *Imagined Communities* by Benedict Anderson (1991), as well as other studies of nationalism (Balibar 1988; Borneman 1992; Briggs 1996; Comaroff 1987; Sommer 1991). Also, anthropologists in recent years have analyzed affective aspects of the state, its "modern bureaucracy" that is infused with affect—desire, apathy, irony, cynicism (Navaro-Yashin 2006). Michael Taussig (1993) and Michael Herzfeld

(1997) illustrate aspects of the state and its officials, respectively, that relate individuals affectively to the state.

This understanding of nation as a unit of belonging with a clear boundary that draws individuals together affectively is an important basis of the notion of the global because the notion relies on crossing such boundaries (Doerr 2012). Researchers of globalization focus on disjunctive flows of people, media images, technology, finances, and ideologies *across* national borders (Appadurai 1990) as well as the channeling (Broad and Orlove 2007), interrupting, and resisting of such flows (Tsing 2005). Examination of changing perceptions (Robertson 1992; Wilk 1995) and practices (Appadurai 1986; Howes 1996) does not escape the assumption that the unit of focus—whether crossing it or overcoming it—is that of nation-state.

Because the notion of culture has been linked to the nation-states (though it came to be used to challenge the ideology by "ethnic groups")—in its ideologies, one nation, one people, one culture—some discussions of the notion warrant some space here. Culture is a "take" on human variations that needs to be situated in the context of changing anthropological theorizations: "race" (the nineteenth century), "culture" (the twentieth century), and "ethnicity" with a revised notion of "culture" (late twentieth century). While the earlier approach viewed culture as a given without consideration of power politics, an approach emerged in the 1960s that viewed culture as a new way to stake out claims to precedence and power—the way of life as rooted in the particular place—as cultural particularity has become a major ideological weapon in political struggles (Wolf 1994).

Here, culture came to be viewed as a strategy for groups to mobilize, shape, and reshape self-images and elicit participation. Culture became objectified—aspects of a social world get interpreted as typifying that world and represented as detached, object-like "traits" that are believed to be possessed by the bearer of the culture (Handler 1985)—and analyzed as such (see theme issues in *Mankind,* 1982; *Oceania,* 1992; and *Anthropological Forum,* 1993). Once culture is objectified and named, people take a variety of stances towards it, including using it as a strategy to challenge the one-nation, one-people ideology of the nation-state (Kearney 2004), or to claim authority (Oakdale 2004) and authentic existence as an indigenous group (Clifford 1988; Povinelli 1998), or to gain self-determination (Henze and Davis 1999; Warner 1999), or to intermittently express a sense of belonging when convenient (Gans 1999), or to understand themselves and guide their subsequent behavior (Holland et al. 1998).

Research on study and volunteering abroad often uses the objectified notion of culture without critical analyses about such objectification. The notion of culture is also used to measure the interpersonal skills of individuals who "cross cultural borders"—study and volunteering abroad participants—and is a basis for establishing the desired skills to be taught through these activities, evoked in the notion of "intercultural competence."

In this volume, we do not focus on the notion of culture as an object of study nor as an analytical tool because of its political nature as described above. We are interested instead in maintaining critical distance from the notion of culture and also the notion of intercultural competence, all the while remaining aware of their importance in the field of international education, in order to reflect on how these notions play a role in the evocation of desired affective states for students and volunteers abroad.

Research about the process of globalization is critiqued as itself being part of the ideologies that portray global connections as always positive, progressive, and universally accessible (Friedman 2003; Tsing 2000). What is rarely discussed is its affirmation and perpetuation of the national as the most relevant unit of difference through its analytical privileging of the crossing of the national borders—methodological nationalism (Wimmer and Glick Schiller 2002)—over other kinds of borders. This is also the case for research on study abroad: it relies on a valorization of global connection and the existence of difference based on which the experiential learning of another culture becomes meaningful (Doerr 2012, 2013, 2015a).

We then seek to analyze how students' romantic images of the destination draw on and perpetuate (Doerr, Kumagai), ignore (Rink), or subvert (Taïeb et al.) the imagining of the nation as having unique and homogeneous culture. How does urban-rural difference frame differently the power relations between volunteers and those they serve, complicating the notion of crossing borders (Li)? Chapters in this volume further examine kinds of sameness and difference, commonality and separation, that students/volunteers feel and how this is interpreted in light of national borders and the notion of the global (Taïeb et al., Doerr). That is, we show that globalist ideologies mobilize affect around the crossing of national borders and that affect nurtured by various nationalist ideologies is managed through study abroad practitioners' wish for encouraging critical thinking in students (Taïeb et al.), students' wish to succeed in schooling (Kumagai), and volunteers' own anticolonial critiques (Li), creating various types of subjectivities.

Through these analyses, we open up new fields of inquiry, asking: How does the discourse of culture and interculturality interpret, mobilize, and manage affect, and to what end? What kinds of belongings are being created? Does the notion of the interculturally competent global citizen suggest a new kind of belonging, to a world imagined community? If so, how is affect mobilized and managed to create this new kind of community? What light is shed through this process, and what shadows are cast?

Encounter with Cultural Difference: Power and Affect

Encounters with difference have been analyzed extensively in colonial contexts. Edward Said (1978) argues that Orientalism, a style of thought based upon a distinction made between the "Orient" and the "West," shows a prevalent way of knowing the cultural Other in the context of relations of power. With an assumption that the Orient cannot represent itself, the West gained authority over the Orient by making observations about it, making statements about it, authorizing views of it, and teaching about it. At the same time, the West defined itself in contrast to the Orient. Said argues that this is how cultural domination operates.

In these colonial relations of power, people of the non-West were displayed in zoos, freak shows, circuses, and museums as spectacles (Fusco 1995). These exoticized people embody the audience's anxieties about the cultural Other while also affirming the spectators' mastery over them (Koritz 1997). Such exhibitions helped forge a special place for nonwhite peoples and their cultures in the Euro-American affective imagination, as also discussed by Rink with the case of Hottentot Venus (this volume). The legacy of this colonial exoticism remains in the present day, especially in the form of various "cultural performances" by ethnic minorities (Fusco 1995) but with added implications (Doerr 2008, 2009).

Analyzing imperial travel writing, Mary Louise Pratt (1992/2008) argues that discourses in eighteenth-century Europeans' travel writing on non-European places "produced 'the rest of the world' for European readerships" (4, emphasis in original) and constructed "the imperial order" for these readers, nurturing in them a sense of ownership, entitlement, curiosity, adventure, and moral fervor about their colonies. Debbie Lisle (2006) argues that today's travel writing carries this legacy in two intertwining visions: colonial visions that resuscitate the hierarchy by which the dominant Western writer judges the "less civilized," and cosmopolitan visions that distance themselves from the legacy of empire by celebrating cultural difference yet impose a universal standard by which to judge others, as well as creating an illusion that "globalization" has produced a world where everyone can move freely. Both visions presume aforementioned natural differences between cultures marked by stable boundaries, ignoring the relations of power that structure, mobilize, and mark such differences. Lisle argues that the reemergence of travel writing hinges on its ability to let readers reimagine clear-cut, contained, stable differences, thus alleviating the anxieties of globalization.

These works on colonial relations analyze affect toward the cultural Other—desire and fear, longing and disdain, and surrender and control—as emerging in and perpetuating power relations. In this volume, we will look at some cases in which affect is mobilized and managed in relations of power when students and volunteers encounter the cultural Other. Rink's chapter discusses students' exoticization of the African continent. Jakubiak's chapter portrays contours of affect that simultaneously distance and connect volunteers to those receiving their service. Li's chapter compares different ways volunteers working in the rural areas and urban areas frame themselves to the locals in the context of (neo) colonial relations between the United States and the Marshall Islands. We also look at cases where there is no clear-cut status differential, such as when American study abroad students visit European countries with varying degrees of romanticization of the destination (Taïeb et al., Doerr), or when historically hierarchical relations become more complex, when American study abroad students visit Japan (Kumagai). We then examine how affect is mobilized and managed and new subjectivities get constituted as they intersect with study abroad practitioners' intent, more specific relations between countries, and discourses of schooling.

Analyzing cases where relations of power are explicit and apparent and cases where such relations of power are more ambiguous, we extend the question of affect and the constitution of otherness to a wider frame of cultural Others, to the question of border crossing more generally. Especially, border crossing in general and between those in less-visible relations of power have not been approached yet in the field of the anthropology of affect; this volume can offer new insight in that area.

This volume further asks what happens when the encounter with the Other is interpreted in terms of "intercultural education" or experiential learning through "immersion," as we discuss in the next section.

Learning and Affect

Affect has been examined in the field of education from various angles. Some focus on the classroom, for example, discussing how peer dynamics can produce emotions like alienation, embarrassment, or belonging (Doerr and Lee 2012, 2013; Frekko 2009; Krashen 1998; Yamasaki 2011). Others examine the role of affect in out-of-class learning, such as how culturally specific categories of affect are passed on in linguistic socialization of young children (Schieffelin and Ochs 1987) and how interactions with the "native speakers" of the language outside the classroom, the cultural capital of the target language, and the language-learners' investment in the social position they wish to occupy—such as mother-figure or immigrant—play a crucial role in the language-learners' desire to learn and speak the language (Heller 2003; McEwan-Fujita 2010; Pierce 1995; Whiteside 2009).

Another line of research focuses on the management of affect in education, particularly in advanced capitalism. Lynn Fendler (1998) argues that the rhetoric in current US education suggests the need for reflective teachers with understandings of critical and culturally relevant pedagogy and character education. These emphases point to new types of things that are teachable. Besides intellect and disciplined behavior, motivation and attitudes—desire for education—have become something that teachers aim to teach. Love, pleasure, feelings, wishes, fears, and anxieties—in other words, "soul"—all became teachable and things that educated subjects should have. The educated subject that critical pedagogies aim to create is a subject with a desire for social justice and moral commitment to democracy (Fendler 1998).

Similarly, the idea that study abroad can create global citizens with "intercultural competence" involves believing that it is possible through education to bring into being particular attitudes, such as openness and willingness to interact with cultural Others. This process involves work on the self, and reinterpretation of one's own affect and that of others through new kinds of educative processes. As will be detailed in Chapter 2 of this volume (Taïeb and Doerr), affect and learning have been discussed for many years in the literature on study abroad in terms of the practical issues involved in making "intercultural learning" smooth and helping students adjust to the destination. The focus of discussion moved from handling "culture shock" and its discomforts to include how these can be turned into learning experiences, how to improve students' openness to and understanding of others, and how to increase students' confidence and ability to navigate new environments. More recently, the field has developed new ways of thinking about emotions, with the emergence of the idea of fostering "emotional resilience" in students, and an increasing fine-tuning and development of the process of transforming affect from discomfort and fear into "intercultural competence" and "cultural self-awareness." Study abroad research takes these approaches for granted and thus has not approached them as objects of examination and analyses.

Chapters in this volume contribute to a broadening of how affect and learning can be viewed in these fields. As mentioned above, first we do so by problematizing and analyzing the ideology of globalism prevalent in higher education generally and in study abroad in particular. The ideology is linked to the desire to be "interculturally competent" (though the two are not identical). The search for "intercultural competence" also intersects with other, differently inflected notions of learning, such as moving away from the "mother tongue" to the new social order of the new language (Rodriguez), critical understandings of social issues (Taïeb et al.), learning through immersion (Doerr), learning through academic work (Kumagai)—with varying effects.

We also consider in detail particular emotions, including those of romance, and discuss their mobilizing and transformative effects. Rodriguez's chapter takes a fresh look at the passions associated with language learning for study abroad students, considering how they are "sublimated" (i.e., modified in order to fit into the social order while modifying the social order creatively also) and thus linked in a creative way to the specificities of the host society. Rink's chapter discusses some of the affective reactions to the idea of "Africa"—nostalgia for a lost, pristine nature; fear; desire; and also desire to correct perceived wrongs. He brings in the idea of affective learning to propose how professionals can bring about an "entanglement" between the student and the specific site (not the reified, imagined continent), and shows how affect can become mutual, an engagement. Taïeb et al.'s chapter suggests that on-site professors can join with students in observing, analyzing, and rethinking the very processes of study abroad with which they are involved—rethinking romantic journeys underway, and working towards dialogic and critical learning. Doerr's chapter compares different affective investment in the destinations reflecting the relationships between the students' host and home countries and examines how they shape the students' learning and other experiences during studying abroad. Kumagai's chapter contrasts the kinds of learning—through class work and through extracurricular immersion—that emerge from and further reinforce different student affective experience.

We thus hope to bring the question of study abroad into the discussion of learning and affect, and bring a critical and analytic approach to the discourses of international education, thus contributing to both these domains. We also seek to bring the discussion of affect into the field of volunteering abroad as we discuss in the next section.

Helping and Affect

Volunteer/service work has become increasingly popular in the 1990s (Sherraden et al. 2006). A shift away from the Cold War to "life politics" that focuses on individual morality and sense of self, from the politics of production and social class to consumption and individual identity, and from public politics to a form of therapy for individuals, volunteer/service work came to provide a sense of morality to participating individuals (Butcher and Smith 2010). Neoliberal transformations normalized the privatization of social services by the state, encouraging the development of NGO-run volunteer/service opportunities to fill that gap (Conran 2011). Also, the current tightening of the job market due to the economic crash in the late 2000s in the United States made students increasingly anxious to create a distinguishing edge in their CVs, and volunteer work became a popular choice (Hickel 2013).

Current volunteer/service abroad can be divided into three types. The first emphasizes technical skills to help developing societies to modernize that are (1) altruistic to fight poverty and disease, (2) political to promote a positive image of the West, and (3) manned by skilled people (Butcher and Smith 2010), as in the Peace Corps and the WorldTeach program that Li describes in this volume. The second type, sometimes called International Service Learning (ISL), connects the volunteer work or service with learning, and intends mutual benefit to local partners and to student volunteers who seek engagement in the host society

(Bringle and Hatcher 2011; Plater 2011). The third type is volunteer tourism developed as an alternative to mass-packaged holidays aiming at both enhancing the well-being of the host community and nurturing the volunteer tourists' self-development and academic credit, or "ego-enhancement" (Callanan and Thomas 2005: 196; also see Mowforth and Munt 2009), as Jakubiak discusses in this volume.

Volunteering abroad involves various romanticized notions: the world of cultural Others as an arena of problems to be solved, occluding the problems that exist in students' home country; the notion of "the local community" as a primordial and authentic entity, occluding the fact that local communities are usually heterogeneous with diverse interests; "sharing of knowledge" as the automatic result of volunteering, occluding the fact that volunteers do not always have significant levels of technical knowledge; equal partnership between volunteers and the community they work in, occluding the fact that their relationships are hierarchical at various levels; a romanticized conception of what it takes to "change the world," occluding the difficulty involved in liberal art students without training achieving significant results as volunteers; and a vision of the universality of humanitarianism, occluding the US-specific view of individuals as equal units entitled to pursue their interests as civic participation, and occluding the ways in which this may involve an evasion of political responsibility (Cororation and Handler 2013).

Despite their humanitarian goals, these volunteer abroad programs are critiqued for perpetuating the hierarchical relationship between the volunteers and their recipients by suggesting "privileged" volunteers have power to change situations by "giving" to the "less-privileged" hosts viewed as needy, passive, and incapable of helping themselves (Conran 2011; Manzo 2008; Sin 2009); evading transforming structural inequality by its focus on seeking to improve basic needs—food and shelter— of impoverished communities (Butcher and Smith 2010; Kahne and Westheimer 2003); imposing the idea of what constitutes an ideal state of being onto the community being helped (Gray and Campbell 2007; Munt 1994; Sinervo 2011); and serving primarily volunteers' need to gain "soft skills"—communication, organization, and team working skills—to give an edge in the competitive educational market (Heath, 2007; also see Gray and Campbell 2007; Munt 1994; Stewart 2013).

Those working towards critical and egalitarian projects abroad have sought to respond to these critiques in several ways. There is a growing literature working to develop ethical standards for practice (e.g. Hartman et al. 2014, Strait and Lima 2009), proposing community

direction with multiple stakeholders, long-term interdependent partnerships between volunteer organizations and NGOs (see also Nenga
2011), funding transparency, sustainability, deliberate diversity, and "dual
purpose" with a refusal to prioritize student goals or to view students
as consumers of experience. Framing classes are increasingly seen as
necessary tools, problematizing power relations, raising awareness of
privilege, and fostering dialogue between volunteers and local partners
(Hartman et al 2014); they can also be used to link notions of service
to local conceptions such as solidarity (Taïeb et al 2015). Jacoby (2009)
emphasizes the importance of linking practice to reflection not only for
students, but also for service-learning professionals, who should fore-
ground social justice concerns and resist the rush to set up programs
without considering their duration, sustainability, accessibility, and
long-term consequences including the possible obscuring of the root
causes of problems (Jacoby 2009: 99-103). Innovative program design
can include credit-bearing learning opportunities, teaching, traveling,
and "soft skills" for local partners as well as volunteers; questions of affect can also be raised with local partners as well as volunteers (Taïeb
et al. 2015).

Affect in volunteering abroad is discussed in various ways. "Caring"
is discussed as (re)producing unequal structural arrangements of pater-
nalism (Sin 2009) as in the notion of charity, "a superior class achieving
merit by doing things gratuitously for an inferior class" (Dewey 1908/
1996: 166). The sense of duty as responsible citizens is seen to be cul-
tivated through service work, drawing on John Dewey's vision that it is
a matter of justice rather than altruism (Barber 1994; Saltmarsh, 1996;
Taylor, 2002). Empathy with the less unfortunate through crossing so-
cioeconomic borders and interacting with them is increasingly viewed
as a goal of volunteer/service work (Chesler et al. 2006; Rhoads and
Neururer 1998). Intimate attachment is seen as part of volunteering's
moral economy, "a tangled circulation of money, people, labor, and
emotions that creates complex webs of possibility and connection, but
which also contains points of friction and disillusionment" (Sinervo 2011:
6), as intimate connections developed between volunteers and volunteered is commodified for the former as "authentic" experience (Conran
2011) and regarded as opportunities for further economic interactions
for the latter (Sinervo 2011). Confidence, altruism, and sensitivity that
volunteers develop through their volunteering experience is discussed
by some as positive (McGehee and Santos 2005) and by others as negative for benefiting mainly the privileged volunteers (Gray and Campbell

2007; Heath 2007; Munt 1994) and, as it came to be purchased through signing up for volunteer projects, depoliticizing the political urge for social justice into consumerism for self-transformation (Hickel 2013). The emotional difficulties students experience through volunteering are discussed as a starting point towards self-transformation, learning, and the fostering of successful reciprocal projects (Nickols et al. 2013; Pagano and Roselle 2009).

Some point out the dangers of focusing on intimate emotions while volunteering abroad as it overshadows and obscures—or normalizes—larger structural inequalities, depoliticizing power relations and reframing structural inequality as a question of individual morality (Conran 2011). Our intention in this volume is to investigate the links between affect—which drives individuals to connect with those in communities they work in and gives meaning to their acts—and wider economic and structural inequities at the societal level. In Jakubiak's and Li's chapters here, we see an approach that views the volunteer's romantic motivations and on-site affective responses in this way. How does affect reflect the various motivations for volunteering abroad, and their contradictions? How do volunteers manage the emotions that arise during their activity, including emotions like guilt, disappointment, and doubt? How are these affective responses linked to the construction of subject positions via volunteering? What kinds of affect arise for local partners who are the intended recipients of volunteer activities, and how is this managed and interpreted? What does this suggest about the interconnections between affect and wider relations of power, and about how to develop new kinds of critical reflection on these activities?

The Structure of This Volume

This volume is divided into three parts. Part I consists of this chapter and Chapter 2 and sets out theoretical backgrounds in which the volume can be situated. Entitled "Study Abroad and Its Reasons" and written by Hannah Davis Taïeb and Neriko Musha Doerr, Chapter 2 introduces the overview and history of study abroad and how affect has been treated in the field. We offer a new way to look at study abroad itself, focusing on its genealogies and legitimating discourses as they shift throughout the twentieth and twenty-first centuries, bringing out some of the inherent tensions in the field. We then consider how affect has been brought to bear on the field, considering the processes of orientation and reflection on "cultural shock," "getting out of the comfort zone," and the reinterpretation of the critical incident and the search for "intercultural competence" and "personal leadership."

Part II has five chapters that discuss various cases of affect as it plays out in diverse study abroad contexts. Karen Rodriguez's Chapter 3, entitled "Passionate Displacements into Other Tongues and Towns: A Psychoanalytic Perspective on Shifting into a Second Language," explores the psychic dimension of the second-language learning process, focusing on study abroad students' passion for the Spanish language in Mexico. Based on student reflections, the chapter examines the psychic shifts involved in the transition to the symbolic in one's second language that parallels an infant learning their first language. Drawing on the work of psychoanalyst Julia Kristeva, Rodriguez explores the contradictory affective processes—passionate separations and connections; conflicting feelings of love, desire, and hatred; and narcissism and masochism—of connecting to the destination by taking up a subject position in the local language. Rodriguez illustrates the transformation of study abroad students' subjectivity and its implications for social change through their passionate involvement in another language.

Bradley Rink's Chapter 4, entitled "Sojourn to the Dark Continent: Landscape and Affect in an African Mobility Experience," analyzes the study abroad students' affective responses to the marginalized, patronized, and sexualized Africa—romance, desire, hope/hopelessness, and fear—and considers how such affect influences and is influenced by their institutionalized study abroad experiences. Based on an analysis of the discourses embedded in study abroad literature students are exposed before their travel as well as a series of questionnaires with students during their study abroad experience, this chapter analyzes the complex affective responses that the African city evokes, and suggests pedagogical strategies for affective learning that can be used with students.

Hannah Davis Taïeb's Chapter 5, entitled "Thinking through the Romance" and written with Emily Bihl, Mai-Linh Bui, Hyojung Kim, and Kaitlin Rosenblum, draws on the input of two groups of students in Paris to discuss the enlistment of students in a critical reevaluation of the romantic images that launched them on their study abroad journeys. The discourses students are brought to question include not only the romantic discourse of Paris, but also the somewhat contradictory romantic notions of study abroad adventure, personal transformation, and linguistic immersion. The chapter brings in the particular position of students "studying abroad while studying abroad"—that is, non-US students who come to America for college, and during their college years, study once again "abroad."

Neriko Musha Doerr's Chapter 6, entitled "Falling In/Out of Love with the Place: Affective Investment, Perceptions of Difference, and Learning in Study Abroad," compares two American summer study abroad students' learning experiences in terms of their affective investment (or lack thereof) in the destination, France and Spain, asking how the different degrees of affective investment shaped students' learning experiences and perceptions of difference among people. Doerr argues that the student with an invested, romantic view of the destination highlighted differences between French people and Americans and, when she came to be disillusioned, reflected on her experience critically, whereas the student with fewer romantic preconceptions noticed not only differences between the host and home societies but also differences within each society and similarities between host and home societies; however, she absorbed whatever she encountered though with little critical reflection.

Yuri Kumagai's Chapter 7, entitled "Learning Japanese/Japan in a Year Abroad in Kyoto: Discourse of Study Abroad, Emotions, and Construction of Self," analyzes the interplay between the students' sense of the "success" of their study abroad experience (itself influenced by the discourse of immersion), and their romanticized and exoticized views of Japan. The two students both expressed a romantic fascination with Japan (geisha, Shinto, tea ceremony, etc.), but during their year in Kyoto the student who focused on academic work and experienced more mundane parts of Japanese life viewed her study abroad as wanting, while the other who plunged into many "traditional" cultural activities viewed hers as successful while retaining an exoticized view of Japan.

Part III of this volume consists of two chapters that discuss volunteer abroad experiences. Cori Jakubiak's Chapter 8, entitled "One Smile, One Hug: Romanticizing 'Making a Difference' to Oneself and Others through English Language Voluntourism," illustrates the contradictory link between the discourses of love and caring in teaching, and the encounter with the "exotic" other. Using data collected from the ethnography of English-language voluntourism, where people from the Global North teach English in the Global South as humanitarian aid, this chapter discusses the ways in which voluntourists describe their experience affectively as being helpful and having an important impact, as transformative of self and others, and as an authentic experience of the cultural Other. Her analyses of these affective languages in turn illuminate the ideological underpinning of the voluntourist projects and situate them in terms of North-South power relations.

Richard Li's Chapter 9, entitled "People with Pants: Self-Perceptions of WorldTeach Volunteers in the Marshall Islands," illustrates how the romantic view of Americans as modernizers held by the volunteers as well as Marshall islanders intersect with anticolonialist views, and how this varies geographically between the urban and rural Marshall Islands. The chapter depicts WorldTeach volunteers in the Marshall Islands negotiating a tension between their romantic self-image as modernizers and a desire to avoid imposing their values and beliefs, which evolves faced with the Marshall Islanders own idealized and romantic notions of Americans.

The conclusion written by Hannah Davis Taïeb and Neriko Musha Doerr pulls together arguments and suggestions from all the chapters and discusses how we can use this knowledge for reflecting on study abroad and volunteer abroad practice and discourse, and for thinking about ways to "intervene" in student experience. We also consider what unanswered questions this work has brought up and fruitful directions for future research.

Together, these chapters explore the role of affect in studying and volunteering abroad. While the chapters introduce the reader to individual students and the details of their day-to-day lives while studying and volunteering abroad in particular settings, these quotidian and experiential details are put into the context of the diverse theoretical questions we discussed in this chapter.

Collectively, these chapters contribute to the discussions on globalization and analyses of affect in (re)constituting and crossing borders on which the discourses of globalization rely; to the discussions of power relations in the encounters with the cultural Other cases in which such power relations are not apparent; and to the literature on affect in learning a new examination of the fields of study and volunteer abroad that involve mobilizing and managing affect in specific ways. To the fields of study abroad and volunteering/serving abroad, this volume adds analyses of how affect and wider sociocultural and economic structures relate with each other, as affect is not only mobilized and managed while situated in these wider contexts but also shapes subjectivities and the actions of those involved.

Romantic passions drive us to gaze at maps, pack our bags, and step out of our daily lives to travel. Pushed by strong feelings, we hope for freedom, for new emotions to spring up as we travel into new worlds. However, Althusser (1971) tells us that we are never free: we are always subject in a double sense—subject as author of our own actions but also subjected to ideologies or systems of representation (i.e., categories). Passions rise up inside us, we feel, but we feel as part of wider political, economic, and sociocultural structures. Analyzing such dynamics helps us further examine our experience, perceptions, and feelings, not only in terms of what they can teach us about ourselves personally, but also as they and we are part of our time. Passions for travel thus help us journey into other domains intellectually and affectively.

Postscript: Reflecting on the Genesis of This Project

This project was born out of a conversation that took place in July 2011 in Paris. Neriko Musha Doerr was carrying out fieldwork on study abroad, following a student attending Hannah Davis Taïeb's study abroad program. As we talked about the program and our understandings of study abroad in general, we found our mutual interest in the question of romance—the romance of travel, the romantic attraction of certain destinations and cities, the romance of service. Being ourselves an anthropologist specializing in education (Doerr) and a study abroad director and international educator trained as an anthropologist (Taïeb), we come at the subject from different but related points of view. Though our starting point was the question of romance, as we worked and solicited ideas from colleagues, we expanded our scope to other kinds of passions about travel, learning, and service. We decided to investigate questions of affect in the very specific context of study abroad and volunteering abroad, looking not only at romance, desire, and objectification, but at other passions and emotions such as shame, embarrassment, yearning, and the desire to be of service. We hoped to analyze these themes in an open-ended, context-specific manner, looking at particular places and projects and some of the expressions of affect they elicit. This is a beginning in which our two divergent visions, as detailed below, converged.

> **Neriko Musha Doerr:** I came to do research on study abroad because a friend, Drew Maywar, who was designing a study abroad program for engineering students asked me to work with him as a consultant to understand and support the adjustment of students to their desti-

nation, Japan. Prior to that, my research had been on issues of education, language politics, race relations, and technologies of power in the context of the revitalization of indigenous Maori language in Aotearoa/ New Zealand (2009), English-as-a-Second-Language (ESL) education in the United States (2012), and the education of Japanese-as-a-heritage-language (JHL) in the United States (Doerr and Lee 2012; 2013). The friend felt my expertise would be an asset for the team. Although the program did not materialize due to lack of funding, I was inspired by what is involved in study abroad processes, and I decided to carry out research on study abroad.

For me, the issue of romance was one of the things that made study abroad special. Compared to the areas of education I had studied, in which the students tended to be driven to learn by their ethnic affiliation, the sense of responsibility, and parental and peer pressure (indigenous language revitalization); by the necessity to adjust and increase career opportunities (ESL education); or by the need for communication with extended family, their ethnic affiliation, and future career opportunities (JHL education), study abroad appeared to be driven more by personal romantic views of things the students seek to learn about—the people and culture of a destination. This made me focus on the role of affect, especially romantic sentiment, of the students.

I value collaboration with people I meet in the field. To work together is a way to give back something—documents collected through fieldwork and their analyses from anthropological viewpoints—to the field site. It is also a way to include viewpoints and draw on the expertise of the people in the field site in the research, and to share authorship of knowledge production during research, which has often been claimed solely by the ethnographer (Clifford 1988). Moreover, because many of the people I meet in the field are professionals, working with them often means interdisciplinary collaboration. For example, I have worked with a school administrator, who is also a linguist, of a JHL program where I was doing fieldwork (Doerr and Lee 2012; 2013; 2016; Lee and Doerr 2015). This project is also an interdisciplinary collaboration with a study abroad director I met in the field, who is also an international educator and anthropologist.

I found it fruitful to approach the issue of romance in study abroad from two different viewpoints—that of the cultural anthropologist, and that of the study abroad practitioner/international educator. I feel that anthropology's current focus on affect and the ethnographic method can offer critical tools for study abroad, and the focus on study abroad can offer anthropology the opportunity to analyze affect in new ways.

Hannah Davis Taïeb: I have been working in study abroad since the year 2000, most of that time as resident director of CIEE's Contemporary French Studies program in Paris. My studies, however, were not in the field of international education, but in anthropology, and I did anthropological fieldwork in Morocco in 1988–89, focusing on conceptions of self for unmarried women in a middle-sized town. My interests at that time involved the relationship between conceptions of self and political economy (looking for the links between changing conceptions of the self and of self-control and the fact that women were remaining single longer and entering the labor market). I was also preoccupied by the question of boundaries, of transnational cultural forms and the creating and blurring of boundaries by social actors (Davis 1989), and the projection onto others of our fantasies and desires (Davis 1990, 1993, 1998).

As I learned the profession of international educator, the anthropological approaches that had shaped me were always in the back of my mind. It seemed natural to me to set up classes based on participant-observation, and I launched classes comparing the French and US educational systems. Questions of culture, in constant discussion within the field of study abroad, I saw in terms of long-standing anthropological debates, and I could never feel comfortable when definitions of cultural difference came across as essentialist. Critical anthropological approaches and my own sociopolitical slant also led me towards educational forms that were dialogues or partnerships. I set up seminars that brought French and American scholars and professionals together,[1] co-taught bilingual classes and workshops with mixed student bodies,[2] and set up classes integrating volunteering with a critical shared questioning of notions such as solidarity, service, and diversity.[3]

When I met Neriko Musha Doerr, I saw that we shared common analyses of how study abroad works, and that an explicit return to the anthropological approach could enrich my own professional life. What "culture work" are we doing, are we part of, as practitioners in our fields? How is the movement of American and other students around the world contributing to changing discourses of culture and diversity? What is being achieved when global discourses combine with international organizations that talk more and more about difference, but in more and more standardized ways?

At the same time, as an international educator and program director, the pedagogical, practical, and also ethical questions are never far away. What is the next step with each particular student, professor, program, partnership? What are the paradoxical or contradictory aspects of our mandates, and how can we negotiate them? How can the anthropological perspective inform our own views of our field, inform our decisions, give depth to our practice?

Five years have passed since our first meeting in Paris where this project emerged. This volume is a result of our numerous email exchanges, skype sessions, and in-person meetings whenever either of us crossed the Atlantic, in which our knowledge, theoretical orientations, analytical perspectives, practical concerns, aspirations for the future of study abroad, and personal affective investments diverged, bounced off of each other, converged, and generated something new. This project is a milestone of our own continuing journeys for both of us.

Neriko Musha Doerr received a Ph.D. in cultural anthropology from Cornell University. Her research interests include politics of difference, language and power, and study abroad and alternative break experiences. Her publications include *Meaningful Inconsistencies: Bicultural Nationhood, Free Market, and Schooling in Aotearoa/New Zealand* (Berghahn Books), *The Native Speaker Concept* (Mouton de Gruyter), and *Constructing the Heritage Language Learner* (Mouton de Gruyter), and articles in *Anthropological Forum, Compare, Critical Discourse Studies, Discourse: Studies in the Cultural Politics of Education, Identities: Global Studies in Culture and Power,* and *Journal of Cultural Geography.* She currently teaches at Ramapo College in New Jersey, US.

Dr. **Hannah Davis Taïeb** is an international educator, teacher, and writer who was the director of CIEE's Contemporary French Studies Program in Paris from 2003 to 2015. She has a Ph.D. in anthropology from New York University; her thesis, concerning unmarried women and changing conceptions of the self, was based on fieldwork in a middle-sized city in Morocco. After working with a research team in Lyon, Hannah settled permanently in France in 1992, where she first was the co-editor of a multilingual, multidisciplinary review, *Mediterraneans,* then taught intercultural and interpersonal communication at the American University of Paris before entering the field of study abroad in the year 2000. While at CIEE, she ran Franco-American seminars, joint classes and study trips on subjects like disability, religious diversity and secularism, anti-Semitism and Islamophobia, chaplaincy and religion in prison, and special education. Independently, Hannah continues to teach about popular culture and *métissage,* disabilities, and religious diversity, co-teaches a Franco-American intercultural communication class, and runs volunteer and exchange activities with a Paris youth club.

Notes

We are grateful to Natalie Zemon Davis, Cori Jakubiak, Yuri Kumagai, and Karen Rodriguez for their critical feedback on an earlier draft and to the editor and the anonymous peer reviewers at Berghahn Books for very helpful and stimulating comments we have endeavored to take into account. The text's deficiencies are wholly our responsibility.

1. Hannah Davis Taïeb has led Franco-American seminars on themes such as Islamophobia and anti-Semitism, religion in everyday life through a reflection on the role of chaplains in prisons and hospitals, and disabilities.
2. Hannah Davis Taïeb has co-taught classes with Verena Aebischer of the University of Paris Nanterre (Paris X), with a joint student body including Intercultural Communication students and Social Psychology students; co-led workshops with Ita Hermouet of the Institut Catholique d'Enseignement Supérieur in La Roche sur Yon, with a joint student body of CIEE study abroad students and French students bound for study abroad in the United States; and co-taught classes with Jérémy Arki at the University of Paris Diderot (Paris VII) with a class that was open to CIEE study abroad students and also to Paris-Diderot students.
3. Hannah Davis Taïeb is co-teaching a class entitled Community Service Learning: Social Justice/Solidarité, Diversity/Diversité, in which American students engage in tutoring French youth from a youth club in a low-income, diverse neighborhood. The class also involves joint discussions of topics such as race and "service", and an independently funded voyage by four French high-school students from the club to US universities.

References

Ahmed, Sara. 2004. "Affective Economies." *Social Text* 22: 121–39.

Althusser, Louis. 1971. *Lenin and Philosophy and Other Essays.* New York: Monthly Review Press.

Anderson, Benedict. 1991. *Imagined Communities.* London: Verso.

Appadurai, Arjun. 1986. "Introduction: Commodities and the Politics of Value." In Arjun Appardurai (ed.), *The Social Life of Things: Commodities in Cultural Perspective.* Cambridge: Cambridge University Press, pp. 3–63.

———. 1990. "Disjuncture and Difference in the Global Cultural Economy." *Public Culture* 2(2): 1–24.

Balibar, Etienne. 1988. "The Nation Form: History and Ideology." In Etienne Balibar and Immanuel Wallerstein (eds), *Race, Nation, Class: Ambiguous Identities.* London: Verso, pp. 86–106.

Barber, Benjamin R. 1994. "A Proposal for Mandatory Citizen Education and Community Service." *Michigan Journal of Community Service Learning* 1(1): 86–93.

Besnier, Niko. 1990. "Language and Affect." *Annual Review of Anthropology* 19: 419–451.

Borneman, John. 1992. *Belonging in the Two Berlins: Kin, State, Nation.* Cambridge: Cambridge University Press.

Briggs, Charles L. 1996. "The Politics of Discursive Authority in Research on the 'Invention of Tradition.'" *Cultural Anthropology* 11(4): 435–69.

Bringle, Robert G., and Julie A. Hatcher. 2011. "International Service Learning." In Robert G. Bringle, Julie A. Hatcher, and Steven G. Jones (eds), *International Service Learning: Conceptual Frameworks and Research.* Sterling, VA: Stylus Publishing, pp. 3–28.

Broad, Kenneth, and Ben Orlove. 2007. "Channeling Globality: The 1997–1998 El Nino Climate Event in Peru." *American Ethnologist* 34(2): 285–302.

Buda, Dorina Maria. 2015. *Affective Tourism: Dark Routes in Conflict.* New York: Routledge.

Butcher, Jim, and Peter Smith. 2010. "Making a Difference: Volunteer Tourism and Development." *Tourism Recreation Research*, 35(1): 27–36.

Callanan, Michelle, and Sarah Thomas. 2005. "Volunteer Tourism: Deconstructing Volunteer Activities within a Dynamic Environment." In Marina Novelli (ed.), *Niche Tourism: Contemporary Issues, Trends and Cases.* Oxford: Elsevier, pp. 183–200.

Chesler Mark A, Joseph A. Galura, Kristie A. Ford, and Jessica M. Charbeneau. 2006. "Peer Facilitators as Border Crossers in Community Service-Learning." *Teaching Sociology* 34(4): 341–56.

Clifford, James. 1988. *The Predicament of Culture: Twentieth-Century Ethnography, Literature, and Art.* Cambridge, MA: Harvard University Press.

Comaroff, John. 1987. "Of Totemism and Ethnicity: Consciousness, Practice and the Signs of Inequality." *Ethnos* 52(3–4): 301–23.

Conran, Mary. 2011. "They Really Love Me! Intimacy in Volunteer Tourism." *Annals of Tourism Research* 38(4): 1454–73.

Cororation, Claire, and Richard Handler. 2013. "Dreaming in Green: Service-Learning, Global Engagement and the Liberal Arts at a North American University." *Learning and Teaching* 6(2): 72–93.

Davis, Hannah. 1989. "American Magic in a Moroccan Town," *Middle East Report,* July-August 1989.

———. 1998. «'La où vont les femmes': notes sur les femmes, les cafés, et les Fast Food au Maroc,» in *Miroirs Maghrebins : Itinéraires de soi et paysages de rencontre,* S. Ossman, ed. Paris : CNRS.

———. 1993. «Dreams of Another Kind of Woman,» in *Who's Afraid of Femininity? Questions of Identity,* M. Brügmann et al, eds., Amsterdam, Atlanta; Rodopi.

———. 1990. «Des femmes marocains et 'La chaleur de St. Tropez',» in *Cahiers de l'Orient* (20), pp. 191–199.

Dewey, John. 1996/1908. *Theory of the Moral Life.* New York: Irvington.

d'Hauteserre, Anne-Marie. 2015. "Affect Theory and the Attractivity of Destinations." *Annals of Tourism Research* 55: 77–89.

Doerr, Neriko Musha. 2008. "Global Structures of Common Difference, Cultural Objectification, and Their Subversions: Cultural Politics in an Aotearoa/New Zealand School." *Identities: Global Studies in Culture and Power* 15(4): 413–36.

———. 2009. *Meaningful Inconsistencies: Bicultural Nationhood, Free Market, and Schooling in Aotearoa/New Zealand.* London: Berghahn Books.

———. 2012. "Study Abroad as 'Adventure': Construction of Imaginings of Social Space and Subjectivities." *Critical Discourse Studies* 9(3): 257–68.

———. 2013. "Do 'Global Citizens' Need the Parochial Cultural Other? Discourses of Study Abroad and Learning by Doing." *Compare* 43(2): 224–43.

———. 2014. "Desired Learning, Disavowed Learning: Scale-Making Practices and Subverting the Hierarchy of Study Abroad Experiences." *Geoforum* 54(July): 70–79.

———. 2015. "Volunteering as Othering: Understanding A Paradox of Social Distance, Obligation, and Reciprocity." *Partnerships: A Journal of Service-Learning and Civic Engagement* 6(2): 36–57.

Doerr, Neriko Musha, and Kiri Lee. 2012. "'Drop-Outs' or 'Heritage Learners'? Competing Mentalities of Governmentality and Invested Meanings at a Japanese Language School in the United States." *Discourse: Studies in the Cultural Politics of Education* 33(4): 561–73.

———. 2013. *Constructing the Heritage Language Learner: Knowledge, Power, and New Subjectivities.* Berlin: Mouton de Gruyter.

———. 2016, "Heritage Language Education without Inheriting Hegemonic Ideologies: Shifting Perspectives on 'Korea' in a Weekend Japanese Language School in the United States." *Diaspora, Indigenous, and Migrant Education* 10(2): 112–126.

Fendler, Lynn. 1998. "What Is It Impossible to Think? A Genealogy of the Educated Subject." In Thomas S. Popkewitz and Marie Brennan (eds), *Foucault's Challenge: Discourse, Knowledge, and Power in Education.* New York: Teachers College Press, pp. 39–63.

Frekko, Susan. 2009. "Social Class, Linguistic Normativity and the Authority of the 'Native Catalan Speaker' in Barcelona." In Neriko Musha Doerr (ed.), *The Native Speaker Concept: Ethnographic Investigations of "Native Speaker Effects".* Berlin: Mouton de Gruyter, pp. 161–84.

Friedman, Jonathan. 2003. "Globalizing Languages: Ideologies and Realities of the Contemporary Global System." *American Anthropologist* 105(4): 744–52.

Fusco, Coco. 1995. *English Is Broken Here: Notes on the Cultural Fusion in the Americas.* New York: New Press.

Gans, Herbert J. 1999. *Making Sense of America: Sociological Analyses and Essays.* Lanham: Rowman and Littlefield Publishers.

Geertz, Clifford. 1963. *The Interpretation of Cultures.* London: Fontana Press.

Good, Byron. 2004. "Rethinking 'Emotions' in Southeast Asia." *Ethnos* 69(4): 529–33.

Gray, Noella J., and Lisa M. Campbell. 2007. "A Decommodified Experience? Exploring Aesthetic, Economic and Ethical Values for Volunteer Ecotourism in Costa Rica." *Journal of Sustainable Tourism* 15(5): 463–82.

Grünzweig, Walter, and Nana Rinehart, eds. 2002. *Rockin' in Red Square: Critical Approaches to International Education in the Age of Cyberculture.* Piscataway, NJ: Transaction Publishers.

Handler, Richard. 1985. "On Having a Culture: Nationalism and the Preservation of Quebec's Patrimoine." In George W. Stocking, Jr. (ed.), *Objects and Others: Essays on Museums and Material Culture.* Madison: University of Wisconsin Press, pp. 192–217.

Hartman, Eric, Cody Morris Paris, and Brandon Blache-Cohen. 2014. "Fair Trade Learning: Ethical Standards for Community-Engaged International Volunteer Tourism." *Tourism & Hospitality Research* 14(1–2): 108–16.

Heath, Sue. 2007. "Widening the Gap: Pre-University Gap Years and the 'Economy of Experience'." *British Journal of Sociology of Education* 28(1): 89–103.

Heller, Monica. 2003. *Crosswords: Language, Education and Ethnicity in French Ontario.* Berlin: Mouton de Gruyter.

Henze, Rosemary, and Kathryn A. Davis. 1999. "Authenticity and Identity: Lessons from Indigenous Language Education." *Anthropology and Education Quarterly* 30(1): 3–21.

Herzfeld, Michael. 1997. *Cultural Intimacy: Social Poetics in the Nation-State.* New York: Routledge.

Hickel, Jason. 2013. "The 'Real Experience' Industry: Student Development Projects and the Depoliticisation of Poverty." *Learning and Teaching* 6(2): 11–32.

Hochschild, Arlie Russell. 2003. *The Managed Heart: Commercialization of Human Feelings.* Berkeley and Los Angeles: University of California Press. First publication 1983.

———. 2004. "Love and Gold." In Barbara Ehrenreich and Arlie Russell Hochschild (eds), *Global Woman: Nannies, Maids, and Sex Workers in the New Economy.* New York: Henry Holt, pp. 15–30.

Holland, Dorothy, Debra Skinner, William Lachicotte Jr., and Carole Cain. 1998. *Identity and Agency in Cultural Worlds.* Cambridge, MA: Harvard University Press.

Howes, David. 1996. "Introduction: Commodities and Cultural Borders." In David Howes (ed.), *Cross-Cultural Consumption: Global Markets Local Realities.* New York: Routledge, pp. 1–16.

Jacoby, Barbara. 2009. "Facing the Unsettled Questions about Service-Learning." In Jean R. Strait and Marybeth Lima (eds.), *The Future of Service-Learning: New Solutions for Sustaining and Improving Practice,* Sterling, VA: Stylus, pp. 99–105.

Johnson, Martha. 2009. "Post-reciprocity: In Defense of the 'Post' Perspective." *Frontiers* 28(Fall): 181–86.

Kahne, Joseph, and Joel Westheimer. 2003. "Teaching Democracy: What Schools Need to Do." *The Phi Delta Kappan* 85: 34–40, 57–61, 63–66.

Kearney, Michael. 2004. *Changing Fields of Anthropology: From Local to Global.* Lanham, MD: Rowman & Littlefield.

Koritz, Amy. 1997. "Dancing the Orient for England: Maud Allan's 'The Vision of Salome'." In Jane Desmond (ed.), *Meaning in Motion: New Cultural Studies of Dance.* Durham, NC: Duke University Press.

Krashen, Stephen. 1998. "Language Shyness and Heritage Language Development." In Stephen D. Krashen, Lucy Tse, and Jeff McQuillan (eds), *Heritage Language Development.* Culver City, CA: Language Education Associates, pp. 41–49.

Kristeva, Julia. 2011. *Hatred and Forgiveness,* trans. J. Herman. New York: Columbia University Press.

Lewin, Ross, and Greg Van Kirk. 2009. "It's Not About You: The UConn Social Entrepreneur Corps Global Commonwealth Study Abroad Model." In Ross Lewin (ed.), *The Handbook of Practice and Research in Study Abroad: Higher Education and the Quest for Global Citizenship.* New York: Routledge, pp. 543–64.

Leys, Ruth. 2011. "The Turn to Affect: A Critique." *Critical Inquiry* 37(Spring): 434–72.

Lee, Kiri, and Neriko Musha Doerr. 2015. "Heritage in the Making: Policies of Old Homeland, Discourse in New Homeland, and Heritage Language Education for 'Japanese' in the United States." In Horiguchi Sachiko, Imoto Yuki, and Greg Poole (eds.), *Foreign Language Education in Japan: Exploring Qualitative Approaches.* Rotterdam: Sense Publishers, pp. 19–34.

Lisle, Debbie. 2006. *Global Politics of Contemporary Travel Writing.* Cambridge: Cambridge University Press.

Manzo, Kate. 2008. "Imaging Humanitarianism: NGO Identity and the Iconography of Childhood." *Antipode* 40(4): 632–57.

Massumi, Brian. 1995. "The Autonomy of Affect." *Cultural Critique* 31, The Politics of Systems and Environments, Part II (Autumn) : 83–109.

———. 2010. "The Future Birth of the Affective Fact: The Political Ontology of Threat." In Melissa Gregg and Gregory J. Seigworth (eds), *The Affect Theory Reader.* Durham, NC: Duke University Press, pp. 52–70.

McEwan-Fujita, Emily. 2010. "Ideology, Affect, and Socialization in Language Shift and Revitalization: The Experiences of Adult Learning Gaelic in the Western Isles of Schotland." *Language in Society* 39: 27–64.

McGehee, Nancy Gard, and Katheleen Andereck. 2009. "Volunteer Tourism and the 'Volunteered': The Case of Tijuana, Mexico." *Journal of Sustainable Tourism* 17(1): 39–51.

McGehee, Nancy Gard. and Carla Almeida Santos. 2005. "Social Change, Discourse and Volunteer Tourism." *Annals of Tourism Research* 32(3): 760–779.

Mowforth, Martin, and Ian Munt. 2009. *Tourism and Sustainability: Development, Globalization and New Tourism in the Third World,* 3rd ed. London: Routledge.

Munt, Ian. 1994. "Eco-Tourism or Ego-Tourism?" *Race and Class* 36(1): 49–60.

Navaro-Yashin, Yael. 2006. "Affect in the Civil Service: A Study of a Modern State-System." *Postcolonial Studies* 9(3): 281–94.

Nenga, Sandi Kawecka. 2011. "Volunteering to Give up Privilege? How Affluent Youth Volunteers Respond to Class Privilege." *Journal of Contemporary Ethnography* 40(3): 263–89.

Nickols, Sharon Y., Nancy J. Rothenberg, Lioba Moshi, and Meredith Tetloff. 2013. "International Service-Learning: Students' Personal Challenges and Intercultural Competence." *Journal of Higher Education Outreach and Engagement,* 17(4): 97–124.

Oakdale, Suzanne. 2004. "The Culture-Conscious Brazilian Indian: Representing and Reworking Indianness in Kayabi Political Discourse." *American Ethnologist* 31(1): 60–75.

Pagano, Monica, and Laura Roselle. 2009. "Beyond Reflection Through an Academic Lens: Refraction and International Experiential Education." *Frontiers* 18(Fall): 217–29.

Pierce, Bonny Norton. 1995. "Social Identity, Investment, and Language Learning." *TESOL Quarterly* 29(1): 9–31.

Plater, William M. 2011. "The Context for International Service Learning: An Invisible Revolution Is Underway." In Robert G. Bringle, Julie A. Hatcher, and Steven G. Jones (eds), *International Service Learning: Conceptual Frameworks and Research.* Sterling, VA: Stylus Publishing, pp. 29–56.

Povinelli, Elizabeth A. 1998. "The State of Shame: Australian Multiculturalism and the Crisis of Indigenous Citizenship." *Critical Inquiry* 24(2): 575–610.

Pratt, Mary Louise. 1992/2008. *Imperial Eyes: Travel Writing and Transculturation.* London: Routledge.

Ramos-Zayas, Ana Y. 2009. "Urban Erotics and Racial Affect in a Neoliberal 'Racial Democracy': Brazilian and Puerto Rican Youth in Newark, New Jersey." *Identities: Global Studies in Culture and Power* 16(5): 513–547.

Rhoads, Robert A., and Julie Neururer. 1998. "Alternative Spring Break: Learning through Community Service." *NASPA Journal* 35(2): 100–118.

Richard, Analiese, and Daromir Rudnyckyj. 2009. "Economies of Affect." *Journal of the Royal Anthropological Institute* 15(2): 57–77.

Robertson, Roland. 1992. *Globalization: Social Theory and Global Culture.* London: Sage.

Rosaldo, Michelle Z. 1984. "Toward an Anthropology of Self and Feeling." In Richard A. Sweer and Robert A. LeVine (eds), *Culture Theory: Essays on Mind, Self, and Emotion.* Cambridge: Cambridge University Press, pp. 137–57.

Rose, Nikolas. 1996. "Governing 'Advanced' Liberal Democracies." In Andrew Barry, Thomas Osbourne, and Nikolas Rose (eds), *Foucault and Political*

Reason: Liberalism, Neo-Liberalism, and Rationalities of Government. Chicago: University of Chicago Press, pp. 37–64.

Said, Edward. 1978. *Orientalism.* New York: Vintage Books.

Saltmarsh, John. 1996. "Education for Critical Citizenship: John Dewey's Contribution to the Pedagogy of Community Service Learning." *Michigan Journal of Community Service Learning* 3(1): 13–21.

Savicki, Victor. 2008. *Developing Intercultural Competence and Transformation: Theory, Research, and Application in International Education.* Sterling, VA: Stylus Publishing.

Schieffelin, Bambi, and Elinor Ochs. eds. 1987. *Language Socialization across Cultures.* Cambridge: Cambridge University Press.

Seigworth, Gregory J., and Melissa Gregg. 2010. "An Inventory of Shimmers." In Melissa Gregg and Gregory J. Seigworth (eds), *The Affect Theory Reader.* Durham, NC: Duke University Press, pp. 1–25.

Sherraden, Margaret Sherrard, John Stringham, Simona Costanzo Sow, and Amanda Moore McBride. 2006. "The Forms and Structure of International Voluntary Service." *Voluntas* 17: 163–80.

Shouse, Eric. 2005. "Feeling, Emotion, Affect." *M/C Journal* 8(6): December 2005. Retrieved 22 November 2015 from http://journal.media-culture.org.au/0512/03-shouse.php.

Sin, Harng Luh. 2009. "Who Are We Responsible to? Locals' Tales of Volunteer Tourism." *Geoforum* 41: 983–92.

Sinervo, Aviva. 2011. "Connection and Disillusion: The Moral Economy of Volunteer Tourism in Cusco, Peru." *Childhoods Today* 5(2): 1–23.

Sommer, Doris. 1991. *Foundational Fictions: The National Romances of Latin America.* Berkeley: University of California Press.

Stewart, Kearsley A. 2013. "The Undergraduate Field-Research Experience in Global Health: Study Abroad, Service Learning, Professional Training or 'None of the Above'?" *Learning and Teaching* 6(2): 53–71.

Strait, Jean R. and Marybeth Lima. 2009. *The Future of Service-Learning: New Solutions for Sustaining and Improving Practice.* Sterling, VA: Stylus.

Taïeb, Hannah, Isabelle Jaffe, Rosie McDowell, Gregory Spear, and Senzeni Steingruber. 2015. "Civic Engagement in Multicultural Europe: American Students and Europeans in Dialogue." In Eliza J. Nash, Nevin C. Brown, and Lavinia Bracci (eds), *Intercultural Horizons Vol. III. Intercultural Competence: Key to the New Multicultural Societies of the Globalized World.* Newcastle upon Tyne: Cambridge Scholars Publishing, pp. 207–23.

Taussig. Michael. 1993. *Mimesis and Alterity: A Particular History of the Senses.* New York: Routledge.

Taylor, Joby. 2002. "Metaphors We Serve By: Investigating the Conceptual Metaphors Framing National and Community Service and Service-Learning." *Michigan Journal of Community Service Learning* 9(1): 45–57.

Tsing, Anna. 2000. "The Global Situation." *Cultural Anthropology* 15(3): 327–60.

——. 2005. *Friction: An Ethnography of Global Connection*. Princeton, NJ: Princeton University Press.

Warner, Sam L. Noʻeau. 1999. "Kuleana: The Right, Responsibility, and Authority of Indigenous Peoples to Speak and Make Decisions for Themselves in Language and Cultural Revitalization." *Anthropology and Education Quarterly* 30(1): 68–93.

Whiteside, Anne. 2009. "'We Don't Speak Maya, Spanish or English': Yucatec Maya-Speaking Transnationals in California and the Social Construction of Competence." In Neriko Musha Doerr (ed.), *The Native Speaker Concept: Ethnographic Investigations of "Native Speaker Effects."* Berlin: Mouton de Gruyter, pp. 215–32.

Wilk, Richard. 1995. "Learning to Be Local in Belize: Global Systems of Common Difference." In Daniel Miller (ed.), *Worlds Apart: Modernity through Prism of the Local*. London: Routledge, pp. 110–33.

Wimmer, Andreas, and Nina Glick Schiller. 2002. "Methodological Nationalism and Beyond: Nation-State Building, Migration and the Social Sciences." *Global Networks* 2(4): 301–34.

Wolf, Eric R. 1994. "Perilous Ideas: Race, Culture, People." *Current Anthropology* 35(1): 1–7.

Woolf, Michael. 2007. "Come and See the Poor People: The Pursuit of Exotica." *Frontiers: The Interdisciplinary Journal of Study Abroad* 13: 135–46.

——. 2010. "Another Mishegas: Global Citizenship." *Frontiers: The Interdisciplinary Journal of Study Abroad* 19: 47–60.

Yamasaki, Yuri. 2011. "Conflicted Attitudes toward Heritage: Heritage Language Learning of Returnee Adolescents from Japan at a Nikkei School in Lima, Peru." In Neriko Musha Doerr (ed.), *Heritage, Nationhood, and Language; Migrants with Japan Connection*. New York: Routledge, pp. 25–42.

Zemach-Bersin, Talya. 2009. "Selling the World: Study Abroad Marketing and the Privatization of Global Citizenship." In Ross Lewin (ed.), *The Handbook of Practice and Research in Study Abroad: Higher Education and the Quest for Global Citizenship*. New York: Routledge, pp. 282–302.

——. 2011. "Entitled to the World: The Rhetoric of U.S. Global Citizenship Education and Study Abroad." In Vanessa Andreotti (ed.), *Postcolonial Perspectives on Global Citizenship Education*. New York: Routledge, pp. 87–104.

CHAPTER 2

Study Abroad and Its Reasons
A Critical Overview of the Field

Hannah Davis Taïeb and Neriko Musha Doerr

What is "study abroad"? Why do people do it? To travel for one's studies, to travel to learn: these activities cover a vast terrain. Here, as in contemporary usage, by "study abroad" we refer to a certain kind of student travel. In this volume, we focus on short-term (one year or less) travel by US undergraduates, taking place during their university careers (credits achieved are validated afterwards by the home university), and framed by a study abroad program—some kind of institutional home base on foreign soil (ranging from a tiny one-person office providing some guidance through enrollment at a foreign university, to a massive, well-staffed study center complete with in-house courses, faculty, and computer center). We focus on the United States because "American initiatives have often been in the forefront of this form of educational outreach" (Hoffa 2002: 57).

Study abroad in this sense dates back to the 1920s. Over the last century, it has evolved in many ways, with an overall movement from longer stays to shorter stays, with a decreasing focus on language study (in the context of the rise of English as an International Language or EIL) and an increasing focus on the study of culture, and an increasing institutionalization of the process in line with an internationalization of the educational field as a whole (Hoffa 2007; Hoffa and DePaul 2010).

The goal of this chapter is to situate this book's approach to romance and affect by first looking at the spirit in which study abroad has emerged—the genealogies and legitimating discourses of this practice. This means looking not so much at the affect expressed by young travelers in the past (though this would be an excellent research project), but rather at that suggested by these genealogies and legitimating discourses that existed as the backdrop of their journeys. We will then consider approaches to affect in the literature on study abroad, and certain contemporary debates, in order to place this volume in that context.

Genealogies

Quests and Rites of Passage

How can we characterize the precursors of study abroad? Some see this kind of travel as foreshadowed by vision quests and journeys of initiation and discovery (Hoffa 2007). This genealogy sees the young person's movement through space as a kind of odyssey, a testing of the mettle of the youth against the wild transformations of the dangerous but exciting world outside. The study abroad student here is following in the footsteps of all those who traveled to learn, and, perhaps most importantly, to change themselves. This vision of study abroad brings forth a reflexive, critical perspective, a self-searching involving journaling and careful observation of difference, questioning of motives, on this "hero's journey" (Chisholm 2000).

In this volume, we will be discussing how affect frames the experience of students abroad in two types of destinations—"traditional" and "nontraditional." Each of them has its own genealogy—traditional ones in the European Grand Tour and the nontraditional in colonial travel—with specific historically precedented frameworks of emotions that shape experience and perceptions. Both types can be seen as rites of passage (Van Gennep 1960). American undergraduate life as a whole has also been analyzed in these terms (Moffatt 1991). Rites of passage, like the four-year undergraduate period and like the semester of study abroad, involve a break with previous identities, a liminal period characterized by *communitas* with a new, intense cohort, and a return with a (somewhat) new status. While Taïeb et al.'s chapter discusses this explicitly, other chapters in this volume also imply this aspect of study abroad.

The Genealogy of Study Abroad to "Traditional" Destinations: The Grand Tour

Historians of American study abroad trace its direct origins back to the Grand Tour of Europe: a voyage of cultivation, intellectual and artistic training for European (mainly British) gentlemen in various parts of Europe such as Italy, from the late Middle Ages and Renaissance onward. In the seventeenth and eighteenth centuries, newly founded American colleges and universities sought to develop their own forms of education, but it was still considered necessary for young people to cross the Atlantic and master what the Old World had to offer. By the nineteenth century, foreign study by American college students consisted either of "a Grand Tour ... a year of unmatriculated study at a German or British University, or a postgraduate degree" (Hoffa 2007: 30).

Not only men but some women from women-only institutions such as Smith College pursued language or scientific learning in foreign universities, and some more or less carefully chaperoned gentlewomen traveled independently in a female version of the Grand Tour. Both Henry James and Edith Wharton have portrayed the tensions of American "innocence, energy and ambition," faced with European "experience, sophistication, and history" (Hoffa 2007: 37). Europe offered "high culture" and perhaps also threatened a certain corruption (Lewin 2009; Woolf 2011).

It is in the context of this history of American exploration of Europe that we can place the current predominance of Europe as a destination for US college students, and this continent's definition as the traditional destination as opposed to nontraditional destinations. In this volume, chapters by Taïeb et al. and Doerr discuss this type of study abroad experience.

The Genealogy of Study Abroad to "Nontraditional" Destinations: Colonial Travel

The above genealogies focus on the opening of the travelling students to the learning experiences of the wide world, and do not bring in questions of power relations between the student and local people. In contrast, the genealogy of colonial travel positions itself in terms of stark, institutionalized relations of power. A clear manifestation of the social dynamics of such colonial travels can be seen in the eighteenth-century travel writing by Europeans who visited the "non-West," which Mary Louise Pratt (1992/2008) argues to have constructed "the imperial order" in which the Europeans developed a sense of ownership, entitlement, curiosity, adventure, and moral fervor about their "non-Western" colonies.

This legacy can be seen in the notion of the "colonial student." Anthony Ogden (2007) coined this phrase to refer to the US study abroad student in a nontraditional destination who wants to be abroad and to take full advantage of all the benefits studying abroad offers, but is not necessarily open to experiencing the less desirable side of being there. Ogden traces the outlook of the "colonial student" back to that of colonial families in the nineteenth and early twentieth centuries—wives joining husbands, for example, who travelled from Britain to India, with a certain amount of curiosity and desire for adventure, nonetheless limited to a very confined and isolated sphere. "Like children of the empire, colonial students have a sense of entitlement, as if the world is theirs for discovery, if not for the taking" (Ogden 2007: 38). Michael Woolf (2006: 136) suggests a different way that this power hierarchy is suggested, through a developed-developing binary: some students studying in nontraditional destinations are driven by "attraction to the exotic allied with a quasi-missionary zeal to engage with poverty."

In this volume, chapters by Rodriguez, Rink, Kumagai, as well as Jakubiak and Li touch on some of these themes, looking at what is sometimes termed as "West vs. non-West" power relations. Of course, students do not necessarily come from the former mother countries of the host society. Still, these chapters show how we can see traces of entitlement, curiosity, desire for adventure, and moral fervor in various combinations, common in West–non-West relations, shaping their study/volunteer abroad experiences and their perceptions and interpretations of their own affective responses.

These varying genealogies evoke various kinds of motivations for young travelers, which in turn suggest certain emotions: a drive for self-transformation, to move from youth to adulthood; the desire for wisdom and transformation through the voyage to a spiritual or intellectual center; the desire to free oneself from local concerns and ties; a drive for cultivation of the spirit and a mastery of the past; an equivocal passion, attraction to luxury and/or the exotic with their threat of possible corruption; and the feeling of entitlement, a desire to know and master the world, derived from and perhaps further perpetuating a sense of power.

Now we will look further at the history of study abroad and its legitimating discourses, which took shape in the evolving sociopolitical and economic context of the twentieth and twenty-first centuries, looking for tensions within these discourses and also for the ways in which these discourses suggest accompanying affect.

Twentieth- and Twenty-First-Century Study Abroad and Its Legitimating Discourses

The mobilizing discourses that surround and legitimate study abroad overlap and intertwine, and also exist in tension with each other. We have separated out the following discourses: (1) study abroad as a way to combat American isolation; (2) study abroad as a way to work towards understanding others, helping others, creating partnerships, and building world peace; (3) study abroad as a way to work towards American leadership in the world, through training young leaders, through spreading American ideologies and combating competing ways of thought, through understanding one's enemies; and, (4) various discourses linked by the notion of the global. In what follows, we trace the emergence of these discourses in the context of the development of the study abroad domain.

Starting in the early twentieth century, there was an explicit belief that launching study abroad projects would work against American isolation, would combat "the narrowness of students being confined to one national culture" (Ogden, Soneson, and Weting 2010: 179). Young Americans had to emerge from the "confinement" of their national culture, to understand "the rest of the world," its dangers and opportunities, in order to "qualify for leadership positions in government, business, finance, science, law" (Ogden, Soneson, and Weting 2010: 179). Even the nomenclature—the use of the term *abroad*—emphasizes this distinction between us at home and those elsewhere, abroad. The study abroad program would provide a starting point—an American contextualization of this learning, and possibly a safe haven from its dangers.

In these early years, university-run study abroad programs were the rule. The University of Delaware is usually credited with launching the first study abroad program in 1923; a young professor and World War I veteran, Raymond Kirkbridge, pushed this project through, motivated by the grim image of the destruction he had seen in French countryside, as well as his enjoyment of the French and his belief that travel could lead to cultural understanding (http://www.udel.edu/global/studyabroad/information/brief_history.html, accessed 7 June 2012). The University of Delaware's "Junior Year Abroad" model was successful and followed by other universities, starting notably with Smith College during the interwar years, as mentioned. An early institution for international education in the larger sense of the word (integrating foreign students, internationalizing the curriculum and also projects abroad) was the Institute for International Education (IIE), founded in 1919 (Hoffa 2007: 67).

World War I and its aftermath shaped this emergence of the study abroad field; World War II and its aftermath propelled its growth. Here we see the second of the discourses that we are examining: world peace and understanding, which would be furthered "if, during their formative years, young people were given opportunities to live and learn in each other's countries" (Hoffa 2002: 57). In the 1950s and 1960s, there was a renewed commitment to bridging the distances between the nations, and also to spreading American ideals. "If the values of American democracy had won the war, now was the time to help the rest of the world ... understand those values for the sake of continued peace" (Hoffa 2007: 108).

More and more universities set up one-year programs on the Junior Year Abroad model, and linguistic goals began to share the stage increasingly with geopolitical and cultural goals. This period also saw the birth of the first study abroad "providers." The Council on International Educational Exchange (CIEE), originally a travel organization, extended its activities: in the 1950s, American Friends Service Committee members developed and led orientation sessions that took place on board ship and that prepared students linguistically and culturally for their "ambassador" role. Also in the 1950s, American students boarded the SS *Volendam* to travel to Vienna in the first Institute of European Studies (IES) program; from this beginning evolved another major provider, IES Abroad.

As the Cold War intensified, the postwar sense of mission segued into a different form, with a rise in the importance of political propaganda and concerns of national security. Here we see the third discourse that we are examining: that of world leadership. Both the USSR and the United States saw the domains of culture and education as fruitful fields to build support: "brains" could be more important than muscle in winning the Cold War. At the first international conference of the CIEE in 1965, one participant said that "development of educational exchanges could mean much more than international disagreements in the politics of the Cold War; that brains in education are much more important than muscles in war" (Dick Miller, cited by Sideli 2010: 372).

The independence of colonies, another important new world context, led to the emergence of government funding for language and area-studies learning, international exchange, and service, deriving from a desire to increase American knowledge of what became known as "the Third World." The 1958 National Defense Education Act, designed to boost the United States' competitiveness in the race for space, also funded university research and study in foreign languages and area study in regions deemed important for national security. Though the act did not fund study abroad, it inspired generations of students to pursue studies in these areas (Keller and Frain 2010).

This led to a change in the destinations chosen for study abroad. Alongside the "traditional" destinations—France, Italy, Spain, Germany, and the United Kingdom—"nontraditional" locations, "developing" or "Third-World" countries, became popular (Ogden, Soneson, and Weting 2010). Study abroad providers and US universities focused on opening study centers and programs in Asia, the Middle East, Africa, and Latin America.

We can see here the tension and also intertwinement between the discourse of world peace and understanding, and the discourse of American world leadership. Goals such as service to the "developing world" and a less-politicized goal of understanding can be seen in the launching of the Fulbright program in 1946 and the establishment of the Peace Corps in 1961 (Keller and Frain 2010). For some, these were apolitical academic and cultural exchanges geared towards better understanding of, or service to, or connection with the newly postcolonial world; East-West exchanges could be a way for the two contenders in the Cold War to come to a better understanding of each other, not just as a way for each to push an ideology. For others, the young person abroad is an ambassador of his or her country, winning "hearts and minds" through "soft power," (Nye 2004: x, cited in Keller and Frain 2010: 20). The tension between these views sometimes flared up, becoming evident, for example, with the 1967 *Ramparts* magazine articles revealing CIA funding for the National Student Association including for their participation in the International Student Conference (Keller and Frain 2010).

With the Vietnam War and ensuing international developments in the 1970s and 1980s, including the oil crisis of 1973, the dichotomies of the Cold War era gave way to a more complex and less assured view of the US place in the world. For international education, these developments were linked to the rise of the discourse of globalization, which emphasized economic interdependence and the importance of US knowledge of the world. The development of non-English language competence and "intercultural competence" was emphasized. This global discourse was to rise to predominance in the decades that followed.

In this period, there was a decline in the numbers of American students studying languages at a university level. The Junior Year Abroad model, which had focused on linguistic and cultural immersion in Western European sites, was being questioned, over time giving way to a new model in which larger issues of national diplomacy played a more powerful role (Keller and Frain 2010). Individual educational institutions sent their own students abroad, but along with the aforementioned CIEE and IES developed other providers of study abroad, such as the Institute for the International Education of Students Abroad (Keller and Frain 2010: 23) and the Experiment in International Living (see http://www.exper imentinternational.org/20343.cfm for this institution founded in 1932 and involved in training of Peace Corps volunteers). This professionalization and extension of the field of study abroad continued throughout the late twentieth and early twenty-first centuries (Sideli 2010).

As study abroad numbers soared (doubling in the decade 1991–2001) in the period after the fall of the Berlin Wall in 1992, a new set of legitimating discourses emerged, all linked to the idea of the global: global competence, global skills, and global citizenship. These global discourses coexisted with the ongoing national security discourse, with fears shifting from Cold War enemies to the Middle East with the eruption of the Persian Gulf War in 1991.

With the rise in prevalence of the notion of globalization (Appadurai 1990; Friedman 2003; Tsing 2000), study abroad encouraged students to become "global citizens," able to function in a world described by Appadurai (1990) as now traversed by disjunctive flows of people, finance, media images, ideologies, and technologies. This meant a diversification in terms of the majors of students studying abroad, with a new push to include students in mathematics, science, business, medicine, economics and education; more and more young people of more kinds needed to develop global skills to confront this new world (Keller and Frain 2010; Currier, Lucas, and Saint Arnault 2009; Cushner 2009; Friedman 2007 cited in Keller and Frain 2010: 41; Wainwright et al. 2009). The notion of global interdependence was linked to economics, but also to other factors coming to light in the 1990s and in the twenty-first century. Not only are nations interdependent economically, but health challenges know no borders (as demonstrated by the SARS and AIDS epidemics) nor do ecological problems.

The 2001 attacks on the World Trade Center added a new dimension to this trend: the perception of a need not only for *national* security but *global* security. Study abroad numbers did not diminish after the attacks, but continued to rise (Keller and Frain 2010).

Critical discussions of the ideologies surrounding the globalizing processes have emerged in various disciplines since the 1990s. Political scientists, anthropologists, and others have discussed globalization in terms of its universalist aspect (Eriksen 2003), its ironic differentiation processes while standardizing the criteria of differentiation (Hannerz 1996; Wilk 1995), and types and contours of flows (Appadurai 1990; Tsing 2005). The discourse of globalization has been criticized as valorizing the global flow and thus masking unequal access to such global mobility and masking the different ways people relate to the areas in the world outside one's own (Friedman 2003; Glick Schiller and Salazar 2013; Tsing 2000). That is to say, the discourse of globalization masks the extremely different ways that people move through space and perceive the parts of the world they think of as away from home: as a playground for those in search of adventure (Doerr 2012; Zemach-Bersin 2009); as underdeveloped communities in need of saving (Sin 2009; Woolf 2007); as a place to find work unavailable in the domestic economy (Glick Schiller and Salazar 2013; Wimmer and Glick Schiller 2002) or to find possibilities for peace and escape oppression or war.

Study abroad literature, with some exceptions (Doerr 2012; 2014; Grünzweig and Rinehart 2002; Johnson 2009; Woolf 2007; 2010; Zemach-Bersin 2009, 2012), is largely uncritical of these ideological aspects of the discourse of globalization. Discourses of global competence and global citizenship continue to prevail in the field. There is a tendency to proceed as if globalization were evenly occurring everywhere and were unquestionably a progressive and desirable situation (Tsing 2000).

Since the 2000s, study abroad has been going through three types of transformations. First, study abroad, once seen as an attractive option for *some* students, is increasingly seen as something important for *all* students, reflecting the belief that study abroad is indispensable for everyone to survive and thrive in this globalizing world. There is a push for growth and diversity. This means more and more students abroad, more kinds of students traveling, more destinations including so-called nontraditional destinations, and more kinds of "real-world" experiences through internships, experiential learning, and service-related or volunteering projects. Efforts have been made to encourage *access* to study abroad for all underrepresented students, such as students of color; first-generation college students; gay, lesbian, bisexual, transsexual, and other gender-nonconforming students; low-income students; and students with disabilities. This also means reaching out to other groups that are minorities within study abroad, though not in society—male students, and those from the STEM disciplines of science, technology, engineering, and math. The 2005 report of the Commission on the Abraham Lincoln Study Abroad Fellowship Program, entitled *Global Competence and National Needs,* set a goal of one million Americans studying abroad by 2020 (Keller and Frain 2010).

The second is the changing profile of higher education as a whole, and of study abroad within it, with the emergence of the notion of "comprehensive internationalization." The idea is that in the current globalizing world, in which American dominance is no longer a given, higher education as a whole has to include intercultural and international elements (Keller and Frain 2010). The increasingly well-defined goals of intercultural competence and global citizenship are important for all students (Li, Olson, and Frieze 2013), so educational institutions as a whole need to develop international components. Study abroad is a key part of this comprehensive internationalization but is not the only part: this new approach involves "infusing an international or intercultural dimension into the teaching, learning, research and service functions of higher education" (Olson, Green and Hill, 2005, cited in Keller and Frain 2010: 42). Home universities should become global, it is argued, and more and more young people should go abroad, for one-year or one-semester stints, or, increasingly, for shorter trips, sometimes to multiple sites, or integrated in home university classes, accompanied by US professors. This has led to a decline in semester- and year-long study abroad programs and a rise in short-term, faculty-led, and customized programs, some of them multisite, and increasingly geared to needs arising from the structure of American universities (as opposed to the integration of American students into foreign universities).

The third transformation is the emergence of larger US-based international institutions conceived of as global academic networks. New York University has spearheaded this trend, with the establishment of NYU Dubai and NYU Shanghai. The NYU web site shows a map of the world, with large blue dots in New York, Dubai, and Shanghai, and smaller red and green dots sprinkled through the map showing the many "international academic centers" making up a "global network" managed from the NYU's "primary location" in New York (https://www .nyu.edu/global.html, accessed on 25 April 2015). These new institutions are degree granting, and therefore do not fall within the definition of study abroad that we are using here; but NYU's approach illustrates an important new reach of the field. CIEE has set up four Global Institutes in Berlin, Paris, Rome, and London, allowing students to "customize" their academic experience by mixing and matching destinations for six-week periods with program focuses not just on the traditional theme of "language, literature, and culture" but also options like business, health science, communications, and international relations (http://www.ciee .org/study-abroad/global-institutes/ accessed on 15 December 2015). These institutions dispense their own courses, largely in English; earlier study abroad programs of this sort described themselves as "island programs" (as opposed to direct enrollment or immersion in local universities); the term *global institute* has dropped the slightly apologetic tone. More CIEE global institutes are planned throughout the world, which points towards a model of short-term, English-language, multisite study abroad.

To some extent, these three trends—the generalization of study abroad as desirable for all students, "comprehensive internationalization," and the emergence of global academic networks—are not purely American phenomena. Universities throughout the world seek to internationalize their classrooms and launch their students on international travel, and professors and university administrators throughout the world work to handle the mixtures of kinds of people in the classroom and on campuses. Furthermore, universities throughout the world are competing to attract foreign students, including Americans. It remains to be seen where these trends will lead, and how the new trends in US-based international education will fit in with other non-US-based transformations in international education, in terms of new institutions and movements of students throughout the world.

In the notion of "the global" as used in US international education, there is an attempt to move away from the "here vs. abroad" model, and to develop partnerships with institutions throughout the world, create joint degrees, and so on. This attempt exists in tension with an ongoing tendency for decision-making and logistical structures to be more and more US-based, with this being often justified by the concern for student safety and security. There is a kind of paradoxical movement; on the one hand, everything must be global, and this means decentering, removing the United States from the center, seeking partnerships; on the other hand, everything must be safe, accessible to all, and uniformly structured according to US norms, and this tends to place the United States back in center stage.

We have identified above four interwoven discourses that justify and surround study abroad: combating American isolation, working towards world peace and understanding, working towards American leadership, and training for global citizenship or global engagement. As we have shown, within and among these discourses are overlapping elements and diverse tensions. The notion of learning about others as an end in itself coexists with the idea that one should "know thy enemy" for national security reasons; the political agenda of spreading American ideologies to gain soft power coexists with the idea of dialoguing with respected others for mutual understanding; the search for world peace coexists with the search for American leadership and the terms of peace may emerge from American conceptions; the global discourse involves a decentering of the United States but also the contradictory notion of a new US-centered range.

The emergence and convergence of these discourses illustrates how the history of study abroad in the United States is tightly intertwined with the changing political economy in the world and the place of the United States within it. For this volume, we ask: how are shifting world politics reflected in the mobilizing affect that pushes students to study abroad, and influencing students' experience and their reflections during and after it? If there are tensions running through these discourses—and tensions between these discourses and the discourses of transformation and quest discussed earlier—will we find conflicting emotions? Conflicting policies or conflicts about policies? Diverse ways of managing emotions? How would these manifest themselves in American students studying abroad in "traditional" destinations (Taïeb et al., Doerr), studying abroad (Rodriguez, Rink, Kumagai) or volunteering abroad (Jakbiak, Li) in "nontraditional" destinations? One could imagine finding emotions such as the desire to leap out of one's (isolated) American home environment to confront a thrilling and possibly dangerous Other; a (contradictory) hope to be protected and safe; a longing to help, to save, to repair the world, to calm violence; a desire to master it ... We can predict that the proposed interventions to manage student affect will perhaps suggest links to one or another of these contradictory goals.

Throughout this volume, as we look at affect in many contexts, we can think back on these possible forms that link to the context in which the field of study abroad, and volunteering abroad, emerged.

Affect in Study Abroad Literature

We have discussed many beliefs about why study abroad is valuable and good; yet clearly the basic underlying belief, shared by all its practitioners, is that study abroad leads to learning and self-transformation. This belief shapes how international education literature treats student affect. Emotion is considered in terms of learning: How can the positive and negative emotions linked to travel and to "immersion" in a new culture be transformed into learning experiences? How do emotional predispositions facilitate learning and development? What emotional or psychological strengths or weaknesses come into play?

Affect, Cultural Difference, and Learning

The emotional ups and downs elicited by travel and cultural difference were characterized by Lysgaard (1955) and later by Gullahorn and Gullahorn (1962) as taking the form of a *U*, consisting of (1) a "honeymoon" stage when excitement about new sights and sounds takes precedence, forming the top left part of the *U*; (2) a "culture shock" phase of disillusionment and hardship when faced with innumerable cultural differences, large and small, forming the bottom part of the *U*; and (3) an adjustment stage when sojourners' sense of well-being goes up, forming the top-right part of the *U*. This *U*-curve model was elaborated to include return to the home culture, which in turn would create "reverse culture shock" with an emotional downswing, leading to another rise to adjustment: the *W*-curve. In these models, emotions were conceived as predictable, regular, and as part of a developmental process progressing to a desired outcome (also, see Spitzberg and Changnon 2009; Ward, Bochner, and Furnham 2001).

These theories were conceived to help sojourners cope, and were designed for a wide variety of travelers, such as those on international business assignments. In the study abroad context, what is added to this is the use of discomfort and emotional experience as a tool for learning. The student needs the challenge of facing the emotional difficulty of culture shock: culture shock, "although inevitably stressful and disorienting, can have positive results if handled effectively, including a sense of well-being, heightened self-esteem, cognitive openness and flexibility, increased tolerance for ambiguity, and increased confidence in social interactions" (Cushner and Karim 2004: 292, summarizing Ting-Toomey). The commonly evoked notion of "leaving one's comfort zone" brings out this idea of a desired level of discomfort that will facilitate learning; Senninger (2000) suggests three "zones": the comfort zone, the learning zone with an optimal amount of discomfort, and the panic zone where stress is overwhelming and learning no longer occurs.

These approaches were developed out of learner-centered education and experiential learning, influenced by a model of intercultural
training developed by Edward T. Hall, who is usually credited as the
founder of the field of intercultural communication (Hall 1959; also, see
Rogers, Hart and Miike, 2002; M. J. Bennett 2010 for a history of intercultural learning in study abroad). The learner-centered intercultural
paradigm is based on the idea that students need to find a "balance of
challenge and support" (Sanford's "Challenge and Support" hypothesis
cited in Vande Berg 2009: 12) where discomfort or stress is optimal and
can lead to learning, rather than being overwhelming. As Victor Savicki
explains in an article on student affect, "disequilibrium need not lead
to dissatisfaction" (Bennett 2008: 17, cited in Savicki 2012: 223–24), but
may on the contrary be "dynamic" (Joyce 1984), allowing students to
"unfreeze their typical mindsets in order to encourage alternate points
of view"; facing and overcoming "acculturative stress," "overcoming
hardship and culture clashes," which will lead students to transformation (Savicki 2013: 131).

A key aspect of this process is "immersion" in the host country. Immersion in the other culture is valued not only for its providing holistic
experience involving learning at "intellectual, psychological, and emotional" (Laubscher 1994: xiv) levels, but also for providing a sense of
disorientation, which allows students opportunities to learn to navigate
unknown environments, to develop an "ability to fail," and to confront
their personal limitations. This confrontation is to lead to self-confidence,
increased adaptability, persistence, risk taking, empathy to others, and
the ability to interpret ideas from different perspectives (Brockington and
Wiedenhoeft 2009; Currier, Lucas, and Arnault 2009; Cushner 2009).

However, mere immersion is not enough: "[a]s John Dewey (1897)
began to discuss more than a century ago … experience is simply not
the same thing as learning" and educators have to intervene (Vande
Berg, Paige, and Lou 2012: 20). In particular, study abroad researchers
and practitioners suggest, in order to make emotional difficulty useful,
to transform it into learning, students need to be guided by international educators. Intercultural and reflexive practices should start before student travel, with orientation sessions on the home campus;
on-site intercultural educators should perform appropriate interventions throughout the student's stay; and more guided reflection should
take place after return. The pain of homesickness, which if left to fester
could lead to "a failed educational experience" such as a student returning home precipitously, can be reevaluated with guidance, leading to

connection with the host culture rather than alienation (Whalen 1996). An embarrassing, troubling, or confusing intercultural event can be reframed using the technique of the "critical incident," a reflexive process that brings out not only the "awareness that culture is an issue in everyday practice" but also elicits empathy, the ability to "see the world through another's eyes" (McAllister et al. 2006). The technique of the "critical incident" involves focusing with students on moments that were of particular difficulty for them, eliciting their emotional content and encouraging a "still" and "mindful" observation of those emotions rather than a mindless, unquestioning reaction. This is to lead to transformation of the emotion and, in the long run, to an ongoing practice of observing emotions and body sensations in order to practice "intercultural competence" and "work across difference" throughout life, not just in terms of nationally defined cultural differences and not just in the context of study abroad (Tara Harvey, personal communication, see also for example Schaetti, Ramsey, and Watanabe 2008).

The notion of "intervention" is an important example of how complex and troubling emotions aroused during study abroad are interpreted and managed. International education practice emerged in the context of intercultural communication theory, which linked cultural difference with different kinds of "ethnophysiological states" and advocated increasing awareness of the body and emotion as a way to come to "cultural self-awareness" and work against ethnocentrism (Bennett and Castiglioni 2004: 262). Rather than controlling one's feelings, one can be "willing to feel the widest possible range of emotions and value the maintenance of a 'witness' of consciousness"; this allows for connection and self-enrichment due to the experience of "different ethnophysiological states" (Bennett and Castiglioni 2004: 261–62). A similar kind of self-awareness was also advocated by intercultural communication specialist Stella Ting-Toomey discussing the context of conflict, and calling for "mindful management of emotional frustrations and conflict interaction struggles due primarily to cultural or ethnic group membership differences" (Ting-Toomey 2009: 101). Schaetti, Ramsey, and Watanabe spoke of "moments made vibrant by the differences in values, worldviews and behaviors of those involved" and the importance of choosing "self-reflection, self-development and creative collaboration" (Schaetti et al. 2008: xxvii). Interculturalists emphasize that the process is not only cognitive but is embodied and related to feeling: for example, Milton Bennett and Ida Castiglioni suggest the use of empathy and breathing work "to reestablish connection with our bodies so that we are (a) aware of our embodied experience in our own culture and (b) able to shift body boundaries into the forms that elicit the feeling of the other culture" (Bennett and Castiglioni 2004: 260).

The idea that culture and cultural difference had embodied and affective dimensions thus was built upon by international educators who were looking for practical pedagogical strategies. The fostering of intercultural competence in students was defined as a holistic educational process, which means that it should engage "multiple learning domains," including affective as well as perceptive, behavioral, and cognitive (Vande Berg, Quinn, and Menyhart 2012: 401). Affect is managed as educators help students bring new learning domains into awareness; practicing mindfulness, students "attend to the affective dimension; in describing sensations of emotional or physical discomfort, they may over time come to understand that such feelings or sensations often signal the presence of a challenging cultural difference" (Vande Berg, Quinn, and Menyhart 2012: 401). Emotions in themselves are paradoxically blocks but also opportunities (Schaetti et al. 2008), and it is through "taking leadership" of emotion and internal experience, through a kind of neutrality and self-witnessing, that one can find the insight at the source of the emotion, and in so doing, transform it (Schaetti et al. 2008: 49–51). Even the disorienting moments arising from navigating a new environment without a guide can be eased through techniques of mindful attention focusing "on increasing students' sense of awareness and presence, and ability to regulate emotion and creatively channel stress" (http://www.huffingtonpost.com/kyle-david-anderson/mindful-study-abroad-1_b_8277872.html, accessed 11 January 2016). These recent pedagogical strategies are implemented in forms like CIEE's Seminar on Living and Learning (Vande Berg, Quinn, and Menyhart 2012) and Intercultural Communication and Leadership Course (http://www.ciee.org/study-abroad/advisors/intercultural-studies/, accessed 10 January 2016), the American University Center of Provence Experiment in Holistic Intervention (Engle and Engle 2012), and the University of Minnesota's Global Identity online course (Paige, Harvey, and McCleary 2012).

Psychological Predispositions and "Intensity Factors"

Along with looking at the transformative potential of affect when handled with attention, study abroad literature focuses on predicting and handling stress through examining "intensity factors" and through considering students' emotional predispositions and emotional strengths and weaknesses in adjusting to the host society. "Intensity factors" include large cultural distance between home and host culture, ethnocentrism in the sojourners or in the society visited, degree of cultural immersion, degree of isolation from home country peers, lack of language skills, lack of prior intercultural experience, exaggerated expectations of the site or of oneself, physical difference as compared to people in the host country or invisibility of certain aspects of the sojourners identity, changes in status (e.g., unexpected rise or fall in perceived status), and loss of power and control (Paige 1993, adapted by Bruce LaBrack http://www2.pacific.edu/sis/culture/pub/1.5.4_-_intensity_factors .htm). All these factors are used as predictors of stress.

Student dispositions as well may be favorable or unfavorable to cultural learning and a "successful" study abroad experience; they may be suggestive of needs for more profound interventions on the part of educators; they may predispose students to study abroad. Li, Olson, and Frieze identify students with "achievement motivation," "neophilia" (the love for the new), "migrant personalities" and the desire to help others as those with "personality factors" motivating them to study abroad (Li, Olson, and Frieze 2013). Janice Arbanel shows the power of "emotional resilience" and "tolerance for ambiguity" to facilitate movement through cultural space (Arbanel 2009). V. Savicki shows that students have "a range of psychological readiness to face study abroad uncertainties" and points out that as more and more students go abroad, and as mental health difficulties increase overall on US campuses, educators must learn how to deal with more students who are psychologically vulnerable with "lower mood states" (Savicki 2013: 143).

For Students' Well-Being

This brings us to another context in which study abroad literature deals with student affect: in terms of promoting student well-being and taking care of student mental health issues. International educators must be able to handle students' emotional states, not just to facilitate learning, but also to provide a supportive backdrop to the potentially stressful experience the student is having away from home, away from support networks and well-known ways of being, faced with a society with different norms about intimate subjects such as gender and sexuality, different mental health systems, and different attitudes about health, psychic troubles, and disability.

Operating between US and non-US educational systems, study abroad professionals must be aware of the legal frameworks and expectations of the American college student, including the Americans with Disabilities Act (ADA), the Family Educational Rights and Privacy Act of 1974 (FERPA), and Health Insurance Portability and Accountability Act (HIPAA), and must live up to the study abroad programs promise of ensuring safety and well-being (Robinson, Teague, and Walker 2014; Lindeman 2006). This mental-health and well-being-related literature does not have the same orientation as the literature related to student learning; the concern here is the successful treatment of problems and the providing of appropriate support.

These goals may sometimes be in tension with the goal of maximizing student learning through dynamic discomfort and immersion, so the international educator has a delicate balancing act to maintain. While promoting well-being and supporting students with mental health issues may be primary activities for professionals, and are often discussed in professional conferences and training workshops, the professional literature (for example, the online journal *Frontiers*) nonetheless is dominated by questions concerning student learning abroad, with questions of affect framed in the terms we discussed above.

Contemporary Debates and Concepts

Contemporary study abroad literature has included debates about how to define and assess desired outcomes of the process and how to intervene to achieve those outcomes; among the desired outcomes are the key concepts of "global citizenship" and "intercultural competence," which we also discuss in detail. After examining these debates and concepts, we ask how our focus on the management of affect can shed new light on them.

Assessment and Intervention

The *assessment* of the results of study abroad involves the definition of the correct goals of the process and the identification of the means to evaluate whether they have been achieved. This means defining and measuring language learning and, perhaps more centrally at this time, skills and attitudes defined as "intercultural competence," "intercultural sensitivity," "global competence," "global awareness," "cross-cultural adaptability," etc. (M.J. Bennett 1986, 1993, 2012; Carlson et al. 1990; Cohen et al. 2005; M/Deardorff 2008, 2009; Hammer 2005a, 2005b, 2009, 2010; Hammer et al. 2003; Jackson 2005; Laubscher 1994; Paige et al. 2002, 2003; Savicki 2008; Spitzberg and Changnon 2009; Stuart 2012; Vande Berg, Paige, and Lou 2012).

The question of *intervention* involves the identification and propagation of key practices that will maximize these desired results. As more and more Americans travelled, and as heftier structures came into being to welcome them, life became easier for the students, but access to cultural alterity (and, with the rise of English as an international language, even linguistic alterity) became more elusive. The benefits of salutary discomfort receded. At the same time, along with the push for more and more people studying abroad came the need to prove that desired assessable results were being obtained and to identify key practices to achieve those results. Suggested are practices like program design and length for immersion (Engle and Engle 2003, 2004); journal writing and encouraging student reflection (Chen 2002; Chisholm 2000); ethnographic projects (Jurasek, Lamson, and O'Maley 1996; Ogden 2006; Roberts et al. 2001) and service-learning during the stay (Bringle and Hatcher 2011; Lewin and Kirk 2009; Plater et al. 2009) and other kinds of engagement (Bennett 2008); "cultural mentoring" (Paige and Goode 2009); predeparture and postreturn programming (Bathurst and La Brack 2012; Zemach-Bersin 2009), and other kinds of interventions in student experience as described in detail above (Chen 2002, Vande Berg 2009; Vande Berg, Connor-Linton, and Paige 2009; Vande Berg, Quinn, and Menyhart 2012).

How do these new approaches, focusing on assessment and intervention in student experience, relate to the question of affect that concerns us in this volume? How do our questions intersect with these themes?

First of all, in the study abroad field there is a new and increased skepticism about student self-reporting of positive results. The exhilaration that students feel about studying abroad, their perception that they have been transformed, is no longer taken at face value. In theory at least, all student emotions—include the desire for the exotic or authentic, the passion of wanderlust—are subjects of reflection and possible reevaluation. In this volume, several chapters (Rodriguez, Rink, Taïeb et al.) discuss ways study abroad professionals have launched discussion with their students about these kinds of questions.

The focus on assessment and intervention involves an increased attention to the emotional make-up and learning predispositions of students, conceived of as measurable and identifiable—e.g., through Kolb's Learning Style Inventory (Passarelli and Kolb 2012; Vande Berg, Quinn, and Menyhart 2012)—and to their psychic and intercultural development, conceived as in stages and also measurable (e.g., through the intercultural development inventory, Hammer 2009, 2012), and subject to intervention.

Lastly, the question of the purposeful management of student affect is of particular importance in the field at this time (though it is not talked about in these terms). What is this achieving? What reassessments of emotion, what changes occur? What notions of difference, of boundaries, are suggested by the practice itself? What kinds of subjectivities are being fostered? We approach these questions throughout this volume; below, we begin by examining tensions within two of the concepts that are goals of these interventions: "global citizenship" and "intercultural competence."

Tensions in Key Concepts: "Global Citizenship" and "Intercultural Competence"

In line with the tensions in the field of study abroad as a whole, there are tensions around different interpretations of concepts like "global citizenship" and "intercultural competence." The discourse of the global citizen can be inflected in many ways; one dominant form of the discourse is global connectedness under American leadership (see for example the analysis of President Obama's 2016 state of the union address, Blackburn-Dwyer 2016). Other inflections focus more on the promotion of social justice on a global scale (usually without problematizing First-World notions of "justice"), resistance to neoliberalist forms of globalization, or the abolition of poverty (sometimes focusing on poverty-stricken Third World nations and ignoring poverty in the First World, others creating less of a dichotomy and considering poverty also in the First World) (https://amizade.org/globalcitizenresourceguide/; Larsen 2014).

In international education, the discourse of the global citizen has been commercialized and is very important in marketing, as has been pointed out in recent critical studies (Zemach-Berstin 2008, 2009; Streitwieser and Light 2009). The idea may work to inspire students, but on site student affect often demonstrates confusion or conflict about its achievement, with many students returning to a sense of American particularity and/or privilege, which can be self-congratulatory or critical (Zemach-Berstin 2008; Rink, Li, Jakubiak in this volume). In arguing against an uncritical deployment of the "global citizen" discourse, Zemach-Berstin writes: "American students who travel abroad cannot be expected to transcend historical, political, social, and global systems of power in order to become cross-culturally immersed 'global citizens.' We can, however, be asked to become internationally conscious and self-aware American citizens who are responsible for thinking about those critical issues" (2008: 34).

The notion of "intercultural competence" also contains internal tensions and varying inflections. It is closely related to affect and to a certain desired way of managing affect. There may be some disagreement about what the term in fact means (Deardorff 2004) but most advocates agree that it is a practical ability to navigate in different contexts, to empathize with others, to shift out of one's engrained worldview. It involves recognition of difference wherever it takes place (not just in national cultural terms) and advocates detachment from negative emotional reactions in order to adapt smoothly and serenely, thus facilitating amicable relations and cooperation in diverse groups. It suggests a desired subject who is flexible, aware of but untrammeled by deep physical, psychic "cultural" selves.

One of the tensions linked to the idea of "intercultural competence" concerns the perception of "culture": viewing it as hybrid versus viewing it as reified distinct "cultures" that, in the study abroad context, are usually based on national boundaries. (When the concept is used in other contexts, the "cultures" may be conceived as ethnic, religious, etc.) On the one hand, the field of intercultural communication includes an evocation of multiple and hybrid identities (Ting-Toomey and Dorjee 2014), an acknowledgement of the danger of reifying cultural difference (Bennett and Castiglioni 2004: 250). At the same time, there is also a reassertion of the importance of seeing "culture" as the key category with which to understand difference. Thus the discourse of "intercultural competence" works to create subjects who can handle difference in a flexible way, but paradoxically, and somewhat in spite of itself, also reasserts continually the boundaries of "cultures."

Another tension within the discourse of intercultural competence concerns the goals of the cooperation that this competence will achieve. The intercultural online series "Cultural Detective" offers their services in this way: "Cultural Detective … will help you increase performance, productivity and profits through loyalty, teamwork, and return on investment. It is a tool you and your employees can use immediately to achieve the bottom-line results that intercultural competence can bring to your organization" (https://blog.culturaldetective.com/2013/10/21/ building-leadership-resilience-with-cultural-detective/). On the other hand, the well-known interculturalist Darla Deardorff expresses goals in a very different way on the web site of NAFSA: "As we continually search for ways to get along together as human beings sharing this one planet, the need to transcend boundaries, to bridge and transform our differences, to be in relationship with one another, to join in the oneness of our humanity while accepting our differences—these needs will continue to drive us as we seek to overcome differences that may divide us" (https://www.nafsa.org/_/File/_/theory_connections_intercul tural_competence.pdf).

Our work in this volume suggests that the contradictions in understandings of such terms will be expressed in tensions not only in study abroad and volunteer abroad policies but also in the affect experienced by students and volunteers and by educators ourselves. Furthermore, some study abroad practices may be interpreted as more geared towards one or another of the different inflections enumerated above: American leadership vs. social justice inflections of the "global citizen," critical vs. self-congratulatory reaffirmations of American particularity in the context of that discourse, hybrid vs. reifying inflections of "intercultural competence," increasing productivity vs. transcending boundaries interpretations of "intercultural competence." We can begin to look closely at particular kinds of interventions, asking what implicit or explicit goals are aimed at and achieved.

Our goal is to use the theoretical approach from the field of the anthropology of affect to shed light on tensions within concepts and practices within international education concerning the management of affect. Therefore, we look at key concepts within this field with a certain distance, from the perspective of another discipline that views them as "folk categories," constructs with different inflections. How can we use the "management of affect" approach to analyze and better understand interventions in the context of study abroad that are often based on the assumptions behind these key concepts? What are educators aiming to achieve and are actually achieving through such interventions? How do the underlying tensions described above emerge in the practice of the management of emotion? These are some of the questions asked throughout this volume and discussed further in the concluding chapter.

New Ways of Looking at Affect in Study Abroad

Study abroad literature currently mainly concerns itself with students' learning and adaptation to the study abroad destination, or how to support students through difficulties, or the transformation of emotion to achieve goals like "intercultural competence." Here, in this volume, we seek to provide a different perspective on affect, looking at the breadth of student emotion and its multiple possible implications; how such varied affect came to be mobilized and managed in what wider sociocultural and political and economic environments; and what kind of subjects study abroad students became through experiencing such affect. Through these analyses, in our concluding chapter, we suggest implications for practical and pedagogical questions concerning interventions and other managing of student experience in the study abroad context.

We situate our book in the context of emerging debates in the field, which examine study abroad from a multidisciplinary and critical perspective, addressing issues like power relations between study abroad students and host societies, consumerism, and exoticism (Beaudin 2013; Bolen 2001; Doerr 2013, 2014, 2015; Feinberg 2002; Ogden 2007; Woolf 2006, 2010; Zemach-Bersin 2009), or proposing nuanced, nondichotomized ways of looking at difference, cosmopolitanism, diversity, and self and other (Gristwood and Woolf 2013; Johnson 2009; Rodriguez 2006; Taïeb et al. 2016). A critical approach to study abroad as a whole has been advocated by Walter Grünzweig and Nana Rinehart (2002: 241) and more recently by Doug Reilly and Stefan Senders (2009), who launch a plea that the domain not be reduced to catch-phrases about internationalization and global competency. It is in the context of these multidisciplinary and critical debates that this book finds its place.

Our volume brings out the exhilaration and (sometimes frustrated) longing involved in border crossing that is defined as inherently enlightening, in a world with some borders confusingly blurred and others (class, perhaps, being one of them) increasingly hard to cross. We illustrate fascination that can become damaging, desire that leads to alienation, disinterest that may generate deep love, yearning that may or may not contradict with learning, moral fervor that turns into guilt, a longing for otherness that turns in unexpected ways, and more. Through these discussions, we hope to launch some questions about the link between affect and contemporary discourses of difference, of culture, and of the global—questions of interest to those within and outside of the sphere of study abroad.

Dr. **Hannah Davis Taïeb** is an international educator, teacher, and writer who was the director of CIEE's Contemporary French Studies Program in Paris from 2003 to 2015. She has a Ph.D. in anthropology from New York University; her thesis, concerning unmarried women and changing conceptions of the self, was based on fieldwork in a middle-sized city in Morocco. After working with a research team in Lyon, Hannah settled permanently in France in 1992, where she first was the coeditor of a multilingual, multidisciplinary review, *Mediterraneans,* then taught intercultural and interpersonal communication at the American University of Paris, before entering the field of study abroad in the year 2000. While at CIEE, she ran Franco-American seminars, joint classes and study trips on subjects like disability, religious diversity and secularism, anti-Semitism and Islamophobia, chaplaincy and religion in prison, and special education. Independently, Hannah continues to teach about popular culture and *métissage,* religious diversity, and disability, co-teaches a Franco-American intercultural communication class, and runs volunteer and exchange activities with a Paris youth club.

Neriko Musha Doerr received a Ph.D. in cultural anthropology from Cornell University. Her research interests include politics of difference, language and power, and study abroad and alternative break experiences. Her publications include *Meaningful Inconsistencies: Bicultural Nationhood, Free Market, and Schooling in Aotearoa/New Zealand* (Berghahn Books), *The Native Speaker Concept* (Mouton de Gruyter), and *Constructing the Heritage Language Learner* (Mouton de Gruyter), and articles in *Anthropological Forum, Compare, Critical Discourse Studies, Discourse: Studies in the Cultural Politics of Education, Identities: Global Studies in Culture and Power,* and *Journal of Cultural Geography.* She currently teaches at Ramapo College in New Jersey, US.

References

Appadurai, Arjun. 1990. "Disjuncture and Difference in the Global Cultural Economy." *Public Culture* 2: 1–24.

Arbanel, Janice. 2009. "Moving with Emotional Resilience Between and Within Cultures." *Intercultural Education* 20, supplement 1.

Bathurst, Laura, and Bruce La Brack. 2012. "Shifting the Locus of Intercultural Learning: Intervening Prior To and After Student Experiences Abroad." In Michael Vande Berg, R. Michael Paige, and Kris Hemming Lou (eds), *Student Learning Abroad: What Our Students Are Learning, What They're Not, and What We Can Do About It.* Sterling, VA: Stylus, pp. 261–83.

Beaudin, Giselda. 2013. "Selling Study Abroad: Cosmopolitanism as Commodity." In Anthony Gristwood and Michael Woolf (eds), *Cosmopolitanism and Diversity Concepts, Practices and Policies in Education Abroad.* Capa International Education Occasional Publications No. 2. Boston: CAPA International Education, pp. 59–62.

Bennett, Janet M. 2008. "On Becoming a Global Soul: A Path to Engagement During Study Abroad." In V. Savicki (ed.), *Developing Intercultural Competence and Transformation: Theory, Research, and Application.* Sterling, VA: Stylus, pp. 13–31.

Bennett, Milton J. 1986. "A developmental approach to training for intercultural sensitivity." *International Journal of Intercultural Relations* 10(2): 179–196.

———. 1993. "Towards Ethnorelativism: A Developmental Model of Intercultural Sensitivity." In R. Michael. Paige (ed.), *Education for the Intercultural Experience* 1. Yarmouth, ME: Intercultural Press, pp. 21–71.

———. 2010. "A Short Conceptual History of Intercultural Learning in Study Abroad." In William W. Hoffa and Stephen DePaul (eds), *A History of U.S. Study Abroad: 1965–Present.* A Special Publication of *Frontiers: The Interdisciplinary Journal of Study Abroad,* pp. 419–50.

———. 2012. "Paradigmatic Assumptions and a Developmental Approach to Intercultural Learning." In Michael Vande Berg, R. Michael Paige, and Kris Hemming Lou (eds), *Student Learning Abroad: What Our Students Are Learning, What They're Not, and What We Can Do About It.* Sterling, VA: Stylus, pp. 90–114.

Bennett, Milton J., and Ida Castiglioni. 2004. "Embodied Ethnocentrism and the Feeling of Culture: A Key to Training for Intercultural Competence." In Daniel Landis, Janet Bennett, and Milton Bennett (eds), *Handbook of Intercultural Training.* Thousand Oaks, CA: Sage, pp. 249–65.

Blackburn-Dwyer, Brandon. 2016. "12 Times President Obama Called on Global Citizens in the State of the Union." Retrieved 13 January 2016 from https://www.globalcitizen.org/en/content/12-times-president-obama-called-on-global-citizens/.

Bolen, Mel. 2001. "Consumerism and U.S. Study Abroad." *Journal of Studies in International Education* 5: 182–99.

Bringle, Robert G. and Julie A Hatcher. 2011. "International Service Learning." In Robert G. Bringle, Julie A. Hatcher, and Steven G. Jones (eds.), *International Service Learning: Conceptual Frameworks and Research.* Sterling (VA): Stylus Publishing, pp. 3–28.

Brockington, Joseph L., and Margaret D. Wiedenhoeft. 2009. "The Liberal Arts and Global Citizenship: Fostering Intercultural Engagement Through Integrative Experiences and Structured Reflection." In Ross Lewin (ed.), *The Handbook of Practice and Research in Study Abroad: Higher Education and the Quest for Global Citizenship.* New York: Routledge, pp. 117–32.

Carlson, Jerry S., Barbara B. Burn, John Useem, and David Yachimowicz. 1990.

Study Abroad: The Experience of American Undergraduates. New York: Greenwood Press.

Chen, Leeann. 2002. "Writing to Host Nationals as Cross-Cultural Collaborative Learning in Study Abroad." *Frontiers: The Interdisciplinary Journal of Study Abroad* 8(4): 143–164.

Chisholm, Linda. 2000. *Charting a Hero's Journey.* New York: International Partnership for Service Learning.

Cohen, Andrew D., R. Michael Paige, Rachel L. Shively, Holly A. Emert, and Joseph G. Hoff. 2005. *Maximizing Study Abroad Through Language and Culture Strategies: Research on Students, Study Abroad Program Professionals, and Language Instructors.* Minneapolis: Center for Advanced Research on Language Acquisition, University of Minnesota.

Currier, Connie, James Lucas, and Denise Saint Arnault. 2009. "Study Abroad and Nursing: From Cultural to Global Competence." In Ross Lewin (ed.), *The Handbook of Practice and Research in Study Abroad: Higher Education and the Quest for Global Citizenship.* New York: Routledge, pp. 133–50.

Cushner, Kenneth. 2009. "The Role of Study Abroad In Preparing Globally Responsible Teachers." In Ross Lewin (ed.), *The Handbook of Practice and Research in Study Abroad: Higher Education and the Quest for Global Citizenship.* New York: Routledge, pp. 151–69.

Cushner, Kenneth, and Ata U. Karim. 2004. "Study Abroad at the University Level." In Daniel Landis. Janet M. Bennett, and Milton J, Bennett (eds), *Handbook of Intercultural Training,* 3rd ed. Thousand Oaks, CA: Sage, pp. 289–308.

Deardorff, Darla K. 2004. "Internationalization: In Search of Intercultural Competence." *International Educator* 13(2).

———. 2008. "Intercultural Competence: A Definition, Model, and Implications for Study Abroad." In Victor Savicki (ed.), *Developing Intercultural Competence and Transformation: Theory, Research, and Application in International Education.* Sterling, VA: Stylus, pp. 32–52.

———, ed. 2009. *The Sage Handbook of Intercultural Competence.* Thousand Oaks, CA: Sage.

Dewey, John. 1897. "My Pedagogic Creed." *School Journal* 54: 77–80.

Doerr, Neriko Musha. 2012. "Study Abroad as 'Adventure': Construction of Imaginings of Social Space and Subjectivities." *Critical Discourse Studies* 9: 257–68.

———. 2013. "Do 'Global Citizens' Need the Parochial Cultural Other? Discourses of Study Abroad and Learning by Doing." *Compare* 43: 224–43.

———. 2014. "Desired Learning, Disavowed Learning: Scale-Making Practices and Subverting the Hierarchy of Study Abroad Experiences." *Geoforum* 54: 70–79.

———. 2015. "Learner Subjects in Study Abroad: Discourse of Immersion, Hierarchy of Experience, and Their Subversion through Situated Learning." *Discourse: Studies in the Cultural Politics of Education* 36: 369–82.

Engle, Lilli, and John Engle. 2012. "Beyond Immersion: The American University Center of Provence Experiment in Holistic Intervention." In Michael Vande Berg, R. Michael Paige, and Kris Hemming Lou (eds), *Student Learning Abroad: What Our Students Are Learning, What They're Not, and What We Can Do About It.* Sterling, VA: Stylus, pp. 115–36.

Eriksen, Thomas Hylland. 2003. "Introduction." In *Globalization: Studies in Anthropology.* London: Pluto Press, pp. 1–17.

Feinberg, Ben. 2002. "What Students Don't Learn Abroad." *Chronicle of Higher Education: The Chronicle Review* (3 May).

Friedman, Jonathan. 2003. "Globalizing Languages: Ideologies and Realities of the Contemporary Global System." *American Anthropologist* 105: 744–52.

Friedman, Thomas L. 2007. *The World Is Flat: A Brief History of the Twenty-First Century.* New York: Farrar, Straus and Giroux.

Glick Schiller, Nina, and Noel B. Salazar. 2013. "Regimes of Mobility Across the Globe." *Journal of Ethnic and Migration Studies* 39: 183–200.

Gristwood, Anthony, and Michael Woolf. 2013. *Cosmopolitanism and Diversity Concepts, Practices and Policies In Education Abroad.* CAPA International Education Occasional Publications No. 2. Boston: CAPA International Education.

Grünzweig, Walter, and Nana Rinehart, eds. 2002. *Rockin' in Red Square: Critical Approaches to International Education in the Age of Cyberculture.* Piscataway, NJ: Transaction.

Gullahorn, John T., and Jeanne E. Gullahorn. 1962. "An Extension of the U-Curve Hypothesis." *Journal of Social Issues* 3: 33–47.

Hall, Edward T. 1959. *The Silent Language.* New York: Doubleday.

Hammer, Mitchell R. 2005a. *Assessment of the Impact of the AFS Study Abroad Experience Executive Summary.* New York: AFS, International.

———. 2005b. The Intercultural Conflict Style Inventory: A Conceptual Framework and Measure of Intercultural Conflict Approaches. *International Journal of Intercultural Research* 29: 675–95.

———. 2009. "The Intercultural Development Inventory: An Approach to Assessing and Building Intercultural Competence." In M. Michael Moodian (ed.), *Contemporary Leadership and Intercultural Competence.* Thousand Oaks, CA: Sage, pp. 203–18.

———. 2010. *The Intercultural Development Inventory Manual.* Berlin, MD: IDI.

———. 2012. "The Intercultural Development Inventory: A New Frontier in Assessment and Development of Intercultural Competence." In Michael Vande Berg, R. Michael Paige, and Kris Hemming Lou (eds), *Student Learning Abroad: What Our Students Are Learning, What They're Not, and What We Can Do About It.* Sterling, VA: Stylus, pp. 115–36.

Hammer, Mitchell R., M.J. Bennett, and R. Wiseman. 2003. "Measuring Intercultural Sensitivity: The Intercultural Development Inventory." *International Journal of Intercultural Relations* 27: 421–43.

Hannerz, Ulf. 1996. *Transnational Connections: Culture, People, Places.* London: Routledge.

Hoffa, William W. 2002. "Learning about the Future World: International Education and the Demise of the Nation State." In Walter Grunzweig and Nana Rinehart (eds), *Rockin' in Red Square: Critical Approaches to International Education in the Age of Cyberculture.* Piscataway, N.J.: Transaction.

——. 2007. *A History of US Study Abroad: Beginnings to 1965.* A Special Publication of *Frontiers: The Interdisciplinary Journal of Study Abroad* and the Forum on Education Abroad.

Hoffa, William W., and Stephen C. DePaul, eds. 2010. *A History of U.S. Study Abroad: 1965–Present.* A Special Publication of *Frontiers: The Interdisciplinary Journal of Study Abroad.*

Jackson, Jane. 2005. "Assessing Intercultural Learning through Introspective Accounts." *Frontiers: The Interdisciplinary Journal of Study Abroad* 11: 165–86. Retrieved 7 January 2011 from http://www.frontiersjournal.com/Frontiers backissaug05.htm.

Johnson, Martha. 2009. "Post-reciprocity: In Defense of the 'Post' Perspective." *Frontiers: The Interdisciplinary Journal of Study Abroad* 28 (Fall): 181–86.

Joyce, B.R. 1984. "Dynamic Disequilibrium: The Intelligence of Growth." *Theory into Practice* 23: 26–34.

Jurasek, Richard. Howard Lamson, and Patricia O'Maley. 1996. "Ethnographic Learning While Studying Abroad." *Frontiers: The Interdisciplinary Journal of Study Abroad* 2.

Keller, John M., and Maritheresa Frain. 2010. "The Impact of Geo-Political Events, Globalization, and National Policies on Study Abroad Programming and Participation." In William W. Hoffa and Stephen DePaul (eds), *A History of U.S. Study Abroad: 1965–Present.* A Special Publication of *Frontiers: The Interdisciplinary Journal of Study Abroad,* pp. 15–53.

Larsen, Marianne A. 2014. "Critical Global Citizenship and International Service Learning." *Journal of Global Citizenship & Equity Education* 4(1).

Laubscher, Michael R. 1994. *Encounters with Difference: Student Perceptions of the Role of Out-of-Class Experiences in Education Abroad.* Westport, CO: Greenwood Press.

Lewin, Ross. 2009. "Introduction: The Quest for Global Citizenship through Study Abroad." In Ross Lewin (ed.), *The Handbook of Practice and Research in Study Abroad: Higher Education and the Quest for Global Citizenship.* New York: Routledge, pp. xiii–xxii.

Lewin, Ross, and Greg Van Kirk. 2009. "It's Not About You: The UConn Social Entrepreneur Corps Global Commonwealth Study Abroad Model." In Ross Lewin (ed.), *The Handbook of Practice and Research in Study Abroad: Higher Education and the Quest for Global Citizenship.* New York: Routledge, pp. 543–64.

Li, Manyu, Josephine E. Olson, and I. H. Frieze. 2013. "Student's Study Abroad

Plans: The Influence of Motivational and Personality Factors." *Frontiers* 23(Fall): 73–89.

Lindeman, Barbara A. (ed.). 2006. "Best Practices in Addressing Mental Health Issues Affecting Education Abroad Participants." NAFSA Association of International Educators. Retrieved from http://www.valdosta.edu/academics/international-programs/dept/documents/study-abroad/mental-health.pdf.

Lysgaard, Sverre. 1955. "Adjustment in a Foreign Society: Norwegian Fulbright Grantees Visiting the United States." *International Social Science Bulletin* 7: 45–51.

McAllister, Lindy, Gail Whiteford, Bob Hill, Noel Thomas, and Maureen Fitzgerald. 2006. "Reflection in Intercultural Learning: Examining the International Experience through a Critical Incident Approach." *Reflective Practice* 7: 367–81.

Moffatt, Michael. 1991. *Coming of Age in New Jersey: College and American Culture*. New Brunswick, NJ: Rutgers University Press.

Nye, Joseph. 2004. *Soft Power: The Means to Success in World Politics*. New York: Public Affairs.

Ogden, Anthony C. 2006. "Ethnographic Inquiry: Reframing the Learning Core of Education Abroad." *Frontiers: The Interdisciplinary Journal of Study Abroad* 13: 87–112.

———. 2007. "The View from the Veranda: Understanding Today's Colonial Student." *Frontiers* 15(Winter): 35–55.

Ogden, Anthony C., Heidi M. Soneson, and Paige Weting. 2010. "The Diversification of Geographic Locations." In William W. Hoffa and Stephen DePaul (eds), *A History of U.S. Study Abroad: 1965–Present*. A Special Publication of *Frontiers: The Interdisciplinary Journal of Study Abroad,* pp. 161–98.

Olson, Christa L., Madeline F. Green, and Barbara A. Hill. 2005. *Building a Strategic Framework for Comprehensive Internationalization*. Washington DC: American Council on Education.

Paige, R. Michael. 1993. "On the Nature of Intercultural Experiences and Intercultural Education." In R. Michael Paige (ed.), *Education for the Intercultural Experience*. Yarmouth, ME: Intercultural Press, pp. 1–19.

Paige, R. Michael, A.D. Cohen, B. Kappler, J.C. Chi, and J.P. Lassegard. 2002. *Maximizing Study Abroad: A Student's Guide to Strategies for Language and Culture Learning and Use*. Minneapolis: Center for Advanced Research on Language Acquisition, University of Minnesota.

Paige, R. Michael, and M.L. Goode. 2009. "Cultural Mentoring: International Education Professionals and the Development of Intercultural Competence." In Darla K. Deardorff (ed.), *The SAGE Handbook of Intercultural Competence*. Thousand Oaks, CA: Sage, pp. 333–49.

Paige, R. Michael, Tara A. Harvey, and Kate S. McCleary. 2012. "The Maximizing Study Abroad Project: Toward a Pedagogy for Culture and Language Learning." In Michael Vande Berg, R. Michael Paige, and Kris Hemming Lou (eds),

Student Learning Abroad: What Our Students Are Learning, What They're Not, and What We Can Do About It. Sterling, VA: Stylus, pp. 308–34.

Paige, R. Michael, M. Jacobs-Cassuto, Y.A. Yershova, and J. DeJaeghere. 2003. "Assessing Intercultural Sensitivity: An Empirical Analysis of the Hammer and Bennett Intercultural Development Inventory." *International Journal of Intercultural Relations* 27: 467–86.

Passarelli, Angela M., and David A. Kolb. 2012. "Using Experiential Learning Theory to Promote Student Learning and Development in Programs of Education Abroad." In Michael Vande Berg, R. Michael Paige, and Kris Hemming Lou (eds), *Student Learning Abroad: What Our Students Are Learning, What They're Not, and What We Can Do About It.* Sterling, VA: Stylus, pp. 137–61.

Plater, William M., Steven G. Jones, Robert G. Bringle, and Patti H. Clayton. 2009. "Educating Globally Competent Citizens through International Service Learning." In Ross Lewin (ed.), *The Handbook of Practice and Research in Study Abroad: Higher Education and the Quest for Global Citizenship.* New York: Routledge, pp. 485–505.

Pratt, Mary Louise. 2008 (1992). *Imperial Eyes: Travel Writing and Transculturation.* London: Routledge.

Reilly, Doug, and Stefan Senders. 2009. "Becoming the Change We Want to See: Critical Study Abroad for a Tumultuous World." *Frontiers: The Interdisciplinary Journal of Study Abroad* 18(Fall): 241–67.

Roberts, Celia., Michael Byram, Ano Barro, Shirley Jordan, and Brian Street. 2001. *Language Learners as Ethnographers.* Clevedon: Multilingual Matters.

Robinson, Jamie, Thomas Teague, and Jeanne Walker. 2004. "Supporting Students' Emotional Well-Being While Studying Abroad." Retrieved from http://www.ceastudyabroad.com/educators/global-education/academic-team/publications.html.

Rodriguez, Karen. 2006. "Re-Reading Student Texts: Intertxtuality and Constructions of Self and Other in the Contact Zone." *Frontiers: The Interdisciplinary Journal of Study Abroad* 8(Fall): 43–64.

Rogers, Everett M., William B. Hart, and Yoshitaka Miike. 2002. "Edward T. Hall and The History of Intercultural Communication: The United States and Japan." *Keio Communication Review* 24: 1–5.

Savicki, Victor. 2008. *Developing Intercultural Competence and Transformation: Theory, Research, and Application in International Education.* Sterling, VA: Stylus.

——. 2012. "The Psychology of Student Learning Abroad." In Michael Vande Berg, R. Michael Paige, and Kris Hemming Lou (eds), *Student Learning Abroad: What Our Students Are Learning, What They're Not, and What We Can Do About It.* Sterling, VA: Stylus, pp. 215–38.

——. 2013. "The Effects of Affect on Study Abroad Students." *Frontiers* 22 (Winter/Spring): 131–47.

Schaetti, Barbara F., Sheila J. Ramsey, and Gordon C. Watanabe. 2008. *Making a*

World of Difference: Personal Leadership: A Methodology of Two Principles and Six Practices. Seattle: Flying Kite.

Senninger, Tom. 2000. Abenteuer Leiten—in Abenteuern Lernen [Facilitating adventures—Learning in adventures]. Münster: Ökotopia Verlag.

Sideli, Kathleen. 2010. "The Professionalization of the Field of Study Abroad." In William W. Hoffa and Stephen DePaul (eds), *A History of U.S. Study Abroad: 1965–Present.* A Special Publication of *Frontiers: The Interdisciplinary Journal of Study Abroad,* pp. 369–418.

Sin, Harng Luh. 2009. "Who Are We Responsible to? Locals' Tales of Volunteer Tourism." *Geoforum* 41: 983–92.

Spitzberg, Brian H., and Gabrielle Changnon. 2009. "Conceptualizing Intercultural Competence." In Darla K. Deardorff (ed.), *The Sage Handbook of Intercultural Competence.* Thousand Oaks, CA: Sage, pp. 2–52.

Streitwieser, Bernhard, and Greg Light. 2009. "Study Abroad and the Easy Promise of Global Citizenship: Student Conceptions of a Contested Notion." Comparative and International Education Society (CIES) Annual Meeting, Charleston, SC. March. Retrieved from http://www.northwestern.edu/searle/research/docs/study-abroad-global-citizenship.pdf.

Stuart, Douglas K. 2012. "Taking Stage Development Theory Seriously." In Michael Vande Berg, R. Michael Paige, and Kris Hemming Lou (eds), *Student Learning Abroad: What Our Students Are Learning, What They're Not, and What We Can Do About It.* Sterling, VA: Stylus, pp. 61–89.

Taïeb, Hannah, Isabelle Jaffe, Rosie McDowell, Gregory Spear, and Senzeni Steingruber. 2016. "Civic Engagement in Multicultural Europe." In Eliza J. Nash, Nevin C. Brown, and Lavinia Bracci (eds), *Intercultural Horizons Vol. III—Intercultural Competence: Key to the New Multicultural Societies of the Globalized World.* Newcastle upon Tyne: Cambridge Scholars Press, pp. 207–23.

Ting-Toomey, Stella. 2009. "Intercultural Conflict Competence as a Facet of Intercultural Competence Development." In Darla K. Deardorff (ed.), *The Sage Handbook of Intercultural Competence.* Thousand Oaks, CA: Sage, pp. 100–120.

Ting-Toomey, Stella, and T. Dorjee. 2014. "Language, Identity, and Culture: Multiple Identity-Based Perspectives." In T. Holtgraves (ed.), *The Oxford Handbook of Language and Social Psychology.* New York: Oxford University Press, pp. 27–45.

Tsing, Anna. 2000. "The Global Situation." *Cultural Anthropology* 15: 327–60.

———. 2005. *Friction: An Ethnography of Global Connection.* Princeton, NJ: Princeton University Press.

Vande Berg, Michael. 2009. "Intervening in Student Learning Abroad: A Research-Based Inquiry." *Intercultural Education* 20(4): 15–27.

Vande Berg, Michael, J. Connor-Linton, and R.M. Paige. 2009. "The Georgetown Consortium Project: Interventions for Student Learning Abroad." *Frontiers: The Interdisciplinary Journal of Study Abroad* 18: 1–75.

Vande Berg, Michael, R. Michael Paige, and Kris Hemming Lou. 2012. *Student Learning Abroad: What Our Students Are Learning, What They're Not, and What We Can Do About It.* Sterling, VA: Stylus.

Vande Berg, Michael, Meghan Quinn, and Catherine Menyhart. 2012. "An Experiment in Developmental Teaching and Learning: The Council on International Educational Exchange's Seminar on Living and Learning Abroad." In Michael Vande Berg, R. Michael Paige, and Kris Hemming Lou (eds), *Student Learning Abroad: What Our Students Are Learning, What They're Not, and What We Can Do About It.* Sterling, VA: Stylus, pp. 383–410.

Van Gennep, Arnold. 1960. *The Rites of Passage.* London: Routledge & Kegan Paul.

Wainwright, Philip, Preetha Ram, Daniel Teodorescu, and Dana Tottenham. 2009. "Going Global in the Sciences: A Case Study at Emory University." In Ross Lewin (ed.), *The Handbook of Practice and Research in Study Abroad: Higher Education and the Quest for Global Citizenship.* New York: Routledge, pp. 381–98.

Ward, Colleen, Stephen Bochner, and Adrian Furnham. 2001. *The Psychology of Culture Shock,* 2nd ed. New York: Routledge.

Whalen, Brian J. 1996. "Learning Outside the Home Culture: An Anatomy and Ecology of Memory." *Frontiers* 2 (Fall 1996): 1–16.

Wilk, Richard. 1995. "Learning to be Local in Belize: Global Systems of Common Difference." In Daniel Miller (ed.), *Worlds Apart: Modernity through the Prism of the Local.* London: Routledge, pp. 110–33.

Wimmer, Andreas, and Nina Glick Schiller. 2002. "Methodological Nationalism and Beyond: Nation-State Building, Migration and the Social Sciences." *Global Networks* 2: 301–34.

Woolf, Michael. 2006. "Come and See the Poor People: The Pursuit of Exotica." *Frontiers: The Interdisciplinary Journal of Study Abroad* 13: 135–46.

———. 2007. "Impossible Things Before Breakfast: Myths in Education Abroad." *Journal of Studies in International Education* 11(3/4): 496–509.

———. 2010. "Another Mishegas: Global Citizenship." *Frontiers: The Interdisciplinary Journal of Study Abroad* 19: 47–60.

———. 2011. "The Baggage They Carry: Study Abroad and the Construction of 'Europe' in the American Mind." *Frontiers: The Interdisciplinary Journal of Study Abroad* 21(Fall): 289–309.

Zemach-Bersin, Talya. 2008. "American Students Abroad Can't Be Global Citizens." *Chronicle of Higher Education* (7 March).

———. 2009. "Selling the World: Study Abroad Marketing and the Privatization of Global Citizenship." In Ross Lewin (ed.), *The Handbook of Practice and Research in Study Abroad: Higher Education and the Quest for Global Citizenship.* New York: Routledge, pp. 282–302.

———. 2012. "Entitled to the World: The Rhetoric of U.S. Global Citizenship Education & Study Abroad." In Vanessa Andreotti and Lynn Maria T.M. de Souza (eds), *Postcolonial Perspectives on Global Citizenship Education.* New York: Routledge, pp. 87–104.

PART II

Studying with(out) Passion

Study Abroad and Affect

CHAPTER 3

Passionate Displacements into Other Tongues and Towns

A Psychoanalytic Perspective on Shifting into a Second Language

Karen Rodríguez

Students studying abroad in Mexico often make reference to their passion for the Spanish language in their application essays and onsite comments. When they say it, of course, they refer to their positive feelings about Spanish: feelings that are wrapped up in their fascination with Mexican culture, their desire to learn, and their increasing ability to communicate with locals, among other things. These passionate feelings can also be connected to media images that paint Latin America as exotic and romantic, as a place of hot nights spent salsa dancing, and as a home to exuberant artists and Latin Lovers, although students are increasingly aware of these stereotyped constructions and perhaps less seduced by them than in the past. What students tend to ignore (in the sense of being ignorant of), however, are the other, darker aspects of their passion for language and place. Experiences shifting into other languages can provoke powerful desires to possess or control the language, as well as feelings of hatred of oneself or others. These aspects of passion are not usually articulated by language learners or facilitators despite the fact that both parties experience them. So while we think about *physical* travel as dramatic and change producing, this essay will argue that it is the *psychic* shift catalyzed by passion, with its moments of love, hatred, longing, and anxiety, that lead the speaker to intense transformation and that could catalyze deep social change as well.

Tracing the passionate relationship with other languages through its happier and darker aspects, I focus on the psychic displacements at hand in the study abroad context. I work from a theoretical perspective. While I use several examples and quotes from former study abroad students in Mexico to pull the theory down to place, this is not an ethnographic study of the student experience and is not based on student data.[1] After a psychoanalytic discussion of language learning and passion, I draw rough parallels between the infant's original move into language and students' later shifts into other languages as they occur in the sojourn abroad. I then examine key moments of desire, love, and aggression embedded in the second learning process. For these passions to be sublimated they must be channeled into and attached to the social order, and because this happens in a specific place, I tentatively sketch out the site-specific nature of this passionate encounter with another language. I argue that it is precisely the connection with the local specificity of place that permits and begins to illustrate what psychoanalyst/cultural theorist Julia Kristeva[2] refers to as this "metabolism" of passion (2011: 89). I conclude by suggesting that this specificity has ramifications for social change post-sojourn, referring to the case of Mexico and the United States in particular, which demands more research.

Psychoanalysis, Passions, and Language

It is well known that moving into a new language is an experience fraught with emotion. The language learner frequently experiences anxiety, embarrassment, fear, desire, and confusion, both in the classroom and, even more so, when immersed into the social world in which it is spoken (Arnold 1999; Valdes 1986; Guiora 1972) While these are common experiences that few learners, if any, can avoid, the process varies by personality. Whether the learner is introverted or extroverted, has a high or low level of self-esteem, tolerates ambiguity well or poorly, and is willing to take intellectual risks has been shown to affect the process (Onwuegbuzie, Bailey, and Daley 1999; Horwitz, Horwitz, and Cope 1991; see Gregerson and Horwitz 2002 on perfectionism). Outside of the classroom, Pavlenko has studied the struggle to express one's emotional self in a second language and examined bilinguals' perceptions of their different personalities in the different languages they speak (2002, 2006) often studying language memoirs and narratives (1998). However, most of these emotion-oriented studies emphasize the self and one's "sense of self" more than the *relationship* with the language per se, or the relationship with other speakers in the new language. They also tend to focus on the debilitating aspect of anxiety rather than the facilitating effect these anxieties that are coiled around the desire to speak might have (Piniel 2006: 40). Passion tends not to get discussed, and the individual dynamic is only weakly linked to the social transformation, if at all.

Psychoanalysis, on the other hand, which studies the emergence of the subject, emphasizes the passionate psychic aspects of the language learning process. Several definitions and clarifications are useful here to explain more about how the speaking subject takes up a position with respect to others in language: First, as Kristeva emphasizes, the subject is always in flux, constituted through his or her changing relationships with the exterior environment and with others. Indeed, the subject is nothing *but* a set of flows and relationships. Psychoanalyst Robert Langan explains: "We exist in the midst of an exchange—indeed, as an exchange—of outside and inside" from conception, to birth, to a lifetime of relationships with exterior sources of physical and affective elements vital to our continued existence (2000: 70). Our borders are thus *"en procès,"* as Kristeva observes, which means both "in process" and "on trial," threatened and refortified by these contacts with the exterior world, which leaves us in a state of permanent becoming. As she notes wryly, "Even the soundest among us knows, just the same, that a firm identity remains a fiction" (1989: 257), and this instability applies not only to the self, of course, but also to the other with whom we speak.

This fluctuating subjectivity is both constituted and challenged through language. Complicating this, however, is the fact that language also finds *itself* in a permanent state of displacement. Languages are never fixed and finished; rather, languages are in constant negotiation with new words, new accents, and new ways of expressing things, something students realize easily if they move between one Spanish-speaking country to another, for example, or if one returns to a speech community many years later to find that the slang has changed. No language (maternal or second) is ever fully learned in this sense, and this makes the goal of "acquisition" even more tenuous. Language will always resist possession and consolidation, and it is never fully or exclusively "ours," much as people speak colloquially of "my French" or "his German."

These changing relationships with and within languages occur in specific sites, even as the places in which one speaks the other language may vary over time, from one country to another, from a personal to

a professional context, or the inverse. These contexts are equally vola-
tile, and geographers have—much like psychoanalysts—recast places,
cities, and other sites previously understood as fixed and immutable
in equally *en procès* terms. Cities are now conceptualized as unstable
conglomerations comprising shifting flows and intersections, energies
and movements (Thrift 2009; Grosz 1998). Because study abroaders
learn language in specific places in particular moments, it is therefore
worth noting the fluctuating nature of the "containing" sites or cities
as well. Thus we find ourselves with a shifting subject in an ephemeral
place attempting to speak a fluid language to equally changing others.
There are few moments of stability; everything is movement!

Passions are what will connect the subject with the social world of
language and others, however tenuously, and in this case, push the subject toward bilingualism. How are passions defined? For Kristeva, "emotions belong to all vertebrates; they express their fluctuating relationship
to their body and environment and have the function of adaptation and
communication ... The passions, on the other hand, are specific to man,
because they suppose the existence of reflexive consciousness" (2011:
80). She means that while both humans and animals experience wordless
attachments and aggressions, in the human subject there exists the possibility of expression in symbolic language. This reflexivity is "the constit-
uent factor of the passions" (80) and makes passion a human experience.

As we know, passions are highly unstable. They must be expressed
or extinguished, and this movement to a more stable ground occurs
via sublimation. In Freud's understanding, sublimation refers to the
transformation of the aim or the object of the drives undertaken in
negotiation with social order: the Freudian subject necessarily curbs
his desire in order to adjust and fit into society. Kristeva (1973) adds that
sublimation involves not only a modification of oneself in order to fit
into the social, but also marks a highly creative moment that shakes up
the social order, demanding *its* modification as well. She understands
sublimation as the process through which the *semiotic* (energies,
drives and instincts, and the rhythms, intonations, and even musical-
ity of the preverbal infant) is discharged and accommodated (or not)
into the *symbolic* (the social order). Moving into language thus necessarily involves a tension between agency and compliance, conformity
and transgression, rule following and creativity. And because not everything in the semiotic "fits" into the social order, there is always an
excess: words always fall just a little short when we try to express our
deepest passions (for example, to speak of love or grief, no matter how

poetically, never fully captures what we feel). This excess is what keeps language alive, flexible, and creative, which means that to speak is to question is to change—both the subject and society are reopened, put on trial, in these interactions. And just as the subject must find a way to accommodate her passion in words (or other communicable symbols), society too must grapple with the otherness and accommodate new voices (accepting, for example, immigrants, or the Spanish language) or decide to reject them.

This not-quite-translatable passion links the semiotic to the symbolic, attaching or inscribing the subject into the social (the symbolic world of the other), because it permits representation. For the infant, this effects a move into his native language. In the second language (L2), the speaker once again lives out a passionate desire to communicate, to connect with the other in the other's words and symbolic world. And once again, only through this sublimation of passion into L2 (the transfer and transformation of the drives, the sensory, the preverbal) will the subject attain full expressive capacity and truly take up a position in the new language. Only then will the subject "transmute the feverish sensation of a passion into the pleasure of mouth and ear" (Kristeva 2004: 9). These displacements of passion are, therefore, essential not only to the infant but also to the later learner attempting to move into a second language. The next section will trace some of these shifts.

The Shift to L2: Passionate Separations and Joinings

Increasingly, the relationship with L2 begins at home (in the family, community, classroom, or virtually); but (at least for study abroad students) the deeper elements of this relationship are still most frequently catalyzed through physical displacement into a speaking community abroad. This separation from home and the maternal tongue mimics the original separation from the mother. While the student ostensibly wants very much to move into L2, the shift is neither easy nor consistently smooth and forward moving. It is, therefore, useful to trace some of the parallels between these two distinct moments without purporting to equate them: in psychoanalysis, repetitions can be understood more as variations on a theme than exact replicas of prior experiences.

In the semiotic realm of our mother tongue, we speak the language of the mother country and experience an easy unity with others. Our needs are effortlessly expressed and met; we are at one with our linguistic-cultural container.[3] Metaphorically, in national and global terms we could posit that to maintain this unity with the mother country and language (to speak only English) is to deny the existence of others, to enter into an incestuous and psychotic state with the maternal (tongue) in which subjectivity—a self that relates to others in the multilingual world via language—is not achieved. For the monolingual speaker, everything exterior to one's native tongue remains unsymbolized; or in other words, the speaking others who are not encountered through language may not be recognized as subjects. At the most unbecoming and ignorant level, we see this when nonnative speakers in the United States are treated as truly alien, i.e. not seen as complex adults, not recognized as fully human (much as the early priests in the Conquest did not view Latin America's indigenous populations as human or as having languages, cultures, and even souls). While it would be unfair to read a student in such dramatic terms, the United States' historical disinclination to learn other languages can be considered in this way.

Separating from the maternal and moving into language and the social world are inherently linked. As Amati-Mehler, Argentieri and Canestri remind us:

> [W]e must take into account that learning to walk also coincides with learning to speak, and therefore with the acquisition of a whole spatial organization regarding separation from the primary object, experiments in detachment, and the possibility of verbal conjunction with the distant object. It is therefore clear that learning to speak in one or more languages means coming to terms with problems of separation at both the interpersonal level and the level of endopsychic caesura and discrimination. (1993: 126)

The shift abroad restages this early experience, and recatalyzes some separation anxiety. In his well-known "Walking in the City," Michel De Certeau hints at this repetition, writing that travel is like exploring the "deserted places of my memory" and "to practice space is thus to repeat the joyful and silent experience of childhood, it is, in a place, *to be other and to move toward the other*" (original emphasis, 1974: 110). The subject must harness the second language, still imperfectly understood and spoken, in order to mourn, cope, and compensate for this rupture.[4] Just a baby employs translinguistic strategies to communicate, students abroad also rely once again on gestures, intonations, and so on to communicate as they struggle to acquire new words and linguistic structures. The nonverbal body takes on new importance.

Kristeva asserts that these separations from the maternal are not only sad or anxiety producing, but also joyful: if they were purely traumatic, why would the infant ever give up his bond with the mother? In her view, through the mother's love the infant is able to perceive that there is something else "out there" to have. Because the mother is loved by others and loves other people/things (e.g. a partner, her work, a Third something), the infant has faith that he too will gain other experiences and objects of love if he separates (1987). This desire to connect to others will ease and make pleasurable the split. For the second language speaker, who has already achieved a successful entrée into L1, is this loving Third the foreign country itself? The somewhat formless "other culture" and its members? A faith in language—a conviction that the other words will indeed eventually permit representations both of things and of one's passions/joys/fears? As Kristeva frequently mentions, it is when our need to believe (that this is possible) meets our desire to know (the other language, culture, people) that we can move forward as subjects (2009). We see this sharply when students describe how the desire for connection to the Mexican culture is what pushed them to learn Spanish. For example, one said, "I hated studying language in school" but longed to enter into Mexican culture. For many students, this desire for connection and the faith that they can indeed form a part of the local social fabric catalyzes the move to speak.[5]

Once this initial break from the maternal figure/tongue is made, however, the process is far from over. Subjectivity is not simply achieved, just as languages are not acquired in a single act. For some, frustration at early or later plateaus in one's ability to speak can occasionally produce a narcissistic retreat. The speaking subject encounters "the difficulty of renouncing the universal narcissistic illusion that one's own language is the best and only one capable of expressing the complexities of life and of reflecting the truth" (Amati-Mehler, Argentieri, and Canestri 1993: 46). For example, in the HBO series entitled *In Treatment*, Sunil, an Indian patient being treated by a psychoanalyst in New York, converses politely and cogently in English yet breaks into Bengali during his more passionate outbursts when he feels deeply about the topic, as if English was simply not large enough to contain his deepest emotions. For others, the dissonance of the second language can provoke a state of melancholy, which is characterized by a loss of interest and a loss of faith in language itself. In his well-known essay "Dialogism and Schizophrenia," Tzvetan Todorov describes it as a falling into silence, remarking on the "silence and insanity looming on the horizon of 'boundless polyphony'" (1994: 214).

Feelings about the mother tongue's value can also be tied to nostalgia and encourage momentary retreats. Kristeva refers to "my maternal memory" of Bulgarian filled with childhood loves and Gregorian music. This provokes some guilt as well; as she laments that "There is matricide in the abandon of a native tongue" (2002: 244), referring to Bulgarian as "the still warm cadaver of my maternal memory" (245). In Kristeva's situation, that of an immigrant moving from a nondominant language into a dominant one, there may indeed be some guilt as the mother tongue is left behind, but in the case of American students abroad (who are not leaving the powerful language of English behind in this more permanent or traumatic way), one often observes feelings of shame or guilt for betraying the *new* language when they return to the native tongue. A bilingual colleague once referred to the "guilty pleasure" of reading and writing in your original tongue when you have lived abroad a long time and have no logistical need to do so. Many avid students also comment that they feel a "time out" watching English language TV or hanging out in an all-American group constitutes a sort of cheating on the new language. (See the chapters of both Doerr and Taïeb, this volume, for examples of students' policing of these degrees of commitment to L2.)

Beyond nostalgia and ambivalent feelings about the native tongue, negative and positive regressions can send the L2 speaker reeling backwards as well. The experience of learning another language is often likened to returning to a childlike state: frequently, students and others complain of feeling like six-year-olds in the second language. In psychoanalytical terms, regression occurs when someone reverts to an earlier stage of psychosexual development as a response to anxiety. There is no doubt that a reduced communicative capacity causes anxiety, and we can observe negative regression when frustrated language learners become upset.[6] However, and ideally, speakers may experience more positive regressions when they become playful, less concerned with mistakes and self-editing, and as open to learning as children often are. For the best language learner is one who is not self-editing, one who sets aside the adult shame of not knowing to take a risk and learn.

If this is achieved, the shift to a new language can then produce a feeling of release or joy, and some speakers throw themselves into a passionate affair with the language at this point. Kristeva notes: "But, to begin with, what an incongruous liberation of language! Lacking the reins of the maternal tongue, the foreigner who learns a new language is capable of the most unforeseen audacities when using it—intellectual daring and obscenities as well" (1991: 31–32). Even a quiet person, she continues, may become "a dauntless speaker" in the new language (31–32). This sense of abandon into what is new can hurtle a speaker into the process as well.

Together, these movements forward and backward, which are experienced differently by different speakers, point to the fact that our shift into L2 is neither solely forward-moving nor permanently finished. Amati-Mehler, Argentieri, and Canestri concur, explaining our good and bad days in the language: "In fact, the linguistic endowment of an individual is not a solid and stable system but, rather, an ever-changing constellation in which the supremacy of one language over the other, the internal hierarchy, and the absolute and relative degree of mastery, vary continuously in time and space" (1993: 101). Cronin echoes this call to conceive of language acquisition as a shifting back and forth:

> The gap of the "entre-deux" here should be conceived of less as a space, a reified entity tending towards stasis than as a constant movement backwards and forwards in which there is no fixated identification with either of the poles. The continuous oscillation ... between home culture and foreign culture, native language and foreign language, define [the] traveler as someone who can embrace the mode of both/and. (2000: 106–7)

What mobilizes these ongoing displacements and moves the speaker to deeper connections with the language and eventual bilingualness? This movement is fueled by passion.

Passions and L2

Even in the most stable, well-adjusted, and otherwise happy and engaged students, the relationship between the subject and the second language is marked by passionate attachments. Quite commonly, language takes the position of an idealized love object: students can fall in love with the new language. In *Powers of Horror,* Kristeva goes as far as to call language "our ultimate and inseparable fetish" as it is a substitute for the maternal (1982: 37). Fetish or not, language is "the Principle Object of the Subject in culture," an object that will call up both love and hatred (Kristeva 2010: 684). The learner in love finds her subjectivity put on trial, and she may suffer for the desire to merge with the language, to be completely absorbed and transformed by it. Indeed, it is not far-fetched to argue that L2 evokes in us the desire for the oceanic feeling

Freud described in *Civilization and Its Discontents*, following Romain Rolland. As second language speakers, we often hope to be contained, engulfed, possessed by the new tongue—to become one with our new linguistic and cultural surroundings, to erase any otherness.

Closely following this, the "perfect native speaker" can represent an embodiment of this idealized love. While in reality, the native speaker is a myth—"a monolingual, monocultural abstraction," someone who represents a standardized, (usually) national culture, versus a member of several discourse communities (Kramsch 1998: 80)—language learners often perceive the native speaker as the ideal performer of the local language. Like the infant in the Lacanian mirror stage, unable to match his imperfectly controlled body to the perfect, coherent image, the L2 subject can also see (hear) the perfection she is unable to perfectly mimic. Hence the tendency to idealize: and to want to become the image. As writer Lisa St. Aubin-Terán succinctly states, the second language learner aches with the desire to hear "but I thought you were French/German/Chinese!" (Cronin 2000: 53).[7]

This wanting to be perfect can provoke not only intense love for L2 and its speakers, but also moments of masochism or self-hatred when perfection is not achieved, and when mistakes appear. While native speakers certainly make mistakes, their mistakes tend not to interrupt the symbolic in noticeable ways; in other words, their imperfections occur in a fairly regulated way and fit into the correct schemes. When locals say "la calor" (instead of "el calor") or "ya desayunastes?" (instead of "ya desayunaste"),[8] it is barely noticeable because these mistakes still follow the rules of permissible deviations. But the foreigner, the L2 subject, disrupts much more noticeably when he misconjugates or mispronounces (for example, saying *ya desayunaron* to an individual instead of *ya desayunastes* marks a glaring mistake which provokes a breakdown of understanding; these two misconjugations are not equivalent). Again, as we know, this can produce acute frustration or a sense of inadequacy on the part of the L2 learner. Kristeva writes that the foreigner takes on the new language like an instrument, becoming a "virtuoso" only to have the whole illusion explode when a mistake or an accent breaks through (1991: 15).

> [T]he melody of your voice comes back to you as a peculiar sound, out of nowhere, closer to the old spluttering than to today's code. Your awkwardness has its charm, they say, it is even erotic, according to womanizers, not to be outdone. No one points out your mistakes so as not to hurt your feelings, and then there are so many, and after all

they don't give a damn. One nevertheless lets you know that it is irritating all the same. Occasionally, raising the eyebrows or saying, "I beg your pardon?" in quick succession lead you to understand that you will "never be a part of it," that "it is not worth it," that there, at least, one is "not taken in." Being fooled is not what happens to you either. At the most, you are willing to go along, ready for all apprenticeships, at all ages, in order to reach—within that speech of other, imagined as being perfectly assimilated, *some day* ... (15)

Are accents and mistakes a return of the repressed maternal (tongue)? And can one get lost in this odd site between languages? In "Bulgaria My Suffering," Kristeva qualifies herself as "the monster of the crossroads" as her native language becomes strange to her, and her anxiety heightens (2000: 168). While students tend to be reluctant to use the word *hatred* when discussing the loved language, some are quick to agree that there is hatred directed toward the self in these moments. As one quipped, "It's not you (Spanish), it's me. I love you, but I'm so frustrated with myself. I'm only here 4 months. Why didn't I take a grammar class?" Elaborating, she notes:

> I hate the fact that I cannot roll my "rrrrrrr"s. I feel like it's a huge barrier to me ever truly being able to speak Spanish and I feel like when I have to try to say a word like "perro" or "guerra" and I obviously can't say it like it is supposed to sound, it's like sticking a huge, giant sticker on my forehead that says GRINGA. And of course, people love to comment on it, and come up in my face, trilling their "rrrr"s and they laugh and say "You really can't do it? But it's so easy!!" Then they want me to try to say every word that has "rrrr" in it. 5 words later, or when I finally refuse to try more, they might finalllllllly get it that I just can't say it and they aren't helping. It makes me angry because my tongue feels like a block of cement and there is nothing I can do about it. Or if there is, PLEASE tell me!!! I guess it makes me mad at language in general, because why does that sound not exist in English??? Then I would be able to do it too! (email communication, 10 February 2012).

We can perceive the passionate nature of the response through the capital letters and the repetition of letters and punctuation marks. As St. Aubin-Terán noted above, the desire to pass and to appear or sound perfect is one that many of us can identify with.[9]

This frustration or desperation can lead to feelings of aggression: on the darker side of one's passion for L2 are the desires to possess or control the language. In the same devouring way that we may wish to possess a lover or control a child—desires not at all unrelated to love—

we can experience these passions with respect to learning. While infrequently articulated, these desires are commonplace to perfectionists and overachievers in all areas, and language is no exception. One can overstudy, obsessively make lists of new vocabulary, attempt to memorize the infamous *500 Verbs* books. A student commented: "When I first began acquiring Spanish, I felt the need to control everything, because I thought this would help me master the language and acquire it more quickly," a practice she later abandoned, switching out these masculine/objectifying/controlling words for a much softer approach. Another student mentioned that she observed in herself a tendency to cling to "set phrases" she heard locals use in an attempt to exert some control over the language, to establish a solid base to which she could always return during conversations. Is this not a move to possess the language, to demarcate some territory? An insecure (or committed) establishing of an "us" (*our* conversation traditions, *our* insider phrases) with the language? These are more aggressive passionate moves motivated by a love of language.

However, as we all know, one can never control the loved object. The child becomes independent, the amorous couple must return to the demands of an exterior daily life that includes others. Relationships are never finally resolved and achieved. In Spanish, students often cite frustrations with the language's own shifting from one place to the next. "I get mad at the differences," said one student, annoyed that vocabulary learned in a previous study abroad site did not work in Mexico. There is the sense that the other of language is not maintaining his side of the bargain; the student in love must keep remaking and adjusting herself to a language that won't commit. One imagines the girl who changes styles and tastes for each new boyfriend ... Language's—or, certainly, Spanish's—elusiveness and seeming refusal to love the loyal learner back by remaining ideal and constant can be heavily felt by students.

These everyday passions, highlighted here, underwrite our attachments to language and connect our instinct and drive to speak to a desire for more knowledge and ability. Through the love for the language and the desire to communicate with the speaking other, these passions must be modulated in order to inscribe us into the new symbolic. This is the pivotal challenge in second language learning. Pavlenko asks: "How does second language socialization into emotion discourses take place? What happens in cases when individuals refuse to readjust their emotion repertoires and, as a result, sound too affectionate, emotional, or high-strung (or, in the reverse scenario, too cold and impassive) in their new speech community?" (2002: 73).

While there is a socialization process implicit in learning ways to express emotion (involving both vocabulary and cultural knowledge about appropriateness); the "readjustment" at stake is fundamentally a result of a psychic process made possible by the sublimation of these passions into language which connect the body to L2. The discharge of the drives into words (symbols, representations) is what will move the speaker from a cold or dull translation (a purely cerebral task), or a faked, overexpressive translation devoid of real passion, to full expression in L2.

Why is this so difficult to engender? For the subject entering L2, the new words are often apprehended at arms-length distance; in a traditional classroom for example, it is hard for a 101 student to bond with the language as it may seem lifeless since there are usually no sensory, sensual, or bodily associations being formed in the classroom. One needs to eat (hear, see, touch) the other language, and to do this within the cultural context, for example, to make a distinction between cheese and *fromage* as Levi Strauss noted famously, or *queso* in Spanish. While the word appears to translate simply, the entire collection of sensory associations between cheese, *fromage,* and *queso* does not. This means that the intellectual disconnects from the corporal—or in Kristevan terms, the symbolic becomes detached from the semiotic, creating a dead language (1986).[10] If such a thing occurs with cheese, it only intensifies with experiences of falling in love or getting angry or being excited. "Sense takes root in the sensory," argues Kristeva (2004: 422), and this is equally true in the context of L2 where the learner strives to link the body to L2, to inscribe L2 with meaning and affect.

Stephanie Delacour, Kristeva's bilingual protagonist in several novels, moves between Paris/the French language and the fictional site of Santa Varvara/the Varvarian language and describes this bodily process of moving into language well. Whenever she returns to Santa Varvara, she feels she is "sleepwalking," noting "Her life was that of a dazed Frankenstein's monster: she did everything but was touched by nothing" (1998: 177). In *Strangers to Ourselves,* Kristeva writes similarly that "In that sense, the foreigner does not know what ... [he is saying]. His unconscious does not dwell in his thought" (1991: 32). Indeed, this disconnection between language and experience explains the ease with which foreigners swear: one can say the dirtiest thing because it does not resonate with memory; it does make you blush or feel tense.[11] Stephanie reflects that the new language must enter not only from above, from the brain, but also from a more sensory *"bottom up"* model.

This was low, lazy, and sensual: a rising movement with the tingle of smells, the flutter of sounds, a few hints of color, all boiled together. Then the mixture cleared and chose words; to put it another way, invented words, or more modestly, overhauled their old meanings. Until Stephanie reached the second stage in this alchemy she was still sleepwalking through that first stage: that of the *top down.*" (1998: 177)

For this reason, study abroad (or other sojourns into the language and culture at hand) offers the subject an ideal opportunity through which to apprehend the sensory, psychical, and passionate aspects of language. Amati-Mehler, Argentieri, and Canestri note that while multilingual minds may be prone to defenses and splittings, these same shifts are what will permit rebirth as a subject now in L2 (1993: 108). Kristeva's Stephanie experiences exactly this as she notes that moving into the Santa Varvarian language constituted "a kind of death followed by resurrection" (1998: 177). Another *petit mort*? Sex, life/death, and language learning become linked ...

At this point, things get more specific.

Specific Sublimations

In her essay entitled "The Impudence of Uttering," Kristeva notes provocatively that it is not the same to sublimate in one language as another, or in one genre as another: "I do not sublimate the same way in Chinese or in French, in the XII century or the XXIth century, in writing a novel, or composing a symphony or designing a dress" (2010: 683). The psychic, therefore, to borrow a term from contemporary public art, is *site-specific.* It depends upon the language, the time and place, and the formal possibilities within the chosen mode of articulation. How can we tease out this specificity that we know exists both theoretically and intuitively? What is specific about a particular language and site for a study abroad student, and how does passion play out along these specific routes? While we can agree intuitively that learning French, Spanish, and Chinese will not feel the same, most of us (including me) lack the vocabulary to articulate this. This final section points to the site-specific nature of this romance with another language and links it suggestively to a social change agenda.

I will leave aside the important questions concerning the specific subject with his or her specific body, early experiences, and psychic make-up to pose several thoughts about the external context, i.e. the language and/in the specific site in which a student sojourns.[12] What are the formal and psychic properties of the L2 language and site? What have been the language's and site's experiences with otherness? What specific sensory "bodies" do *they* have? While one might argue that cultural immersion experiences, like Western romances, follow a general template, each great love of language or place has its own specificity.

To begin, we do not only love language in the abstract. We love particular languages for particular reasons. Kristeva loves the French language for its precision and logic. She writes about "the clarity of language and the clear sky" (2002: 247). "the classical cadences of the argument" (246) in a site where "the fields are cut into neat rectangles" (247), where "every millimeter of landscape seems reflective" (247). She concludes, "I have placed my body in the logical landscape of France" (247). In short, the body is fully present in the new linguistic and cultural context, and this love has its particular contours, or singularity, as Kristeva terms it. Similarly, linguist Jean Zukowski (1997) details what she loves about Turkish:

> I had been living in Turkey for about six years, and my favorite pastime was studying the Turkish language. I loved the consistency and predictability of the language, I loved the music of its vowel and consonantal harmonies, I loved the images possible within the language. ... You would love it too, if you were a student of languages. Why? Because when you learn a rule in Turkish, you know that it has no exceptions and that you will always follow it.

Again the particularities of the qualities of the loved object (Turkish) and how she feels in this encounter (able to play, for example) stand out.

In Spanish, students found their own delights. They mentioned finding Spanish more expressive and liking the sound of the language. One student wrote, "I love the phonology of Spanish. I love the way that sounds are organized and the way that they are pronounced." Writer Michele Morano (2006), identifies a different aspect: she loves the subjunctive in Spanish. While many Spanish learners find the subjunctive to be their Achilles heel, she found that the subjunctive—the language's capacity to build doubt and incorporate a release of control into speaking—helped her loosen her defenses and move into the language.

It is here that the site's own body and previous/customary ways of encountering otherness enter in. Mexico is known for the hospitality extended to foreigners and tendency to accept their differences generously. Like the larger cultural body from which it emanates, Mexican

Spanish also tends to be hospitable, flexible, and spacious. It allows in a seemingly endless parade of Anglicisms, indigenous words, and European vocabulary. It allows the beginner to do a lot with few words, which then intersects easily with people's proclivity to be generous listeners. More locally, in Guanajuato (where these students were), this quirky, hilly city has a baroque body that is filled with *churrigueresque* architecture and nonlinear pathways, which also connects to the body of Spanish. The exuberant detail and layering of the city architecture mesh with the baroque and Arabic aspects of Spanish in which sentences go on forever in strings of coordinate clauses that often emphasize cadence, repetitions, digressions, and rhythm over precision. This is physically embodied in the city and the way one moves through it. One student emphasized something similar. She wrote, "I feel that there is a sort of dichotomy in learning Spanish in Guanajuato, at least from a cultural perspective. Guanajuato is a Mexican city but with a Spanish (from Spain) influence, so I feel that culturally, a student can feel the effects of both the past and the present [in both the city and the language]."

She is alluding to the fact that Mexican Spanish is full of Iberian/colonial archaisms and indigenous languages, in particular Nahuatl. She is beginning to understand the complexity and specificity of Mexico's Spanish. In another comment that links language to place, she writes: "Linguistically, I think that the cobblestone roads are like Spanish phonology. As one walks down the cobblestone streets of Guanajuato, one walks on every stone, just like one pronounces every morpheme in a word in Spanish." The local urban body and language are connecting in her mind; the other of the language connecting to the other of the physical city body. Spanish has now moved from the blurry, bodiless, emotions-less realm of *500 Verbs* and vocabulary lists to having a very particular flesh, history, and singularity within this site. While one does not want to ascribe language's aspects to one topography or geography alone, what is important is that the student is doing so in a specific space and moment. How does this specificity aid sublimation?

To be alive, writes Kristeva, we need a psychic life which connects us to our own body and to others (1995: 6). This happens through language, which means to be alive in another language is to create a psychic life within it, to connect one's body to it. By connecting a more abstract idea of language to the local city body (Guanajuato) and the body of local Spanish itself (the singularity of Mexican Spanish, its expressions, particular vocabulary, intonation, etc.), students discharge the sensory and drive-based elements behind their own bodily desire to speak into the new tongue. The new language becomes "real" (i.e., more than a set of cerebral rules) and specific. It acquires, in short, subjectivity: L2 becomes a subject worthy of love (which prompts desire and passion, but remains uncontrollable, unpossessable, untranslable) versus an object (something one acquires, dominates, or lifeless knowledge on résumé for use in the capitalist global arena). "Spanish" becomes a specific Mexican Spanish spoken in the specific city of Guanajuato, attached to specific foods, sounds, and other sensory experiences, in a specific ephemeral moment.

This accepting of the other language as truly other and unique is matched by an acceptance of self as other as well, or a relinquishing of the passionate desire to become the local. Kristeva notes that her bilingual character of Stephanie Delacour may never speak the French of Proust, but "she writes the melody of the sensory that flows beneath her sentences" (2011: 301). Her full self, with these residues of her maternal tongue, is carried forward into the new French. Identifying with this, Kristeva writes in a more autobiographical essay, "in the neighborhood of the senses and the biological that my imagination has the good fortune to bring to existence in French—suffering comes back to me, Bulgaria my suffering" (2000: 169). In other words, the semiotic of her Bulgarian past, which is tied to the senses and the body, can now be articulated into the French symbolic; yet, she accepts her accent and her occasionally still foreign nuances of French, i.e. her own difference. She is other to French, as French is other to her, yet she is in full dialogue with this and in full bilingualness. Is this not the goal of living and speaking abroad? To be able to acknowledge otherness and dialogue with it without losing the self or forcing the other's assimilation?

Psychic Displacements and Passions: Ramifications for the Social?

For many students, study abroad in another language is this love story, a story that follows Kristeva's (2011) call for the "dispassionizing of passion." She refers to a cycle of attachment and release that includes a temporary loss of the self into love (a passionate fusion with the loved object) followed by a modulation of this passion (a releasing and accepting of the other's alterity), which neither denies/represses passion nor relinquishes love. This ability to modulate passion allows the subject to passionately attach to and let go of an endless cycle of loves/projects/causes, i.e., to keep learning, to keep reaching toward what is new and other. Learning from this passionate and lovestruck point of departure is what makes L2 fluency ultimately possible. As I have attempted to argue in this chapter, there will be no "click" or full coming to life in another language if the process is not imbued with these amorous attachments with their joyful and less joyful moments.

I conclude with three implications for application. First, facilitation of language immersion experiences must continue to make room for passion, not push it away by offering too much disclosure or providing too much comfort. To open to love (of another language and place) is to accept both the pain and the pleasure, and to be convinced that it is worth it, that the expansion of subjectivity that occurs in contact with the unknowable other is a risk worth taking. Second, we must pay more attention to the site-specific nature of language learning and tease out the specificities and oft-ignored role of place. This passionate language process will not, realistically, occur in the classroom at home; students still need to *be there* among the smells of the market, the sounds of the language, the textures of a city's streets. Understanding and learning how to articulate exactly how the cobblestone, postcolonial contours of provincial Guanajuato compare to Buenos Aires' neighborhoods inscribed with its vestiges of State violence or Quito's narrower, Andean physiognomy is as important as knowing that playing a piece of music on the drums, the tuba, or the oboe is not the same thing, or that painters, sculptors, and ceramists do not experience identical creative processes. We are challenged to inquire how to articulate these differences and, certainly, this points to a need to conduct research into places' particularities, temporalities, and materialities as these interact with students' processes of taking up subject positions in L2 in a given site.

Finally, as noted at the beginning of this essay, the shift into language is a radical one that calls not only for the would-be speaking subject to accommodate to the rules of the social world, but also shakes up this world as each individual comes into it with his or her excesses of drives and passions. The passionate language learner, tormented or amorous, is on her way to enacting a psychic shift that is not only personal, but also—potentially—deeply social. A passionate experience abroad could lead to passionate advocacy related to L2 and its speakers back at home, in this case related to Spanish and Mexican immigrants. The amorous process described here parallels any sort of revolution: idealizations of a language, cause, or leader, with their concomitant elements of love and hate, followed by "depassionizings" or metabolizations into sense, logic, commitments, and compromises. In other words, revolutions shake up the social order only to inevitably become institutionalized social change, which then demands further revolutions in a permanent cycle of passionate attachment and release. Students who can embrace these passionate displacements of affect as they shift into Mexican Spanish are thus primed to return home and continue this process, shifting from individual learning to more social action, something we see continually as students' intense love for Mexico and Spanish matures into working in immigrant communities, teaching ESL, pursuing health and social work careers. ... In the process they change the stateside definition of who constitutes a Spanish speaker rather radically, which will affect policies surrounding multilingualism as well. Learning a second language (especially in the case of Americans), therefore, constitutes anything *but* a passive fitting into the social order. Making these passionate shifts toward multilingualism and globalization in which difference is not denied, but used to continually question and put on trial the status quo, is quite a revolutionary act.

The study abroad student is an unstable subject, moving into a changing language in a temporary iteration of a city site. The passions that come to the fore must be sublimated through love into representations, into language. When this happens the self is reasserted, and the other is recognized as fully other, which in turn engender both personal and social transformations. While important attention is paid to students' emotional needs and personal feelings in the experience abroad, more attention to the affective and psychic aspects of the learning processes allow us to consider the larger structures underwriting self and other relations and to mobilize affective processes in the name of both learning and social change.

Karen Rodríguez (Ph.D., Cultural Studies) is a researcher and a writer. Drawing from psychoanalysis, geography, and the arts, she explores how people make sense of their constant contact with difference whether this difference involves other languages, other cities, other texts, objects or people. She has published an academic book and a poetry book, as well as myriad articles and art catalogue texts, and she is currently working on an experimental biography. After working for almost two decades in global education, she is currently serving as Dean of Studies at Bard College's Early College in Cleveland.

Notes

1. Several observations and student quotes are incorporated from American undergraduates who participated on for-credit study abroad programs in Guanajuato, Mexico, at a center that I directed from 2002 to 2012. The majority were collected at a discussion session organized in February 2012, with others collected via emails with students who continued to think about the learning process post-study-abroad experience. These quotes are included solely to illustrate some of the theoretical points in this essay. The reflections here stem from the theory, not a student sample or ethnographic project.

2. Kristeva is a Bulgarian native working in Paris. She has written extensively about subjectivity and the second language process, and she also relates language to revolt and social change.

3. This is in theory only; there are many ways to be uncomfortably *other* within and beyond one's footing in the dominant national language. And true or perfect monolingualism is a myth given language's porosity and variation across time and space.

4. This idea of replacing or compensating for the loss of the maternal with language may play out differently for the current Millennial generation than it did for Baby Boomers or Gen Xers. Travelers from these two prior generations tend to look back upon their early travels and narrate the clean break made from home, a break that, while somewhat imposed by the lack of technology that foreclosed regular communication, is generally not remembered as traumatic (whether or not it was). Millennials, however, maintain closer relationships with the home (Howe and Strauss 2000) and have been raised in a context of increased technology as well as increased risk (or an increasingly articulated and visible risk). As one student opined, today's students are willing to separate *physically* by attending college far from home and then again by studying abroad, but many stay in constant touch via technology (cell phone, texting, Skype, etc.) as many as several times as day. To some extent, the spatial rupture with the maternal (mother, culture, language) can be compensated for or even avoided through intensified communication in the mother tongue in ways previous generations simply did not have access to. More work would have to be done on whether the emotional positives of having support are upset by being held back linguistically through this constant connection to the mother (tongue), if at all; however, for the moment, it is enough to underline that the context of separation within study abroad has changed dramatically from one generation to the next and requires further study.

5. What propels passion—the desire to speak to connect with place (place as the loved object), or the desire for place in order to be able to speak (language being the loved object)? How would the subjectivity process look

distinct? While I have focused on language as the loved object here and am connecting language to place, a subsequent paper based on wider student data might tease these two options apart and illuminate more on the subject's shift into L2.

6. Noticeably, however, the existence of a "language ego," first posited by Alexander Guiora (following Freud) as a way to understand the subject's protective or defensive reaction to speaking a new language, is generally *not* attributed to children under the age of puberty (Guiora 1972). The term *language ego* is frequently used more vernacularly to signify the learner's sense of injured pride during the mistake-making and self-conscious process of learning. It would seem useful to step back and consider this ego not as something the subject possesses but, rather, as a shifting and fluctuating sense of self formed in direct relationship to things external, as language only works when there is an addressee.

7. See also D. Moon (2001) on "passing practices" as they interrupt the binaries of self and other and as they interact with the host culture's power to impede or complicate this process of attempting to fit in.

8. We see the same in English as natives say "Anyways" or "Where are you at," for example; or in French with "Après que tu sois venue" instead of "Après que tu es venue," or "Si vous voudriez me voir" instead of "Si vous vouliez/voulez me voir."

9. As noted in the introduction to this essay, this is not a formal study of students and the cited words here do not represent a planned and statistically significant sample. However, it is worth noting that my respondees were all female, in keeping with the overwhelmingly female student body on the programs I ran, and that this desire to be perfect, to fit into the local L2, may have some important gender nuances that space does not allow me to explore here. However, Cronin (2000) and Amati-Mehler, Argentieri, and Canestri (1993) have much to say about the role of gender, as does Kristeva herself across her oeuvre.

10. Amati-Mehler, Argentieri, and Canestri concur. After citing the *fromage* example, they write, "This is true because the affective and sensory paths and the linking roots that for each individual characterize the learning of language and of separate vocabularies, are too specific. It follows that the unconscious representations relative to 'cheese' and 'fromage' are also potentially different, even though we should ask ourselves how these two areas of thought are able to coexist with, contrast with or modify each other reciprocally during the course of time" (1993: 105)

11. Quite similarly, analysts have long agreed that a patient undergoing therapy in a second language can also find herself detached from the language; recounting early childhood memories in the other tongue provides an emotional distance and can sometimes make the process less real/threatening. In this case, the second language serves as "a form of defense to guarantee

a certain degree of emotional detachment and of control regarding instinctual infantile vicissitudes" (Amati-Mehler, Argentieri, and Canestri 1993: 51). At other times, however, the use of L2 might help an analysand come to terms more gradually with something and provide a safe space in which to rework and reapproach earlier trauma (Amati-Mehler, Argentieri, and Canestri 1993; Hill 2008). As students develop greater language abilities, the question of which language they choose as they discuss their processes will become interesting.

12. The effects of gender, in particular, are enormous in psychic terms. Similarly, studying the relationship between race/ethnicity, sexual preference, and other factors would yield much information about these variations of bodied experiences as students move into L2. Without denying the need for more research on the student side, my goal here is to shine light at the specificity of the language and site and its potential role in this process.

References

Amati-Mehler, Jacqueline, Simona Argentieri, and Jorge Canestri, 1993. *The Babel of the Unconscious: Mother Tongue and Foreign Languages in the Psychoanalytic Dimension,* trans. J. Whitelaw-Cucco. Madison, CT: International Universities Press.

Arnold, Jane, ed. 1999. *Affect in Language Learning.* Cambridge: Cambridge University Press.

Cronin, Michael. 2000. *Across the Lines. Travel. Language. Translation.* Cork, Ireland: Cork University Press.

De Certeau, Michel. 1974. "Walking in the City." In *The Practice of Everyday Life,* trans. Steven Rendall. Berkeley: University of California Press, pp. 91–110.

Freud, Sigmund, James Strachey, and Peter Gay. 1989. *Civilization and Its Discontents.* New York: W.W. Norton.

Gregersen, Tammy, and Elaine K. Horwitz. 2002. "Language Learning and Perfectionism: Anxious and Non-anxious Language Learners' Reactions to Their Own Oral Performance." *Modern Language Journal* 86: 562–70.

Grosz, Elizabeth. 1998. "Bodies/Cities." In H. Nast and S. Pile (eds), *Places Through the Body.* London: Routledge, pp. 42–51.

Guiora, Alexander Z. 1972. "Construct Validity and Transpositional Research, Toward an Empirical Study of Psychoanalytic Concepts," *Comprehensive Psychiatry* 13: 139–50.

Hill, Sarah. 2008. "Language and Intersubjectivity: Multiplicity in a Bilingual Treatment." *Psychoanalytic Dialogues* 18: 437–55.

Horwitz, Elaine Kolker, Michael B. Horwitz, and Jo Ann Cope. 1991. "Foreign Language Classroom Anxiety." In Elaine K. Horwitz and Dolly J. Young (eds), *Language Anxiety: From Theory and Research to Classroom Implications.* Englewood Cliffs, NJ: Prentice Hall, pp. 27–36.

Howe, Neil, and William Strauss, 2000. *Millennials Rising: The Next Great Generation.* New York: Vintage Books.

Kramsch, Claire. 1998. *Language and Culture.* Oxford: Oxford University Press.

Kristeva, Julia. 1973/1986. "The System and the Speaking Subject." In Toril Moi (ed.), *The Kristeva Reader.* Oxford: Blackwell, pp. 24–33.

——. 1982. *Powers of Horror: An Essay on Abjection,* trans. L. Roudiez. New York: Columbia University Press.

——. 1987. *Tales of Love,* trans. L. Roudiez. New York: Columbia University Press.

——. 1989. *Black Sun: Depression and Melancholy,* trans. L. Roudiez. New York: Columbia University Press.

——. 1991. *Strangers to Ourselves,* trans. L. Roudiez. New York: Columbia University Press.

——. 1995. *New Maladies of the Soul,* trans. R. Guberman. New York: Columbia University Press.

——. 1998. *Possessions: A Novel,* trans. B. Bray. New York: Columbia University Press.

——. 2000. "Bulgaria, My Suffering." In *Crisis of the European Subject,* trans. S. Fairfield. New York: The Other Press, pp. 163–83.

——. 2002. *Intimate Revolt,* trans. J. Herman. New York: Columbia University Press.

——. 2004. *Colette,* trans. J.M. Todd. New York: Columbia University Press.

——. 2009. *This Incredible Need to Believe,* trans. B. Bie Brahic. New York: Columbia University Press.

——. 2010. "The Impudence of Uttering: Mother Tongue." *Psychoanalytic Review* 97(4): 679–99.

——. 2011. *Hatred and Forgiveness,* trans. J. Herman. New York: Columbia University Press.

Kristeva, Julia, and Toril Moi. 1986. "The System and the Speaking Subject." *The Kristeva Reader.* New York: Columbia University Press, pp. 24–33.

Langan, Robert. 2000. "Someplace in Mind." *International Forum on Psychoanalysis* 9: 69–75.

Moon, D. 2001. "Interclass Travel, Cultural Adaptation and 'Passing' as a Disjunctive Inter/Cultural Practice." In Mary Jane Collier (ed.), *Constituting Cultural Difference Through Discourse.* Thousand Oaks, CA: Sage, pp. 215–40.

Morano, Michelle. 2006. "Grammar Lessons: The Subjunctive Mood." In Lauren Slater and R. Atwan (eds), *The Best American Essays.* Boston: Houghton-Mifflin, pp. 107–21.

Onwuegbuzie, Anthony, Phillip Bailey, and Christine Daley. 1999. "Factors Associated with Foreign Language Anxiety." *Applied Psycholinguistics* 20: 217–39.

Pavlenko, Aneta. 1998. "Second Language Learning by Adults: Testimonies of Bilingual Writers." *Issues in Applied Linguistics* 9(1): 3–19.

——. 2002. "Bilingualism and Emotions." *Multilingua* 21(1): 45–78.

———. 2006. "Bilingual Minds." In A. Pavlenko (ed.), *Bilingual Minds: Emotional Experience, Expression, and Representation*. Clevedon, UK: Multilingual Matters, pp. 1–33.

Piniel, Katalin. 2006. "Foreign Language Classroom Anxiety: A Classroom Perspective." In M. Nikolov and J. Horváth (eds), *UPRT 2006: Empirical Studies in English Applied Linguistics*. Pécs: Lingua Franca Csoport, pp. 39–58. Retrieved 28 March 2012 from http://www.pte.hu/uprt/1.3%20Piniel.pdf.

Todorov, Tzvetan. 1996. "Dialogism and Schizophrenia." In A. Arteaga (ed.), *An Other Tongue: Nation and Ethnicity in the Linguistic Borderlands*. Durham, NC: Duke University Press, pp. 203–23.

Thrift, Nigel. 2009. "Space: The Fundamental Stuff of Human Geography." In N.J. Clifford, S.L. Holloway, S.P. Rice, and G. Valentine (eds), *Key Concepts in Cultural Geography*, 2nd ed. Thousand Oaks, CA: Sage, pp. 95–107.

Valdes, Joyce Merrill. 1986. *Culture Bound: Bridging the Cultural Gap in Language Teaching*. Cambridge: Cambridge University Press.

Zukowski, Janet. 1997. "Who Am I in English? Developing a Language Ego." *Journal of the Imagination in Language Learning and Teaching* 4: np. Retrieved from http://www.njcu.edu/cill/vol4/zukowski.html.

CHAPTER 4

Sojourn to the Dark Continent

Landscape and Affect in an African Mobility Experience

Bradley Rink

As an education abroad destination and in the popular imagination of outsiders, the African continent is tenuously situated as a site of hope, loss, fear, hate, delight, desire, and pride, among others. As a romantic landscape of animals, tribal mystery, and natural beauty, Africa is at once marginalized, patronized, and sexualized as students engage in academic and volunteer experiences in the "dark continent." Fraught with development challenges, seemingly constant political transformations, and the scourge of HIV/AIDS, Ebola, and other diseases, Africa might seem from an outsider's perspective to be a condition in need of correction. This feeling, in part, may be what draws scores of students from Europe and North America to international mobility experiences in order to learn in the classroom or to volunteer their time and efforts in service projects.

Education abroad experiences provide students with an adventurous, border-crossing experience that allows participants to exercise new ways of thinking and learning. Educators and study abroad alumni would certainly argue that the experience is one that can be transformative and that can provide a unique addition to higher education. International educators help to shape the education abroad experience in Africa for potential students through promotional materials, program design, and learning activities on-site. In this chapter I use the geographical concept of landscape as a point of departure, along with an understanding of international education within the new mobilities paradigm (Sheller and Urry 2006) and Thrift's (2004) notion of affect in order to reflect on learning experiences that promote affective learning outcomes that disrupt preconceptions of Africa. Although they are typically difficult to address in a classroom environment, affective learning objectives target the awareness and growth in attitudes, emotion, and feelings. Using examples from learning activities during student orientation and field-based learning in the context of academic coursework, I discuss the benefits and challenges of affective learning through physical, emotional, and interpersonal experiences during the learning activities. Results from implementation of the activities and assessment involved in the field-based course component (the "Practical") demonstrate the potential for affective learning to enhance undergraduate course design and learning outcomes.

Starting with Landscapes: *The Lion King*

As part of my South African orientation program for international students over the past two decades, I have regularly included a short clip of the Disney animated film *The Lion King*. I feature the clip during the segment of the orientation where I discuss cultural adaptation. In my talk, I explain how the feelings of anticipation and excitement that accompany the prearrival and first several days on-site. At that point I roll the film. Over the lyrics of "Circle of Life," with a chorus of singing and drums beating, the scene is set for Simba's ascendance as "king of the jungle." From his appearance, it would seem he is unsure of his suitability for such a role. He is apprehensive: he doesn't know all of the rules, yet he is excited and willing. Simba is much like our students when they step off the plane. The screening of this clip is always met by roars of laughter at the start. At first, students find the inclusion of a children's film oddly amusing. Soon thereafter, however, they start to understand its meaning. Among a group of students in their twenties, many of them would have learned about Africa through *The Lion King*: a generic place that serves as a stand-in for the entire continent; a place defined by animals instead of humans; a place of stunning natural beauty; a place that is out of time, traditional, and tribal. As the film unfolds before their eyes, the students' memories are awakened. The birds-eye-view scenes that open the film are the same ones that students imagined immediately before touching-down on African soil for an education abroad experience. They have just stepped out of a dream that is now their reality.

The opening scene of *The Lion King* is a technicolor landscape in motion. The image of sweeping African savanna is punctuated by a dramatic score that builds as the landscape unfolds. Landscapes such as this have a long history of being the subject of cinematic and artistic expression. The concept of landscape itself emerges from romanticism and art and presents a sophisticated cultural construction and particular way of composing, structuring, and giving meaning to an external world whose history has to be understood in relation to the material appropriation of land. In its original meaning, *landscape* referred to a portion of the earth's surface that can be seen from one vantage point (Cresswell 2004: 10), and in the case of capitalists of the time, that visual was about capturing more than simply a lovely view: it was about exploitation of resources and extraction of wealth. As Renaissance painters and thinkers sought to represent a visual or literary Arcadia, the landscapes that emerged from their work were characterized by fertile and untouched natural beauty that would be ripe for some Utopian future. Meinig (1979: 33) sketches the scene of a viewer looking over such an Arcadian landscape to illustrate this:

> Such a viewer is ever tempted in his mind's eye to remove man from the scene, to restore nature to her pristine condition, to reclothe the hills with the primeval forest, clear off the settlements, heal the wounds and mend the natural fabric—to imagine what the area is really like. It is an old and deeply rooted view which separates man and nature. Ideologically it had its greatest vogue in eighteenth century Romanticism, in that longing for wilderness, in the view of nature as pure, fine, good, truly beautiful. It can be a seductive view … The romantic view is in fact very much alive, usually, perhaps necessarily, expressed as a kind of nostalgia.

Nostalgia, is after all about pain—a memory that triggers a longing for something else, another time and place. Nostalgia in this case is a longing for an earlier era: one that is more simple and less reliant on technology; one that is closely tied to the land; one that has a clearly defined hierarchy of man and nature. These characteristics should sound familiar, because they map neatly (almost exactly) onto the most widely held feelings of Africa from the American point of view (Keim 2009).

Landscape as a concept in cultural geography serves as a useful entry point to understanding visual, cultural, or natural elements of place (Wylie 2007, 2009; Cresswell 2004). I use a landscape approach in teaching my introductory course on South Africa for international students because landscapes are accessible—and deceptively "knowable"—through seeing. But seeing is informed by experience, education, and feeling. Through gazing, the landscape shapes perception and also acts as Henderson (2003: 192) notes to "[inform] the actual, material making of places." It is within landscape where we take ourselves out of the picture or perhaps dream of ways to insert ourselves within it. Landscapes are easily objectified, held at a distance. As Cresswell puts it, "we do not live in landscapes—we look at them" (2004: 11).

The objectifying position of the viewer outside of landscape makes landscapes themselves problematic, for they are composed not only of what unfolds before our eyes but also from what lies within our heads (Meinig 1979). In this regard, any one landscape is metaphorically painted from a palette that is as unique as the beholding eye. Looking at landscapes is not a neutral activity.

The Romantic Landscape of Education Abroad

If the concept of landscape itself has romantic roots, then so too does the practice and experience of education abroad. Voyages by steam ship that carried the first "study abroad" students from the University of Delaware (Hoffa and DePaul 2010) are nothing if not romantic. Steamer trunks, waiters in dinner jackets, the smell of sea air, and the sound of fog horns on distant shores signal a break from the present and an opportunity to see another world. Study abroad is about exploration, new horizons, and unexpected revelations of the self that emerge from the anonymity of life in a distant landscape and foreign culture. Study abroad involves a romantic tourist gaze embroiled in the search for an essential "other," which both confirms a sense of difference—and perhaps superiority—of their world.

Whatever the case may be, the material and discursive journey involved in education abroad is one taken with reference to a strange, new, sometimes frightening and often seductive landscape. Education abroad becomes an attempt to engage in the landscape, and not just gaze upon it from afar. It is attachment—and affect—materialized in the form of contact with the other. The success of a student mobility experience may be gauged by asking whether the student has engaged with the "other," encountered difference, challenged assumptions, realized new insights ... or, whether the student has remained gazing at the romantic landscape as if from afar, simply inserting or sketching him- or herself into the landscape. The degree to which a student engages is complicated by the notion of mobility itself.

Student Mobilities: A New Paradigm

The concept of mobilities exceeds the movement of students, institutions and programs as it is generally understand in higher education (Guruz 2011: 169). Mobilities can be more broadly understood as the movement of people, objects, capital, and information both locally and across the world (Hannam, Sheller, and Urry 2006). The concept of mobilities encompasses the extraordinary movement of students in pursuit of educational experiences, the movement of tourists and refugees, but may also include the more localized processes of daily transportation, movement through public space, and the travel of material things within everyday life (Hannam, Sheller, and Urry 2006).

A critical reappraisal of the importance of mobility in contemporary social life, which Sheller and Urry (2006) call the "mobilities turn," reinvigorates our understanding of movement and undermines the long-standing static nature of the social sciences. Mobility studies both recenter and destabilize geographical thought, as boundaries, rootedness, territory, and place are called into question. The mobilities paradigm is thus a postdisciplinary field that goes beyond the binary of sedentarist or nomadic conceptions of place (Sheller and Urry 2006). Through the lens of mobilities we can begin to problematize "place" (Hannam, Sheller, and Urry 2006) as a fluid and contingent network of relationships of "hosts, guests, buildings, objects and machines" (Hannam, Sheller, and Urry 2006: 13). Mobility reveals itself in higher education as in tourism (Hannam and Butler 2012), and it does so in many forms as highlighted by Urry (2007) and reinterpreted by Hannam and Butler (2012: 130–32) including (1) the movement of students to their study site (corporeal travel), which is perhaps the most conventional way of understanding mobilities in this context; (2) the movement of "things" (with or without their human companions) involving the movement of luggage, personal belongings, souvenirs, and goods of all kinds; (3) imaginative travel, where perspectives and decisions are shaped through film and other media; (4) virtual travel, through the use of the Internet for experiencing place before any corporeal movement takes place; and (5) communicative travel through the use of mobile telecommunications to keep in touch with family and friends while away. It is in the increased speed and ease of mobilities where our ability to remain physically detached from the landscape and some notion of "reality" on the ground becomes possible.

Experiencing Affect in Student Mobility

Education abroad offers opportunities to engage with the world beyond our everyday borders—of institution, nation, language, culture, and space. Although "affect" is associated with emotional responses such as romance, desire, hope, hopelessness, and fear—the term is not synonymous with emotion (Thrift 2004). Rather, in Thrift's analysis, affect is a dialogue that the subject has with the object. In the case of international student mobility, affect is mediated through the dialogue between student and the space(s) and subjects he/she encounters while abroad, and mobilized through colonial legacies and a range of misperceptions articulated in a broader political economy. Thrift provides useful context when he conceives of affect as related to bodily states and processes, where "a set of embodied practices that produce visible conduct as an outer lining" (2004: 60). It is in the engagement between students and space where affect finds embodiment. A shift in the physical, social, and emotional spaces that a student inhabits is a core element of the education abroad endeavor. When students encounter new spaces and embodied practices in education abroad, they are confronted with affective challenges.

The affective response of the student, in turn, acts to shape the space into a specific "place"—shifting the empty vessel that is space, full of potential, into a place that is inscribed with meaning, memories, cultures, and ideas (Cresswell 2004). It is through affect that we place ourselves *into* the landscape rather than simply remaining detached above it. It is the goal of education abroad to entangle subjects in the multiple landscapes of the host culture—human, natural, cultural, and otherwise. Educators strive to engage students in meaningful, complex, and often uncomfortable ways to elicit learning and growth. In the case of Africa, the space is one composed of perceptions that are deeply rooted in unresolved mysteries, concerns, and old colonial tropes.

Before corporeal travel takes place, the education abroad journey begins on the home campus where students engage in forms of both imaginative and virtual mobility (Urry 2007) as they browse myriad brochures, listen to talks from visiting faculty and program staff, and meet with advisors to plan their overseas learning experience. The planning process, however, does not take place on a tabula rasa. Having taught and advised North American students studying in Africa for more than two decades, I have been keenly aware of the perceptions that drive their choice of African study destinations and influence the ways in which they understand the continent and its people. It is often at the point of choosing a study destination where a variety of perceptions— or at least a conflated geographical awareness—are most evident. Very often this mismatched geography emerges as a choice between cities and a continent: London, Florence, or Africa. As a geographer and international educator, this gives me pause. It also opens the door to a teachable moment. Far too often, however, international educators witness such uneven geographic scalings and remain passive, finding no way to address the misperception of Africa as a single country with a monoculture and singular way of being. The limits of geographical knowledge of the African continent are quickly reached and the continent becomes equated with other notable study abroad "destinations" in Europe. These sites of study abroad are destinations in the sense that they are the end and focal point of students' journeys. The destination is the subject of the students' gaze. The destination in turn gets shaped and consumed. Destinations can be consumed by tourists as they can by study abroad participants.

Understood as a type of "tourist gaze" (Urry 1990), the study abroad grand voyage is "a secular kind of pilgrimage [that] might be seen as a material semiotic process that 'sacralizes' places" (Crang 2009: 763). In planning for an educational experience on the continent, students' African gaze is informed by what Thrift (2004: 65) calls the heavy and continuing mediatization of politics where "societies ... are enveloped in and saturated by the media" (2004: 65). In such media-saturated society, television, film, and books form the milieu where the destination as a complex landscape of meanings is read, interpreted, and understood (Knudsen, Soper, and Metro-Roland 2007). Increasingly both imaginative and virtual mobility precedes the actual corporeal voyage to the study site, allowing ample time for preconceptions to develop in advance of arrival. Years of bearing witness to a range of preconceptions (and misconceptions) led to my interest in exploring perceptions among students engaged in an education abroad experience on the African continent. I therefore set out to survey students studying in programs in Ghana, Senegal, and South Africa.[1] I was interested in learning how students from higher education institutions in the United States understand Africa, and what informs their learning. Having a portfolio of African programs across subregions of the continent under my purview at the time—including Francophone and Anglophone West Africa and Africa south of the Sahara—I was interested in learning more about the perceptions that brought students to the programs.

Keim (2009) reveals that Americans on the whole perpetuate eigh-teenth- and nineteenth-century notions of Africa that are drawn from tales of explorers, missionaries, and hunters. Their perceptions reveal a bias toward thinking of Africa as primitive and backward—even to the point of depravity. Even when probing for positive traits, Keim notes that conceptions of Africa tend to be romanticized versions of premod-ern Africa to the exclusion of modern characteristics of the continent (2009: 63). This is the idea of essentialized Africa, one of a simple, rural life devoid of technology—mysterious, noble, but also perpetually re-tarded in terms of economic growth, intellectual capacity, and global standards—a perception that is only reinforced through films such as *The Lion King*. This is the notion of Africa out of time, kept permanently under the glass of a natural history museum.

Affect and the Experience of Africa

Encountering Africa evokes a range of responses for those who take part in educational programs on the continent. Informed by television, film, and their own classroom-based studies on their home campuses, many students characterize Africa in negative terms as an underdeveloped, hot, poor, and dangerous continent. And, as Johnson (2009: 182) notes, they may come to the experience with notions of the heroic traveler in-formed by nineteenth-century literary tropes. They may also, as Johnson supports through her reading of Pratt (1992), come with a sense of guilt over the relative wealth that they own in comparison to their counter-parts in Ghana, Senegal, or South Africa. Such perceived inequalities are often assuaged through the prospect of volunteering and "giving back" to communities in Africa. Rather than counteracting such expectations, education abroad professionals themselves may reinforce stereotypes through marketing materials and program design (Johnson 2009). How-ever they gather the information and pursue the experiences that inform their understanding of Africa, students nonetheless look at the landscape of Africa and understand it through a variety of affective responses—among them romance, desire, hope and hopelessness, and fear.

Romance

Romantic notions of the postcolonial are part of the discourse of educa-tion abroad experiences in Africa (Johnson 2009). The voyage to Africa even surpasses the romance of the grand voyage to Europe because Africa is conceived of as a place little explored, filled with mystery, and out of time with the rest of the "civilized" world. One doesn't choose to engage in Africa by mistake, but rather by passionate design such as those who came before: explorers, missionaries, and hunters. What they share is passion that finds its outlet in discovery, conversion, and conquest. As Johnson explains,

> Modernist travelers and writers ... idealized the promise of the authentic experience and romanticized the possibility that the enlightened traveler might find the "real" and be rewarded for their efforts. Popular writers such as Ernest Hemingway, E.M. Forster, and Graham Greene wrote stories with characters experiencing people and places in "authentic" ways and attempted to react to the segregated experiences of the elite travelers who preceded them. (2009: 182)

Encountering authentic or "real" Africa is, as Keim (2009) tells us the goal of many Americans who visit the continent. In order to do so, travelers are compelled to explore rural places, because the city is not a site of discovery like the untouched plains of Africa. This points to the attraction toward rural versus urban spaces.

As Keim further notes, American travelers "like to imagine they are explorers discovering Africans who have never seen whites before. They frequently see rural Africans in idyllic terms, as rustics who have captured the basic meanings of life and are unencumbered by the modern world" (2009: 72). Today's internationally mobile student is less likely to be reacting to previous explorers in search of the authentic, but rather as a counter to "easy" study abroad destinations such as those in Europe. An African experience in this way helps to shape them and their experience as "unique" and somehow more challenging than if they swam close to the edge of the pool in a place like London. The affective response of this is to shape the subject and the object as essentially "other." Africa must be different, because I'm pursuing an authentic experience that cannot be had elsewhere. The problem is not with the desire for the authentic in itself, but with the essentialization of Africa that accompanies that desire. This obscures any similarities or resonances between Africa and elsewhere.

Desire

As a place of darkness—in the sense of skin color, civilization, and generally speaking the unknown, Africa is portrayed as a place of corporeal curiosity and heightened sexuality. Portrayed as both less civilized and untouched by Puritanical notions of sex and sexuality, the black African body is a site of unbridled lust. Unbounded by moralities of the "civilized" North, the native (read: black) African subjectivity is one that has long attracted outsiders' gaze since the time of European contact. The case of Saartjie Baartman, the "Hottentot Venus," provides material for fruitful reflection in this regard.

Sara "Saartjie" Baartman was a Khoi woman who was captured and lured under false pretense to London in 1810 only to be put on display as an anthropological curiosity (Hudson 2008). She was the embodiment of perceptions of Africa at the time, and her captive body served as a stand-in for perceptions of the continent as a whole: the proportion of her thighs and buttocks echoed the physical landscape and the curvaceous protrusion of the western flanks of the continent; prominent genitalia suggested sexual abandon that was supposedly characteristic of African morality; and generous breasts confirmed potential for Africa's untapped wealth enriching the rest of the world. As a female alone—not to mention her African origin—Baartmaan was, as Hudson (2008) argues, imbued with that "fleshy and dangerous beauty that needed to be mastered by male reason" (2008: 19). Not only did she suffer the inhumanities of being caged and put on display like an animal, she was also mocked as an object of desire, as seen from the epithet "Venus"—the goddess of love—given to her by her captors. Shaped as she was as the Venus, desire finds an object in Saartjie Baartman. Her curves mirror the shape of Africa, and in turn Baartman becomes the corporeal stand-in the continent itself.

Hope and Hopelessness

Signs of despair surround the African continent, cast as inferior to the civilized North. As a site of disease, conflict, and pestilence, it draws on emotional responses from outsiders who come to "give back" in recognition of something that has previously been taken during colonial times in the form of land, resources, and power. "Helpless" Africans become an object of desire that requires intervention. The statistics often support the concerns: Africa remains ground zero of the HIV pandemic; South Africa ranks among war-torn countries such as Afghanistan and Iraq for violent deaths—while not being at war itself.

There is little doubt that many African states feature gross domestic product and human development index numbers that rank them amongst the lowest levels of human development in the world (UNDP 2015). However, that doesn't account for Africa being cast as a condition in need of correction. Positioning of the continent as slave to its colonial master is hard to abandon. The relationship between aide-giving agencies and those who receive help in the form of international aide and development funding need not permanently undermine Africans' capacity for change. Yet in receiving assistance from abroad, Africa may be cast in terms of pity, helplessness, and the loss of hope.

Fear

Fear has emerged as a key element of the African city—particularly that in postapartheid South Africa. Fear is based on an extreme encounter with difference or the anticipation of that encounter. One respondent reflected on this when noting, "My biggest misperception of Africa was that the continent in general is a lost cause grappling with fears of crime and violence." So why is Africa such a fearful place? The roots of the answer to that question lie in the old tropes of Africa as the "dark continent," yet in more recent times are linked to the loss of control in urban spaces that has characterized postcolonial and postapartheid African cities.

At the same time that cities in Africa—especially South Africa—are increasingly mobile themselves, connected to global networks of commerce, migration, and ideas, some suggest it is also beginning to shutter itself; to turn in on itself, buttressing those citizens who can afford it from the ills that plague the urban world "out there" (Ballard 2005). Fortified cities engage practices and technologies similar to the ever-vigilant panopticon where the fear of crime and the threat of new social orders taking shape within them cause (mostly) upper classes to retreat to exclusive, fortified enclaves. Those enclaves serve as private cities-within-a-city and shatter urban space into disjoined pieces. The enclaves also serve to shield the psyches of (mostly white) South Africans who live in gated communities in order to manage the contradiction between the race/class/culture identity to which they aspire and the place in which they live (Ballard 2005). In public and private settings, citizens in South African cities are isolating themselves through the new architecture of urban built environments whose gated residential areas that segregate themselves from the "other" in order to reaffirm their (white, European) identity (Ballard 2005). Gated communities in particular are read as driven by fear.

Outside of the secure accommodations where many visiting international students live and beyond the gated universities where they study, the US study abroad experience in Africa is also driven by fear. As one student noted in retrospect, what educators need to do more than anything is to address "the crime level and precautions that living here entails [sic]." Orientation programs stress personal safety—particularly when it comes to the most unprotected form of mobility at hand: walking. Women particularly are cautioned against walking—never alone, never at night, always in a group. Coming from a study abroad safety briefing it would seem that to walk is to transgress all of the norms of local culture, where walking is mediated by gender, fear of crime, and weather among others. Yet, walking is how most Africans move in and around the city.

Romance, desire, hope and hopelessness, and fear of the continent are reflected in the responses gathered from students as they reflected on their previous conceptions of Africa (see Table 4.1 below) when they were asked to provide three words they would have used to describe their perception of "Africa" in general. Their reflections of the past were collected while they were in the midst of an education abroad experience in Africa. Responses from 53 students were coded and categorized into seven themes: poverty; war or conflict; disease; development; weather or climate; physical characteristics; and cultural characteristics. In the retrospective responses from students, the majority of responses relate to cultural (35%), development (18%), and physical characteristics (14%) of the continent and express challenges in the face of confounding diversity, colonial pasts that hamper development, and the physical dimensions of an expansive rural continent. Issues of poverty, safety, and to a lesser extent disease also feature in students' reflections.

Table 4.1: Analysis of student responses (retrospective perception)

Theme	Frequency (retrospective)	Percentage of overall responses
Cultural characteristics	55	35%
Development	28	18%
Physical characteristics	22	14%
Poverty	20	13%
War or conflict	16	10%
Weather or climate	12	8%
Disease	3	2%

Learning with Affect

As a lecturer, I am able to shape the learning experiences of my students, and address some of the perceptions and affective responses that I witness in my students, including romance, desire, hope and hopelessness, and fear. Including affective learning goals in course activities allows me to focus learning outcomes as they relate to values, attitudes, and behaviors that engage students' emotions (Shephard 2008: 88). In the following section I will reflect on two learning activities that contribute to affective learning objectives: a field-based experience for a winter-term geography field course organized for South African and study abroad students; and a walking lecture that is a component of a course for a US study abroad program.

"Urban Modernities: Space, Place and Difference" is winter-term geography course that focuses on urban change in South Africa, drawing together historical and contemporary analysis of the South African city. The course is offered to both local (South African) and visiting international students who want to understand South African cities of the past and present. The field-based component of the course (known as the "Practical") is a key component that allows students to contextualize urban modernity in South Africa. Both the Practical and lecture content require students to think about the challenges and opportunities of contemporary urbanism as seen from the specific confluence of Cape Town. Through classroom and field-based learning activities we explore urban modernities by interrogating how they are conceptualized, achieved, and contested.

The brief to students during the Practical is simple: I ask students to open their eyes and query the urban landscape in order to put theory into practice. This involves students looking for evidence of the past, questioning what they see and don't see. They are encouraged to look for ways in which the spaces are contested, and to look for evidence of current urban challenges. The learning experience should allow students to extrapolate conclusions about the South African city from the places we visit. In my design of the Practical, I have included a pre-Practical briefing where we discuss logistics and specific elements of field-based learning such as affective learning outcomes. Within the Practical itself I include three primary activities: a walk up the slopes of Table Mountain to Platteklip Washhouses, a walk through the open expanses of District Six, and a visit to the Langa Pass Office Museum where students are sequestered in the holding cells by the museum curator.

Students are provided with a series of questions that they must answer either during or immediately after the experiences. Answers are to be written in notebooks carried during the visit that are submitted for assessment. Among the questions is one that asks them to consider the affective learning outcomes that have been derived from the visit.

The walk up the slopes of Table Mountain is accompanied by a discussion of the gendered dimension of work since colonial times in South Africa. Platteklip Washhouse was the site to which washer women in the eighteenth and nineteenth centuries carried large bales of linen for hand washing in the streams flowing from Cape Town's iconic mountain. When discussing the physicality of such work in the classroom, the impact is lost on most students. When confronted with the strain of walking up the mountain themselves, students nearly always comment on how difficult the task must have been for washer women, as noted by one participant in 2014:

> The walk to the washhouses is steep and strenuous—and would have been more so before the paths and steps were erected. The work of carrying great loads of washing (including linen and curtains which would have been particularly heavy) would have been physically very grueling—which speaks to the lesser social "value" of the washer-women compared to their employers, who would never be expected to engage in such strenuous physical work. (Practical participant 2014)

Students embody the practice of walking up the mountain, and in doing so are prompted to consider the effort made by washerwomen in the past. On the most recent Practical, as we ascended to the first washhouse I turned to the students behind me gasping for breath, and prompted them to consider the same effort with a bale of washing on their backs. In the same vein, I can discuss during lecture the devastation of a community destroyed through the apartheid-era Group Areas Act that led to the razing of District Six, but the effect is made all that much clearer as students wander through the empty fields that once comprised the main thoroughfares of the former mixed-race neighborhood adjacent to the city center. Having an embodied experience of District Six surfaces important learning outcomes, as noted by one student in her Practical response:

> You see reconstructions, photographs, maps, testimonies, artworks and poems. You can see what thriving District Six looked like, or at least you can get a feel. You can see aspects of personal narrative on a small scale, in other words memory, but you cannot access the landscape of

District Six itself. You cannot see the hurt, pain, humiliation or the residents whose lives were so bitterly torn apart. You also cannot see the
oppressor. You can only see the remnants. (Practical participant, 2014)

Another student reflected on her previous perception of life in District
Six (and present-day South Africa) before coming:

When looking at present-day District Six ... what I see is quietness and
calm as well as tensions underneath ... This is not what I imagined before my actual visit to the city. Through the books I read, plays or films
I watched, I understand [sic] the possible conflicts (in the past or at
present); however, being exposed to this real location, the present day
District Six, I somehow started to understand the tangled and tangible
relations under the macro-narrative of the "rainbow nation." (Practical
participant, 2014)

What students experience by walking and encountering the city through
their own embodiment of it opens pathways to affective learning.

At the Langa Pass Office Museum, the curator of the museum asks
all students to follow him into the back room of the Pass Office, to the
cell where those awaiting hearing would be held, usually in cramped,
uncomfortable conditions without access to a toilet, a place to sit, or
other amenities. Given the size of each group (approximately sixty students), the space in the cell is extremely limited, but very much rep-
resentative of the conditions under which black "Africans" would have
been held. This sequestration proves uncomfortable in both physical
and emotional terms, but once "released" students invariably comment
on the inhumanity of the apartheid pass laws.

Similarly, the walking lecture that I provide each semester for a
group of North American students in Cape Town studying sustainability
addresses a number of affective learning objectives. Coordinated with
the program's director, students have the opportunity to experience different modes of transport through their own bodily experience of it:
local trains, minibus taxi, bus rapid-transit system, and walking. We discuss the informal economy by being present in front of it, and buying
goods from vendors. In the walking lecture students encounter the city
that we discuss in theory. They experience the physical sensations of
mobility that are part of the sustainability curriculum, witness the ways
that inequality plays itself out in urban quarters, and sense the history
of slavery and other forms of subjugation that cannot be denied when
confronted with the bones of the Prestwich Memorial that we visit at
the end of our walk. On our visit to the ossuary at the memorial, where

bones of slaves and other marginalized individuals are interred, students are reminded of the legacies of colonialism and, more importantly, of the enduring effects and new forms of colonialism and marginalization that still characterize urban life in South Africa. Anger and resentment frequently surface when students realize that the ossuary shares space with a popular coffee shop, where students observe patrons paying scant attention to the bones that lay just beyond their coffee and jovial conversations. After their walk through the history—a transect of geographical space and time—their bodily fatigue combined with emotions of surprise, anger, and disgust assist them in reevaluation prior conceptions of South Africa both past and present. Taken together, the walking lecture provides a range of affective encounters with the city that bring material from the course alive, and that undermine misperceptions that may have been informed by distance from the African reality.

Through the experience with my second-year course as well as the walking lecture with North American students, a number of lessons emerge with respect to affective learning in the context of education abroad. First, through the inclusion of field-based learning experiences, I have gained an appreciation for the physical and emotional dimensions of both classroom and field-based learning (and their link to our course content). Second, I have realized the importance of pre-Practical briefings that integrate both logistical and pedagogical considerations: the How? What? and Why? of the field experience. In these briefings, I also begin to prepare students for encountering affective learning, by sensitizing them to the importance of feeling, seeing, and engaging with more than just surfaces. A third lesson that this activity provides me, following Herrick (2010) and Panelli and Welch (2005), is an acknowledgement that field-based activities should be structured according to degrees of autonomy/dependence and observation/participation that correspond to learning goals. In some cases I lead students closely; in others I allow them the independence to explore. Finally, this field-based experience has allowed me to recognize the limits and challenges in field-based learning, not the least of which concerns those students who have physical or learning disabilities that limit the ways in which they can engage in such activities.

As educators we can encourage our students to learn from the embodied practice of the city and its multiple subjects through the simple strategy of walking. Walking challenges the notion that landscapes are to be looked at, not engaged with. Yet in some African cities—such as the city of Cape Town where I live and work—walking is mediated by concerns over crime and safety (Miller 2010). In spite of this, walking can encourage students to become participant-observers and self-conscious performers with their newly adopted urban landscape (Rodriguez and Rink 2011). Reflecting on the experience of studying and living in Africa—on its own terms—opens the possibility of seeing the continent in a different light. Over time, student engagement within the landscape of education abroad allows for new ways of seeing. The change that is evident from student responses reflects less on the object (the African continent) and more on the perspective of the student. The affective response of a deliberate and engaged experience abroad can have profound result in the way the place is shaped. I argue that the perceptual shifts are attributable to students' meaningful engagement with the local context—at street level and in the ivory towers of their host universities. Evidence of this engagement can be found in the responses from students to their current perception of Africa as seen below in Table 4.2.

The largest percentage changes in perception were in the themes of poverty (down 10%) and cultural characteristics (up by 25%). While cultural characteristics informed the largest percentage of perceptions in the retrospective responses from students, in the current perception the words ascribed to culture included more positive and experience-dependent attributes such as diversity, dynamism, friendliness, family, solidarity, and cultural uniqueness. Such characteristics are based on personal, embodied experience of Africans and the spaces of Africa. While there was little change in the frequency of reflections about the theme of development, the words attributed to development appear more complex and nuanced in students' current perceptions. While words like "underdeveloped," "less advanced," and "problem-ridden" characterized earlier perceptions, once students had spent time engaging in

Table 4.2: Analysis of student responses (current perception)

Theme	Frequency (current perception)	Percentage of overall responses	Change
Cultural characteristics	91	60%	+25%
Development	26	17%	–1%
Physical characteristics	21	14%	0%
War or conflict	6	4%	–6%
Poverty	4	3%	–10%
Weather or climate	4	3%	–5%
Disease	0	0%	–2%

affective learning, the theme of development included more complex words with positive and negative developmental connotations including "damaged," "modernizing," "overcrowded," "resiliance," "potential," and "disparity," among others.

Rather than relying on television, film, books, or even lectures on their home campuses, students who engage in an international mobility experience in Africa are confronted with challenging their own ideas, while learning from a variety of local (African) voices. One of the respondents to my survey—a student in Senegal—said it best when asked about what international educators should do to address student perceptions of Africa. The student urged educators to "give students information on local knowledge production and sources [letting them know that knowledge accumulation is often different than in the States] that they will have access to, including professors and non-formal education."

It is in the experience of the student abroad, as above, that can help to inform educators on how to move forward. As I have mentioned previously, the experience of studying and/or volunteering in Africa is one of subject (the student) and object (the African city and continent). When we allow the two to come together in a mutual learning space, the relationship is allowed to develop. As Dewsbury et al. suggest:

> There is a need to move away from speaking of affections and perceptions … to move towards an account that takes seriously the world's own forces. This is a world between potential and determination, between what has happened and what could, a world captured in the tension of its present tense of becoming, a not yet enacted moment where we meet and greet ourselves in the affect that inspires action. In sum, affects and percepts are that through which subject and object emerge and become possible, they speak to the emergent eventuality of the world. (2002: 439)

Here on the continent the face of Africa is emerging every day in new forms of being and new ways of expressing "Africanness." New forms of modernity emerge from the street in terms of fashion, language, music, art, and other forms of expression. Experiencing life from the pedestrian perspective disrupts conventional knowledge of Africa. This means casting aside binary thinking that shapes African subjects as either traditional or modern in their thinking, urban or rural in their place of dwelling, formal or informal in the way they engage with the economy. International educators continually argue for the inclusion of "nontraditional" destinations in the panoply of student mobility offerings, yet much of the field for students and educators alike is tainted by perceptions and misgivings of Africa. It is time, therefore, that the conversation with Africa take a step ahead—beyond the romance of the postcolonial and the thrill of a safari and beyond the seductive mystery of the dark continent. The time for exercising the mutuality of subject and object in rethinking Africa is upon us. By engaging students in educational experiences in Africa, we have only just begun. What comes next is up to the students and their African hosts.

Bradley Rink lectures human geography in the Department of Geography, Environmental Studies and Tourism at the University of the Western Cape (Cape Town, South Africa). He focuses his research and teaching on mobilities, tourism, and urban place making. Having studied abroad in Spain as an undergraduate, Bradley has served in a range of education abroad capacities in South Africa, the United States, and elsewhere. He is a member of the Forum on Education Abroad's Trained Facilitator Team in addition to being in the first cohort of Forum Certified Education Abroad Professionals since 2014.

Notes

1. Based on a survey of 209 students from higher education institutions in the US studying in three African countries (Ghana, Senegal, and South Africa) during the North American spring semester 2007. A total of 209 surveys were distributed with 53 responses received and used to inform this chapter. An online questionnaire was distributed to students via surveymonkey .com. Students were provided with nine questions that were chosen in order to gauge perception of "Africa" before and after their study abroad experience. Perceptions of the past were retrospective in nature and thus demonstrate the students' interpretation of their own feelings toward Africa. In addition, students were asked to record the sources that informed their perception, and to provide suggestions as to how educators could best address perceptions of Africa.

References

Ballard, R. 2005. "Bunkers for the Psyche: How Gated Communities Have Allowed the Privatisation of Apartheid in Democratic South Africa." *Dark Roast Occasional Papers Series* 24. Kenilworth, South Africa: Isandla Institute.

Crang, M. 2009. "Tourism." In D. Gregory, R. Johnston, G. Pratt, M. Watts, and S. Whatmore (eds), *Dictionary of Human Geography,* 5th ed. Chichester, UK: Wiley-Blackwell, pp. 763–64.

Cresswell, T. 2004. *Place: A Short Introduction.* Malden, MA: Blackwell.

Dewsbury, J.D., John Wylie, Paul Harrison, and Mitch Rose. 2002. "Enacting Geographies." *Geoforum* 33(4): 437–41.

Guruz, K., 2011. *Higher Education and International Student Mobility in the Global Knowledge Economy,* 2nd ed. Albany: State University of New York Press.

Hannam, K., and G. Butler. 2012. "Engaging the New Mobilities Paradigm in Contemporary African Tourism Research." *Africa Insight* 42(2): 127–35.

Hannam, K., M. Sheller, and J. Urry. 2006. "Editorial: Mobilities, Immobilities and Moorings." *Mobilities* 1(1): 1–22.

Henderson, G. 2003. "What (Else) We Talk about When We Talk about Landscape: For a Return to the Social Imagination." In C. Wilson and P. Groth (eds), *Everyday America: Cultural Landscape Studies after J.B. Jackson.* Berkeley: University of California Press, pp. 178–98.

Herrick, C. 2010. Lost in the field: Ensuring Student Learning in the 'Threatened' Geography Fieldtrip. *Area* 42(1): 108-116.

Hoffa, W., and S. DePaul. 2010. "Introduction." In W. Hoffa and S. DePaul (eds), *A History of U.S. Study Abroad: 1965–Present.* Carlisle, PA: Frontiers Journal Press, pp. 1–14.

Hudson, N. 2008. "The 'Hottentot Venus,' Sexuality, and the Changing Aesthetics of Race, 1650–1850." *Mosaic* 41(1): 19–37.

Johnson, M. 2009. "Post-reciprocity: In Defense of the 'Post' Perspective." *Frontiers* 18: 181–86.

Keim, C. 2009. *Mistaking Africa: Curiosities and Inventions of the American Mind,* 2nd ed. Boulder, CO: Westview.

Knudsen, D., Anne K. Soper, and Michelle Metro-Roland. 2007. "Commentary: Gazing, Performing and Reading: A Landscape Approach to Understanding Meaning in Tourism Theory." *Tourism Geographies* 9(3): 227–33.

Meinig, D.W. 1979. "The Beholding Eye: Ten Versions of the Same Scene." In J.B. Jackson and D. Meinig (eds), *The Interpretation of Ordinary Landscapes: Geographical Essays.* Oxford: Oxford University Press, pp. 33–48.

Miller, A. 2010. *Slow Motion: Stories about Walking.* Auckland Park, South Africa: Jacana.

Panelli, R. and Welch, R.V. 2005. Teaching Research Through Field Studies: A Cumulative Opportunity for Teaching Methodology to Human Geography Undergraduates. *Journal of Geography in Higher Education* 29(2): 255–277.

Pratt, M.L. 1992. *Imperial Eyes: Travel Writing and Transculturation.* London: Routledge.

Rodriguez, K., and B. Rink. 2011. "Performing Cities: Engaging the High-Tech Flâneur." *Frontiers* 20: 103–19.

Sheller, M., and J. Urry. 2006. "The New Mobilities Paradigm." *Environment and Planning A* 38(2): 207–26.

Shephard, K. 2008. "Higher Education for Sustainability: Seeking Affective Learning Outcomes." *International Journal of Sustainability in Higher Education* 9(1): 87–98.

Thrift, N. 2004. "Intensities of Feeling: Towards a Spatial Politics of Affect." *Geografiska Annaler* 86B(1): 57–78.

UNDP United Nations Development Programme. 2015. *Human Development Report 2015.* Retrieved 23 December 2015 from http://hdr.undp.org/en/2015-report.

Urry, J. 1990. *The Tourist Gaze: Leisure and Travel in Contemporary Societies.* London: Sage.

———. 2007. *Mobilities.* Cambridge: Polity.

Wylie, J. 2007. *Landscape.* London: Routledge.

———. 2009. "Landscape." In D. Gregory, R. Johnston, G. Pratt, M. Watts, and S. Whatmore (eds.), *Dictionary of Human Geography,* 5th ed. Chichester, UK: Wiley-Blackwell, pp. 409–11.

CHAPTER 5

Thinking Through the Romance

Hannah Davis Taïeb, with Emily Bihl, Mai-Linh Bui, Hyojung Kim, and Kaitlin Rosenblum

The romantic notions and the passions of students are what propel study abroad. From the point of view of those of us who are running study abroad programs, a rush of emotion and energy arrives each September and January with each group of young people, buffeting us, rushing past us, and carrying us along. What are these passions? Should we be seeing them as powering a heroic journey (Chisholm 2000), launching students to the unknown? Or do these passions raise students too high, buoying them on euphoric highs that may crash to problematic lows? Should we use a critical lens and see these passions as misguided thrill seeking? Are romantic notions merely part of an illusory search for an imaginary, reified Other, or a nostalgic yearning for a lost "authenticity" or "reality"? And if part of our role is to intervene productively in student experience, then what kinds of interventions can and should we propose?

These questions must be placed in the context of this particular moment in the history of international education. As discussed in Chapter 2, study abroad professionals no longer share the once taken-for-granted idea that student travel automatically will lead to desired positive results—whether these are conceived as language learning, better understanding of others, or transmission of "American values." In an earlier era, it was assumed goals would be achieved through immersion in the other language group and culture—though this word was not always used, since the process was largely taken for granted. In more recent years, "immersion" and "culture learning" and engagement with native speakers have been defined as goals. This was partly a result of close scrutiny and questioning of what actually happens when students travel. But the definition of these terms was also due to the elusiveness of the phenomena themselves—due to increasing movements of people, of images, of objects, throughout the world, due to the rise of English as an International Language, and due to the increasing participation in study abroad of students with varying majors and lower language levels, sometimes studying abroad in island programs and in English. (Study abroad programs are usually identified as falling into three categories: "direct enrollment" programs where students study entirely at local universities, "island" programs where students take in-house courses and do not study side-by-side with local students, and "hybrid" programs combining in-house and direct-enrollment classes.)

So, at this particular moment in time, what are some of the ways study abroad professionals may think they should interact with or "intervene" in student emotional experience?

- We may think our job is to ease students' emotional ride, to smooth over the humps in the ups and downs, to make the roller coaster of exploring cultural difference into a gentle journey. This may include orientation sessions on the up-and-down *W* of culture shock with initial highs followed by disappointing lows and new, more accomplished rises in feeling (see Chapter 2). It may involve as well the task of translating, interpreting, or even watering down differences, while still maintaining them—retranslating or serving up culture in a palatable form. This point of view may be encouraged by the process of assessing study abroad programs based on student evaluations, written just after the end of the program and therefore not taking into account long-term learning and changes in judgement.
- We may think that our job is on the contrary to push the student out of his or her "comfort zone"—to force them, whether or not they so wish, into "immersion" or into activities with local people that might make them uncomfortable, but not so uncomfortable that they will fall back into a refusal to learn. Once again, this can involve a cultural intermediary role for the study abroad professional, who seeks out activities and even particular local people to connect with the students.
- We may think our job is to bring the student's attention to the emotions evoked by cultural difference, since we think these moments of feeling bothered can be reinterpreted as moments of cultural discovery. For example, we can ask students to write about each difficult emotional moment as a possible "intercultural misunderstanding" that could be interpreted through the tech-

nique of the critical incident (McAllister et al. 2006; Apedaile and Schill 2008).

- We may think our job is to bring the student to a new kind of attentiveness to him- or herself and to his or her perceptions, notably of cultural difference—to encourage the student to mindfulness, for example (Pryor et al. 2014; Vande Berg, Quinn, and Menyhart 2012; Schaetti, Ramsey, and Watanabe 2008; http://www.huffingtonpost.com/kyle-david-anderson/mindful-study-abroad-1_b_8277872.html).
- We may see the student's positive emotions (enthusiasm, desire to serve others, passion for connection) as a source of energy we can help the student harness to achieve goals we think useful (for example, to engage in volunteer projects, or to take risks to engage with local society).
- We may think our job is to foster change in the student's emotional being—to influence them so that they feel a desire for social justice, or a new openness to new viewpoints, or greater power and independence.
- We may think we need to urge them along a path towards some organized kind of "intercultural development," determined by external, supposedly objective testing devices such as the Intercultural Development Inventory, which assesses people in terms of six developmental stages: Denial of Difference, Defense against Difference, Minimization of Difference, Acceptance of Difference, Adaptation to Difference, and Integration of Difference (Bennett 1986; Hammer 2009, 2012; Hammer, Bennett and Wiseman 2003; Vande Berg, Paige, and Lou 2012).

This list raises the question of where international educators are themselves situated with regard to "cultural difference." Study abroad directors and staff are astride (at least) two worlds; being bilingual and bicultural are job prerequisites. Whatever has led us to our actual complex positioning, we are by now unlikely to see culture as neat and discrete, unlikely to see authenticity as easy to come by. We are likely to be personally engaged in the project of cosmopolitanism—changing borders, creating new identities, playing with language and self. We may find our own development to be more disconcerting, more individualized, and less linear and evolutionary than the assessment tools suggest; the project of "understanding cultural difference" may seem to us far from straightforward.

We may then balk at the idea that we are supposed to provide an experience that will at once live up to the heightened, vivid expectations of the student and at the same time exempt the student from danger and harm. Though we acknowledge our intermediary position, we do not necessarily see ourselves serving only as moderators, letting through just the right amount of cultural difference (with just the right amount of accompanying discomfort) to keep students happy and satisfied and stimulated.

So if we are not providers of user-friendly cultural difference, if we are not going to cater to or try to satisfy student desires, then how *do* we respond to them? What are the alternatives?

In this chapter, I would like to suggest that we join with students in the observation and interrogation of their passions, pose with them the questions that these passions raise. This means, to the extent that it is possible, that we face squarely with our students the realities of early twenty-first-century travel and study, and that we seek out the theoretical and practical tools to make this possible. Is this a kind of intervention? Yes, just as all teaching is intervention. But it is not a technique designed to achieve a predetermined goal—it is intervention that is also interaction, and a broadening of the field of discussion.

Part of this twenty-first-century reality is just those issues discussed above—intense and constant movement, blurring of cultural boundaries and consequent obsessive refashioning of them, flourishing of diasporic and transnational cultural forms, doubts about authenticity and identity, and consequent searching for that which seems lost. We are part of these phenomena ourselves, as is the increasing volume of student movement in many directions. However, being part of the phenomena does not mean we cannot gain by reflecting on it—on the contrary. As Martha Johnson puts it:

> The terms "authentic" and "real" are perhaps the most widely abused terms in study abroad. Marketing materials and program guides abound with promises to provide the student an opportunity to experience the "real." But perhaps more concerning is the lack of engagement with the complexity of such an idea within the study abroad profession ... [T]he postmodern theoretical base provides the opportunity to enter into a discussion with the student about their own expectations and cultural assumptions that have resulted in this constant desire to seek the "authentic."' (Johnson 2009: 184)

To enter into a discussion with students about their desires: this is what Johnson is proposing. An open-ended discussion that does not presume that we know one path to enlightenment; a critical and self-critical discussion, as all teaching can and should be. And this is what I would like to explore here as a way for international education professionals to respond to student emotion, passion, and romantic notions. The idea is to create opportunities for critical engagement with students about these heightened aspects of their experience. One setting in which I have made this attempt is in teaching intercultural communication to study abroad students in Paris.

In what follows, I will start with an overview of the setting and the students, with a brief résumé of some of the texts and approaches I use in class. I will then present four résumés of student work, written by students in my Intercultural Communication class during the Fall 2011 and Spring 2012 semesters. The first text, by Kaitlin Rosenblum, analyzes the romance of study abroad itself in anthropological terms. The second text, by Emily Bihl, deconstructs one particular romantic image of Paris, and one particular kind of study abroad "tourism" that feeds on the notion of the foreign. The third and fourth texts, by Mai-Linh Bui and Hyojung Kim, are preceded by a brief reflection on the importance of the perspective of multicultural students. Their texts concern "studying abroad while studying abroad"—the particular situation of students who leave their home countries to study in the United States, and from there, join groups of mainly American-born students for a semester in yet another country. Mai-Linh Bui's text compares the romance-driven study quest with that motivated by less starry-eyed considerations, and Hyojung Kim's text compares the difficult immersion of a high-school exchange in a small American town with the pleasures of the Paris stint. After these four student texts, I will conclude with a discussion of the value I believe can be found in developing with students a conversation about study abroad itself, its emotional charge, the romantic notions associated with it and with the destination. I will also return to the questions with which I started this chapter.

The Setting

CIEE is a US-based nonprofit organization focusing on international exchange in education. The activities of CIEE are widespread, including study abroad, gap year programs for youth between high school and college, high school exchanges, faculty seminars, short-term and faculty-led programs, English teaching, and inbound programs for those seeking to work and study in the United States. The study abroad part of CIEE draws on relationships with a wide range of US colleges and universities, including some that are member institutions; however, students from nonmember institutions are also welcomed on CIEE's numerous study abroad programs that exist throughout the world.

The CIEE Paris center houses several programs, including, at the time discussed here, the Critical Studies Program (a direct-enrollment program for students with five semesters or more of French), the Contemporary French Studies Program (a two-track hybrid program with some direct enrollment but mainly in-house courses), and a gap-year program as well as several summer programs. The center, in central Paris, consists of administrative offices, four classrooms, and space for students to study, work on computers, and spend time.

I have a PhD degree in anthropology for Middle East studies from New York University. Prior to working in study abroad, I taught intercultural communication, interpersonal communication, and comparative media at the American University of Paris. I have been working in study abroad since summer 2000, and directed the Contemporary French Studies Program for CIEE Paris and taught within it between fall 2006 and summer 2015.

The Contemporary French Studies Program accepted students enrolled in US universities with a minimum of two semesters of French. This minimum language requirement meant that all students had some prior interest in France or French. However, the relatively low number of required semesters meant that this prior interest could take many forms; some students had taken French throughout high school; others had studied for at least one year in college. A few students each semester had a family connection to France, such as a French parent.

The program size at the time of writing ranged from thirty-five to sixty students a semester, with 10–30 percent of them staying for the year, while the rest stayed only one semester. All students were housed with French people, in Paris itself or, occasionally, in nearby suburbs; this requirement meant that the students who chose the program were interested in taking on the risks and possible rewards of the home stay. Students took six hours a week of French grammar and conversation, and took content classes in English at the CIEE study center (for those with low-intermediate French), in French at the CIEE study center (for those with high-intermediate French), or at a French partner university (for those with advanced French).

This chapter is based on work with students in an intercultural communication class taught in English. The students enrolled had various French levels; though in theory the class was designed for those with low French levels, each semester a few advanced students nonetheless signed up for it.

Pedagogical Approaches

My approach was first to introduce students to the contemporary critique and reflection on the romance of Paris and the romance of study abroad itself, and second to incorporate them into this discussion through reflection on their own experience. Through the establishment of partnerships with French professors and students, I ensured that at least four of the fourteen class sessions took place as joint classes with a mixed French-American student body. The form of the class sessions, whether with all CIEE students or in joint sessions with French students, included not only lecture and discussion but class workshops including skits, role-playing, free association, and the analysis of critical incidents (discussed below). The pedagogical advantages of this joint approach will be discussed in a later section of this chapter.

Required readings for the class included texts on the romance of Paris, of France, and of Europe (Gallant 2004; Kaplan 1994; Woolf 2011), texts on the multiplicity and complexity of identity (Maalouf 2001; Saïd 1999), and sociological approaches to identity and culture as active and created (Goffman 1963; Tracy 2002). The focus was not on "French culture" as an entity but on Frenchness and Amernicanness, on *regards croisés* or views of the other (Carroll 1990; Monneyron and Xiberras 2006; Portes 1990), on how images of self and other are mobilized in discourses of national identity (Shields–Argeles 2004), on how people incorporate aspects of cultures defined as Other in processes of change (Shields-Argeles 2010), on cultural mixing and *métissage*, on different conceptions of difference. Readings for papers include critical recent texts on study abroad (Citron 2002; Engle and Engle 2002; Grünzweig and Rinehart 2002; Ogden 2007; Zemach-Bersin 2008).

Fictional texts, and memoirs like Alice Kaplan's *French Lessons* (1994), can highlight issues for students effectively. One of the desires pulling at the study abroad student is the desire to come in contact with an idealized difference, to create and experience a transcendent "perfect French moment." This can be almost a hunger: Kaplan has written beautifully about the way desire for the other can have a carnivorous quality: "I wanted to breathe in French with André... It was the rhythm and pulse of his French I wanted, the body of it," she writes about the French lover she met during her study abroad year in Bordeaux (94). "I wanted to crawl into his skin, live in his body, be him" (88). Alice Kaplan was passionate about the language itself, which she wants to take on, take in.

If I find few of my students evoking this kind of passion and desire to slip into the other's skin, I do find a common and perhaps more surface desire to create, imitate, or devour something of "Frenchness." The desire to pass as a Parisian, to become fluent, is one of the very frequently expressed, as well as the attempt to create "moments." In my notes from a student trip to Dijon in Spring 2007, I find the following:

> I went around from table to table at the restaurant, making an announcement about the evening's activities. At one table six students had their forks raised, smiling into the camera; they were eating snails. "Don't talk to us right now, we're having a moment."

The desire to participate in and taste the sensations associated with a classic image of a new place can be criticized as shallow and fleeting—as if one wanted to scotch-tape one's photo onto a postcard, or make each travel destination nothing but a pretext for a selfie. But these playful "moments" only become truly objectionable if they involve reducing the locals to extras, to local color. That is why a key strategy of the class was to develop critical approaches to these desires, and also to develop dialogs with French students (through joint classes), including about this very issue.

It is helpful to establish these kinds of discussions in a classroom setting, in which the motivations of the French students participating are similar to those of the American students. In such a context, both the French and the American students are engaged as *thinkers* about culture and difference, as opposed to functioning as *representatives* of their cultures. The reconsideration of romantic notions thus can take place in Franco-American interaction, making it all the more likely that this reevaluation will have a lively, playful quality and a lasting effect. Rather than focusing on the passions and projections of the American student on the French, we can see that these passions and projections run both ways, as Kaplan shows when she looks at Andre's ambiguous passion for his "*petite Américaine*," his little American girl.

Kaplan, in looking back on her own study abroad experience in the 1970s, thus can give students a way to reflect on their own dreams and romantic images. These reflections can be deepened through an intercultural practice that brings in French students as full participants in the classroom. And although Kaplan's love for Frenchness at times leads her astray, the errors in the long run lead her to a very real, down-to-earth connection with the language and the country she loved uncritically at first. Thus she shows that love may be misguided, and frustrating, but it can also be fruitful, as I think these student contributions illustrate.

The Student Papers

American Study Abroad: A Rite of Passage Within the Wake of Globalization—Kaitlin Rosenblum

One of the paper topics I proposed to students was "study abroad as a rite of passage." Kaitlin Rosenblum, then studying anthropology at the College of Charleston, chose to write her final paper on this subject.

Kaitlin Rosenblum's paper starts with an evocation of the magic appeal of study abroad: "Every semester more and more students leave their home universities to join the exodus of those searching for the almost mythical experience of international education. 'A semester abroad'; the rose-tinted phrase ..."

Through interviews with other students, Kaitlin Rosenblum brings out three themes that she sees as characterizing study abroad discourse:

> First, the desire to truly immerse oneself within the culture, ... to become "a seasoned Parisian." Second, the notion that studying abroad is a challenge that the individual must overcome. The third theme is manifested within the idea that studying abroad will lead to complete separation from our native culture; an experience that is often associated with the feeling of being "homesick."

Rosenblum goes on to discuss the historical background of study abroad and its fantasies, including the notion of European study abroad as a "finishing school," and citing John Engle and Lilli Engle's critical analyses of the "almost magical" stories woven around the "life of a student abroad," their supposed unimaginable rapid progress in language, their rapidly developing respect for other cultures, their intuitive ability to make connections between in-class and outside-of-class experience, and their supposed rapid personal growth. Rosenblum evokes Engle and Engle's critical evaluation of how "a visible superficial layer of American-informed global culture, language, and economic values" blurs the cultural landscape, and how students turn to electronic communication and "obsessive weekend travel." She also draws out Ogden's notion of the "colonial student" who crosses "borders and oceans without leaving behind the context, and comfort, of their mother country's customs and regulations ... The world beyond the borders of the fifty states becomes a ware available for purchase that is worn with the same pride as a covetable diamond ring" (Rosenblum paper, citing Ogden 2007: 37–38).

Using the concepts of liminality and *communitas*, Rosenblum discusses the notion of "study abroad as a rite of passage." She identifies the creation of a group with other study abroad students during the period prior to departure, the moment of "separation from the student body of the home campus" as occurring upon the boarding of an airplane, the forming of a new group on arrival in the location, with "stories ... exchanged of struggle and victory as the group grasps for stability within their new environment."

> It is the unstructured nature of *communitas* that drives students to form relationships with one another in order to provide mutual aid and understanding ... Upon completion of the rite, the student is welcomed back into the culture with new respect from both peers and elders. (Rosenblum paper, citing Turner 1969).

Kaitlin Rosenblum makes an original contribution to the analysis of study abroad discourse in her reflection on the contradiction between the "immersion" discourse and the "great adventure" discourse:

> In my opinion ... the discourse on study abroad presents a paradox. The individual is encouraged to completely immerse his or herself within the host culture while also having the greatest adventure of his or her lifetime.

Rosenblum goes on to quote the French expression *Metro, Boulot, Dodo,* suggesting that immersion as a "native" involves an "abandon" of "all illusions of enterprise," a descent into "the monotonous feeling of '*metro*' (subway), '*boulot*' (work), and '*dodo*' (sleep) within one's own daily life." She also points out the contradiction between the search for "the great adventure," which can lead to "traveling out of the host country on a regular basis," and the intention to achieve fluency in the host country's language.

Tourism of Intellect—Emily Bihl

> February eleventh, almost exactly one month after my arrival in Paris, finds me sitting in front of the beloved Hermes typewriter of Shakespeare & Company. ... I remember using my mother's old typewriter to noisily clank out letters to my Grandmother on kitten-clad stationery when I was seven—but I am still decidedly out of practice. Eventually I manage to crank a piece of now-wrinkled paper through its bars and am about to type out the line *I am typing this from Shakespeare & Company in Paris* when I freeze, struck suddenly by a thought: how many others before me—tourists, Americans, students—have sat here and typed out the very same line?

Emily Bihl, a student in the English and Creative Writing Program at Johns Hopkins university, came to Paris full of the images of the writer's Paris. In her final paper for the Intercultural Communication course, she comes up with a term for this: "The Tourism of Intellect."

Her paper expresses a subtle understanding of her own process:

> On my trip I brought with me only three books: The Collected Works of T.S. Eliot, Just Kids by Patti Smith, and A Moveable Feast. Three works by writers who came to Paris from America, like myself—Eliot, who was born in St. Louis where I was raised; Patti Smith who grew up in Camden, New Jersey, not far from where my parents now live; Hemingway, who came of age in Chicago like my father did. Remarkably, I brought with me no French writers.

As Emily started to engage with the city, she noted that she was going "to a café where Americans go." She quotes from her journal entry, where she points out how "funny" it is that "we can pretend we are participating in this city when we meet together like this."

Bihl carefully distinguishes between different motivating passions. Some Americans seek to attain "Frenchness," to become French or to master the language. Emily writes that her goal "was some vague ideal of bohemianism."

> "Americans ... come to France to get themselves some culture," Kaplan remarks—and as someone who came into adolescence alongside a song about adolescents in Paris, whose lyrics go "Hey/let's cross the sea/and get some culture" I can hardly argue with her point (Minus 1). Tourism of the intellect is not about becoming a native in your adopted land—in face it's wholly antithetical to this. The foreign land must remain foreign.

Bihl also raises the question of authenticity. Eating lunch in a site where Hemingway had once lunched, she evokes the Ship of Theseus:

If all parts of an object are replaced, one by one, is it still the same object? Was there anything about the restaurant that was the same as when Hemingway had been there? Would his magic, his essence still be intact even if the floor had been retiled?

Multicultural Students and the Importance of Their Point of View

For some American students, the thrill of studying abroad comes from the novelty of travel, a border crossing that is re-created and relived through continual, ongoing travel during the semester. But other students come from US universities to study "abroad" having already changed countries many times in their lives. These students have much to offer in the context of discussions and interactions about culture, change, and difference.

Students from mixed cultural backgrounds, and in particular those born outside the United States, are less likely to respond to the "rose-tinted" phrases evoked by Kaitlin Rosenblum. Some may be multilingual and are studying French as a third or fourth language; they already know well the difficulties and frustrations of language learning and the real discomfort of cultural "immersion."

The points of view of students of various backgrounds, citizenships, and origins can be elicited and considered in our classroom exchanges, and this allows us to face and analyze the moment in history in which our study abroad projects take shape. As Homi Bhabha puts it in the introduction to *The Location of Culture,* "The very concepts of homogenous national cultures, the consensual or contiguous transmission of historical traditions, or 'organic' ethnic communities—as the grounds of cultural comparativism—are in a profound process of redefinition" (1994: 7).

When we acknowledge with the students that we are in a period of heterogeneity, where national (and other, e.g., religious) identities are in flux, then we can embrace this contemporary period with our students with more integrity. Those students who themselves have experienced many kinds of movement through space, many more kinds of elsewhere, are key players.

The Doors We Open and Close Each Day
Decide the Way We Live—Mai-Linh Bui

Born in Vietnam, Mai-Linh was in the process of studying abroad for her B.A. degree in the United States at Drexel University. So, as a participant in the CIEE study abroad program for one semester in Fall 2011,

Mai-Linh was "studying abroad while studying abroad." The process of choice that she went through contrasts with that of her fellow students, and her reflections on the romance of studying abroad and the cultural changes she faced in her two host countries contributed to class discussions in a significant way. Even the conception of the term *abroad* is repositioned when US students begin to see the United States as "abroad" for visitors.

Mai-Linh focused her paper on a difficult choice she had to make: whether to study abroad in France, or in the United States:

> When my father was young, after high school, he had only two choices: either go to a university in the city or stay at home and take care of my grandfather's farms ... However, we gradually have more and more choices and so we do not know which is the best for us ... I try every day to make choices that I will not regret among those various possibilities, just as when I decided whether to go study abroad in the States or in France.

Mai-Linh's entire life prior to her college years was oriented towards higher education in France. She began learning French at age six. She writes that through "songs, readings, lectures and stories that my teachers gave me throughout primary school, secondary school and high school," she saw in her mind a picture

> about the country where people are jovial, noble and elegant, and where Eiffel Tower always stands as a dream destination for hope and brilliant minds ... All these things came along with every lecture, every French children's song we sang together and every story we heard from our singular teachers. They gradually planted in us a passion to go discover more and more and to enlarge our knowledge in that sparkling country. Studying abroad at that time, for secondary students like us, was a dream of putting our path in the new world of western culture.

The fantasy of France that Mai-Linh experienced shares some elements with the fantasies and images expressed by her US-born fellow students. Like her classmates, Mai-Linh saw the Eiffel Tower gleaming in a city proclaiming the possibility of elegance and hope. But there are many differences as well: the important role of the French teachers, and the notion of a discovery of "Western" culture, for example. The emotional vector of the dream is somehow different.

While her US-born colleagues rarely evoke their parents' fears and attitudes about their studies, Mai-Linh discusses parental concerns about the influence of studying abroad on their children's personalities and the fear that young Vietnamese people abroad might "forget our real traditional culture values or tame them with the western culture since we had learned a foreign language along with our mother tongue since very young." For Mai-Linh Bui, the French classes were "the happiest classes of our childhood," and "comparing France to the US where people are 'too' open and easygoing, our parents claimed that France was a 'safer' destination for their children."

Thus for Mai-Linh Bui, the choice of studying in the United States was a difficult one, and counterintuitive. Clearly, it was France that was the "sparkling destination," full of hope and dreams. The United States was a choice that she thought of as practical, related to the educational system. "I realize that there are things I can get while studying abroad in the States but not in France. The way of teaching and communicating with people are also different."

Mai-Linh Bui then analyses the differences between what she observes seeing her Vietnamese friends who are studying in France, and her own evolution. "I found a new me when studying in the States, the one who is more creative, more dynamic, more 'crazy,' who dares to try new things and who is not afraid of the change." Mai-Linh Bui quotes Flora Whittemore: "The doors we open and close each day decide the lives we live."

Thus, in her paper Mai-Linh Bui reflects on the romance of Paris and also on her unexpected, unromantic choice to study abroad in the United States in Philadelphia rather than in the "sparkling destination." Her emotional and cultural trajectory, presented in class as an oral presentation, made it possible for the questions of choice, or emotional pull, or cultural change to be decentered for the other students in the class as well. There is not only one "abroad," not only one home country to leave. The same "sparkling destination" plays a different role in the imaginations of Mai-Linh Bui and her Vietnamese fellow students than for her fellow students in the CIEE study abroad classroom.

The Way I Have Learned the Cultures—Hyojung Kim

Hyojung Kim, who used the name Tara Kim while studying with us in Paris, is a Korean student who had been studying abroad in the United States since high school. Having "always longed for living in a foreign country" to learn its "language, history and culture," she embarked on a high-school exchange program in a small American town. Her goal was "to learn American culture by heart and to be perfect at English

after the program." There, she was "satisfied with the fact that I was actually living the way other Americans live," in a town where she had
"no contact with other Koreans," as there were no other Asian students
at her high school. "Naturally, I spoke English all the time ... though I
was surrounded by many gentle American friends, I sometimes felt so
lonely and homesick because of difficulty of expressing my feeling and
thoughts on my own language." At the same time, she felt "proud" of
herself "because I constantly thought I had managed well how to live
on my own without any help from my own culture."

Tara Kim then went on to a boarding school in New Hampshire,
and university in Maryland. It was during her university years that she
"studied abroad while studying abroad." When she came to France, far
from feeling homesick, she found herself part of an (American) group
as never before:

> Even though we are not from the same origin, the fact that we came
> from the United States to study abroad in Paris made me feel a sense of
> belonging. Moreover, the big city makes me be able to meet other Ko-
> reans ... I spend most of my time ... speaking English or Korean. How-
> ever, for me who came to Paris with the goal of learning French culture
> and language, this easiness was not good news. At the same time
> when I feel relieved, I become guilty because it seems that I exchange
> this easiness with pain of going through new cultural experience.

Tara Kim also discusses her obligation during her high school exchange to stay in the United States for ten months without travelling.
This meant that she experienced all of the American holidays, which
were presented to her with careful, explicit attention by her host family
who saw themselves as cultural intermediaries. She sees a four-month
semester program in Paris as not enough.

She looks back on her sixteen-year-old self, and calls what she did
then, "total immersion," which was "much more effective to learn even
though it was more painful, and therefore I valued that painful memory
as worthwhile." "After the storm comes the calm," she writes, saying that
the difficulty of her high school exchange period allowed her to settle in
the United States for the following six years.

> But I am not saying that the experience of study abroad in Paris was
> not worthwhile because now I realized which learning method is more
> helpful. Moreover, full of pleasurable memories of Paris encouraged me
> to come back later. I can see I will come back to Paris after my gradu-
> ation with more determined mind to learn the culture and language.

The results for her of her study abroad are unexpected: she told me she "never felt so American" as she did while studying abroad in the program in Paris, and she connected happily and energetically with Koreans in Paris. The changes in identities, identifications, the links made and the discoveries, as students travel and study abroad, clearly cannot be categorized as easily as we might have thought.

Discussion of Student Papers

The four texts here testify to the fact that students can contribute to the reflection about what study abroad is about—and not only through comments on anonymous evaluation forms, not as clients of study abroad, but as full participants, and critical thinkers. Each one of the texts above contributes something to our understanding. Rosenblum's and Bihl's texts help us think through the rite of passage of the study abroad period; the contradictions or possible contradictions in avowed study abroad goals (adventure and immersion); the exoticism involved in certain kinds of particular travel fantasies and the questioning of the desire for the authentic ("Tourism of Intellect"). Bui's and Kim's texts confront us with the profoundly different and sometimes surprising effects of study abroad launched with passion towards "the sparkling destination" as compared to study abroad carried out for practical reasons; of study abroad suffered through in loneliness and hardship as opposed to study abroad without homesickness. They challenge our use of the terms *home* and *abroad* and show us that travel is not always a circular departure and return, and that the connections made and changes in identification may be various and highly particular.

From the point of view of the study abroad staff member, or professor, I am arguing for creating a critical theoretical base with our students. For me, this involved the assignment of readings that analyze the mutual gaze and a social-psychological, anthropological, and/or interactionist approach to discourses of national belonging (e.g., Shields-Argèles 2004 and 2010 concerning French and American images of the Other in terms of food; Lamont 1992 on money; Tracy 2002 on talk; Carroll 1990 on French-American views of the other) and to inequality (Goffman 1963); fictions and memoirs about the romance of the destination (Kaplan 1994 and Gallant 2004 on images of France; Labro 1988 on French study abroad in the United States); works on diversity, inequality, postcolonial identities, and notions of difference (White 2001 on French and American gay men; Rosello 1998 on "Black-Blanc-Beur" films and stereotyping in France, and Rosello 2003 on multiculturalism in France; Maalouf 2001 and Saïd 1999 on complex identities; Stiker 2000 on discourses of the body and disability), and critiques of study abroad (I used Ogden 2007, Grünzweig and Rinehart 2002, Citron 2002, Engle and Engle 2002, and Zemach-Bersin 2008, which was regularly proposed as reading at CIEE centers). The process of interpretation is thus shared with the student. I also integrated into the class activities designed to foster reflection on different positioning in terms of the questions of travel, stereotyping, and romance. For example, I asked students if they have ever lived in a place that was viewed in a romanticized way by visitors; students from places like New Orleans or the rural Midwest shared their experiences of being viewed themselves as "local color." Group work and skits involving stereotypes among the US study abroad students allow for a cathartic and collaborative investigation of how stereotypes work in everyday life, taken out of the France vs. America model. Through questionnaires and essays about their own romances with Paris, I elicited individualized reactions that brought out the fact that each student approached the site in a way that emerged from their own history. Joint classes with French students (discussed below), often involving skits and critical incidents, further integrated into the class the mutual gaze, diversity within France, and the particularity of each individual point of view. Thus I was neither in the role of piercing student illusions, nor in the role of propping up those illusions (e.g., the selection and furnishing of "perfect moments" corresponding to cultural fantasies, the providing of local interlocutors to model cultural phenomena). Instead, I was able to participate in critical group reflection and rethinking with my students and with the French student groups as well.

I have cited student papers at length here as I think they suggest that critical reflection during study abroad can bring students into a conversation with educators and scholars that has content and inherent value—that is both international and educative. As Grünzweig and Rinehart point out, Martin Buber's "dialogical principle of education" can find expression in study abroad (2002:18). Education is the creation of conversations, the initiation of students into conversations already underway, the enlarging and broadening of the group that is able to converse. A focus on student experience should not mean that we abandon the value of teaching critical thought, including about that very experience. This is possible if we trust ourselves, trust our students, trust our local partners, and create respectful, long-term relationships with those around us in the contexts in which we work.

Critical Incidents in Mixed Groups

The extension of our conversation to include our local partners is a key part of the pedagogical strategy I have been exploring. As mentioned earlier, I have consistently integrated into my intercultural communication classes sessions co-led with French professors and a mixed student body. My collaborations have included joint co-led classes with Jérémy Arki of the Université of Paris Diderot (Paris 7); joint co-led classes with social psychologist Verena Aesbicher, in her *Contact de cultures et compétences interculturelles* class at the University of Paris Nanterre (Paris 10); and co-led workshops with Ita Hermouet, then director of International Relations and Communication at the ICES (Institut Catholique d'Etudes Supérieurs) in La Roche sur Yon, working with French students intending to study abroad or returning from studying abroad in the United States. Since these classes were co-taught by an American and a French professor, the mixed group of students had a model of collaboration and of different pedagogical styles. All students were present in their roles as students, all were working towards a grade, and in most cases the American and French students had similar goals and shared readings and approaches; I make this point to distinguish these kinds of dialogues from other contexts in study abroad in which local people, often local students, are brought in as conversation partners or are paid to accompany American students.

In this context, my co-teachers and I used some of the tried-and-true practices of intercultural learning, such as the analysis of the critical incident (Jackson 2002; McAllister et al. 2006; see Turunen 2002: 22–30 for a history of use of the critical incident in experiential learning). Critical incident analysis is a key example of how student affect is managed to facilitate learning, often with a goal of helping American students towards cultural "progress" as defined according to stage models of cultural development, and/or towards "intercultural competence," as discussed in Chapter 2 of this volume. The process as used in study abroad is based on the idea that emotion—which could be intense upset or anxiety, or simply niggling discomfort—can be an indicator of a moment when a student has experienced cultural difference or intercultural misunderstanding. Students are asked to reflect on such heightened moments, and write dispassionate descriptions of the "critical incident" that provoked them, without making value judgements. Then, in a class or workshop, the students reexamine the incident, and through a collaborative process come up with different possible interpretations. Skits can be used purposefully with the goal of rethinking spontaneous reactions.

Working in a mixed group greatly enriches the process of reexamination of emotionally charged critical incidents. This is not to suggest that there is no value to the process in a group composed only of study abroad students; on the contrary, study abroad students share common experiences on site but come from diverse viewpoints, and this kind of session can be valuable. In a mixed group, however, there is a broadening of the kinds of insights shared, and a recognition of the diversity in possible reactions that breaks down the reification of the "French" and the "American."

The critical incidents analyzed in class were provided by both the US study abroad students and by the French students. Topics included flirting and misunderstood intentions, cheating on tests, parental correction of children in public, perceptions of the American political role and American naiveté about this, bystander passivity in reaction to assault on a Paris street, *la bise* (kissing on both cheeks) vs. hugging, helping oneself to food in the refrigerator, questions about origins for people of color, ways of holding and moving while dancing ... Mixed groups produced skits; students could play corresponding to their identities (an American woman playing an American woman) or could choose to take a contrasting role (an American woman playing a French man). The skits were cathartic and allowed for a replaying and expanding of interpretations and roles for all the students (Mason 2006); opening the group to students who are themselves interested in challenging their assumptions works against reification. The process of working together to prepare the skits, and, in many of the joint classes, working together on papers or presentations, integrated practical collaborative processes.

Conclusions

I would like to return now to the more general questions raised at the beginning of this chapter. As study abroad administrators, we may indeed find it necessary and useful to accompany the ups and downs of student emotional experience. In the terms of this book's analytical approach, this means that part of our jobs is the management of affect. Clearly, this process goes beyond the *W* curve, which increasingly seems to be met by students with derision. The shock of culture has changed, now that technology allows for an illusion of permanent connection, a perpetual checking in that changes the role of distance and the nature of the break. Our role as companions to student emotional experience thus needs to evolve, and we need to open our minds to a shifting emotional landscape that we cannot predict and that is not conjured by any letter of the alphabet.

Similarly, I think we need to question developmental models of student change, if we are to fully engage as educators with our students and their world—which is also our world. The stages elaborated by the evolutionary model of the IDI—Denial of Difference, Defense against Difference, Minimization of Difference, Acceptance of Difference, Adaptation to Difference, and Integration of Difference—could in my opinion more fruitfully be viewed as *discourses* about difference. In the study abroad context, we can look at many discourses of difference, not evolutionarily, but as ways of thinking that are called upon at various times.

Rather than focusing uncritically on the predefined goal of "intercultural competence," we can contextualize and problematize such notions (see Chapter 2 for a discussion of different inflections to the term) and by looking at various ways of understanding difference and its handling—including *métissage,* or other local notions depending on the site; we can look at different notions of difference. And rather than focusing on student evolution and increased sensitivity, we can go towards a rich and mutual practice through joint intercultural classes in which professors and students share motivations and question each other's assumptions through collaborative action.

I would also suggest that we should think carefully about the ways we may be led to manipulate student passions. The mobilizing power of affect should not be brought down to the level of a marketing tool. Nor is there value in the study abroad staff member (or teacher, or host family) being put in the position of attempting to live up to student desires, providing safely packaged, consumerized experiences of Otherness that meet student fantasies and that are polished and gleaming to maintain the illusion of heightened experience. This is the kind of mobilization of affect that we should avoid.

However, this is not to say that student passions should be dismissed, derided, or denigrated. Difficult, unsettling emotions indeed can be analyzed and rethought, as is encouraged in the technique of the critical incident. Positive emotions can be fully lived and also questioned; a critique of one's own passions, one's own romantic drives, can yield new understandings.

The desire to find difference, to break with the past, to change—these passions propel people forward. As Alice Kaplan discusses in *French Lessons* (1994), powerful and sometimes misguided passions for France sent her and others into stumbling, difficult, but ultimately rich life trajectories. As we face our study abroad students, I think we can do more than just bemoan the idea that such passions may ebb and safety be chosen over discovery, more than just bemoan the fact that continual weekend travel may seem like a frenetic attempt to re-create the thrill. Instead, I think we need to reiterate the importance of critical thought and analysis and, as I have indicated, to join with our students in the interrogation of our passions. This means engaging with our students as thinking, critical people—returning to the old idea of teaching and the new concept of critical engagement.

This means not only working through emotion, but thinking through emotion—drawing students, and local partners, into this thought process, as equals rather than followers or foils. To the extent that it is possible, we can work towards situations in which thinkers of various backgrounds are communicating, sharing theoretical approaches, building critical approaches together. Once again, I am suggesting respecting ourselves, our peers of all backgrounds, and our students of all backgrounds—we all feel, we experience, we also think critically. This means treating our students as interlocutors, not as clients. While I am in full agreement with the contemporary trend in education that emphasizes experiential learning and out-of-the-classroom activities, I think that the analytical and theoretical basis of all learning needs to be maintained, and wedded to a pedagogy that seeks to pose problems rather than to ease them (Vassallo 2013). I am arguing, as Martha Johnson does (2009), for the creation with our students, and in dialogue with our peers and their peers of all backgrounds, of a useful, contemporary conceptual base from which we can examine our world.

Dr. **Hannah Davis Taïeb** is an international educator, teacher, and writer who was the director of CIEE's Contemporary French Studies Program in Paris from 2003 to 2015. She has a Ph.D. in anthropology from New York University; her thesis, concerning unmarried women and changing conceptions of the self, was based on fieldwork in a middle-sized city in Morocco. After working with a research team in Lyon, Hannah settled permanently in France in 1992, where she first was the co-editor of a multilingual, multidisciplinary review, *Mediterraneans,* then taught intercultural and interpersonal communication at the American University of Paris, before entering the field of study abroad in the year 2000. While at CIEE, she ran Franco-American seminars, joint classes, and study trips on subjects like disability, religious diversity and secularism, anti-Semitism and Islamophobia, chaplaincy and religion in prison, and special education. Independently, Hannah continues to teach about popular culture and *métissage*, religious diversity, and disability, co-teaches a Franco-American intercultural communication class, and runs volunteer and exchange activities with a Paris youth club.

Note

1. Many thanks to Alison McRae who commented on an earlier version of this chapter. All errors are mine. To Emily Bihl, Mai-Linh Bui, Hyojung Kim, and Kaitlin Rosenblum, great thanks for allowing me to use their papers in this chapter, and to all my intercultural communication students over the years, thanks and warm regards for so many inspiring and unexpected conversations. For so many moments of wonderful co-teaching and planning with our students, thanks to Verena Abischer, Jérémy Arki, Ita Hermouet, and Laure Millet.

References

Apedaile, Sarah, and Lenina Schill. 2008. *Critical Incidents for Intercultural Communication.* Norquest College. Retrieved from http://www.norquest.ca/pdf/ edresources/CriticalIncidentsBooklet.pdf.

Bennett, Milton J. 1986. "Towards Ethnorelativism: A Developmental Model of Intercultural Sensitivity." In R. Michael Paige (ed.), *Cross-cultural Orientation: New Conceptualizations and Applications.* New York: University Press of America, pp. 27–70.

Bhabha, Homi. 1994. *The Location of Culture.* London: Routledge.

Carroll, Raymonde. 1990. *Cultural Misunderstandings: The French-American Experience.* Chicago: University of Chicago Press.

Chisholm, Linda A. 2000. *Charting a Hero's Journey.* New York: International Partnership for Service-Learning and Leadership.

Citron, James L. 2002. "Host Culture Integration or Third Culture Formation?" In Walter Grünzweig and Nana Rinehart (eds), *Rockin' in Red Square: Critical Approaches to International Education in the Age of Cyberculture.* Piscataway, NJ: Transaction.

Engle, John, and Lilli Engle. 2002. "Neither International Nor Educative: Study Abroad in the Time of Globalization." In Walter Grünzweig and Nana Rinehart (eds), *Rockin' in Red Square: Critical Approaches to International Education in the Age of Cyberculture.* Piscataway, NJ: Transaction.

Gallant, Mavis. 2004. "The Other Paris." In *The Selected Stories of Mavis Gallant*. London: Bloosmbury.

Goffman, Erving. 1963. *Stigma: Notes on the Management of Spoiled Identity*. Englewood Cliffs, NJ: Prentice Hall.

Grünzweig, Walter, and Nana Rinehart (eds). 2002. *Rockin' in Red Square: Critical Approaches to International Education in the Age of Cyberculture*. Piscataway, NJ: Transaction.

Hammer, Mitchell R. 2009. "The Intercultural Development Inventory: An Approach to Assessing and Building Intercultural Competence." In M. Michael Moodian (ed.), *Contemporary Leadership and Intercultural Competence*. Thousand Oaks, CA: Sage.

——. 2012. "The Intercultural Development Inventory: A New Frontier in Assessment and Development of Intercultural Competence." In Michael Vande Berg, R. Michael Paige, and Kris Hemming Lou (eds), *Student Learning Abroad: What Our Students Are Learning, What They're Not, and What We Can Do About It*. Sterling, VA: Stylus.

Hammer, Mitchell R., M.J. Bennett, and R. Wiseman. 2003. "Measuring Intercultural Sensitivity: The Intercultural Development Inventory." *International Journal of Intercultural Relations* 27: 421–43.

Jackson, Janet. 2002. "Critical Incidents Across Cultures." Retrieved from https://www.llas.ac.uk/resources/paper/1426.

Johnson, Martha. 2009. "Post-reciprocity: in Defense of the 'Post' Perspective." *Frontiers* 28(Fall): 181–86.

Kaplan, Alice. 1994. *French Lessons: A Memoir*. Chicago: University of Chicago Press.

Labro, Philippe. 1988. *The Foreign Student*. New York: Ballantine Books.

Lamont, Michèle. 1992. *Money, Manners and Morals: The Culture of the French and American Upper-Middle Class*. Chicago: University of Chicago Press.

Maalouf, Amin. 2001. *In the Name of Identity: Violence and the Need to Belong*, trans. Barbara Bray. New York: Arcade.

Mason, Paul. 2006. "New Approaches to Role-Play in the Communication Classroom." Retrieved from http://www.ic.nanzan-u.ac.jp/tandai/kiyou/No.34/06-Paul%20Mason.pdf.

McAllister, Lindy, Gail Whiteford, Bob Hill, Noel Thomas, and Maureen Fitzgerald. 2006. "Reflection in Intercultural Learning: Examining the International Experience through a Critical Incident Approach." *Reflective Practice* 7(3): 367–81.

Monneyron, Frédéric, and Martine Xiberras (eds). 2006. *La France dans le Regard des Etats-Unis/France as Seen by the United States*. Perpignan: Presses Universitaires de Perpignan, Publications de l'Université Paul Valéry—Montpellier III.

Ogden, Anthony. 2007. "The View from the Veranda: Understanding Today's Colonial Student." *Frontiers: The Interdisciplinary Journal of Study Abroad* 15 (Winter): 35–51.

Portes, Jacques. 1990. *Une Fascination réticente : Les Etats-Unis dans l'opinion française.* Nancy: Presses universitaires de Nancy.

Pryor, Robert, Mattie Clark, Jamie Robinson, and Denise Cope. 2014. "Mindfulness Training in Intercultural Education." Retrieved from http://www.ceastudyabroad.com/educators/global-education/academic-team/publications.html.

Rosello, Mireille. 1998. *Declining the Stereotype. Ethnicity and Representation in French Cultures.* Hanover, NH: Dartmouth College Press.

——. 2003. "Tactical Universalism and New Multiculturalist Claims in Postcolonial France." In Charles Forsdick and David Murphy (eds), *Francophone Postcolonial Studies: A Critical Introduction.* London: Arnold, pp. 135–44.

Saïd, Edward W. 1999. *Out of Place: A Memoir.* London: Grant Books.

Schaetti, Barbara F., Sheila J. Ramsey, and Gordon C. Watanabe. 2008. *Making a World of Difference: Personal Leadership: A Methodology of Two Principles and Six Practices.* Seattle: Flying Kite Publications.

Shields-Argelès, Christy. 2004. "Imagining the Self and the Other: Food and Identity in France and the United States." *Food, Culture and Society* (Journal of the Association for the Study of Food and Society), Fall.

——. 2010. "Mastering French Cuisine, Espousing French Identity: The Transformation Narratives of American Wives of Frenchmen." *The Anthropology of Food* (December).

Stiker, Henri-Jacques. 2000. *A History of Disability,* trans. Wiliam Sayers. Ann Arbor: University of Michigan Press.

Tracy, Karen. 2002. *Everyday Talk: Building and Reflecting Identities.* New York: Guilford.

Turner, Victor. 1969. *The Ritual Process: Structure and Anti-Structure.* Chicago: Aldine.

Turunen, Hannele. 2002. "Critical Learning Incidents and Use as a Learning Method: A Comparison of British and Finnish Nurse Student Teachers." Ph.D. dissertation, University of Kuopio. Retrieved from http://epublications.uef.fi/pub/urn_isbn_951-781-932-3/urn_isbn_951-781-932-3.pdf.

Vande Berg, Michael, R. Michael Paige, and Kris Hemming Lou. 2012. *Student Learning Abroad: What Our Students Are Learning, What They're Not, and What We Can Do About It.* Sterling, VA: Stylus.

Vande Berg, Michael, Meghan Quinn, and Catherine Menyhart. 2012. "An Experiment in Developmental Teaching and Learning: The Council on International Educational Exchange's Seminar on Living and Learning Abroad." In Michael Vande Berg, R. Michael Paige, and Kris Hemming Lou (eds), *Student Learning Abroad: What Our Students Are Learning, What They're Not, and What We Can Do About It.* Sterling, VA: Stylus.

Vassallo, Stephen. 2013. "Critical Pedagogy and Neoliberalism: Concerns with Teaching Self-Regulated Learning." *Studies in Philosophy and Education* 32(6): 563–80.

White, Edmund. 2001. *The Married Man.* New York: Vintage.

Woolf, Michael. 2011. "The Baggage They Carry: Study Abroad and the Construction of 'Europe' in the American Mind." *Frontiers: The Interdisciplinary Journal of Study Abroad* 21(Fall): 289–309.

Zemach-Bersin, Talya. 2008. "American Students Abroad Can't Be 'Global Citizens'." *Chronicle of Higher Education* (7 March).

CHAPTER 6

Falling In/Out of Love with the Place

Affective Investment, Perceptions of Difference, and Learning in Study Abroad

Neriko Musha Doerr

Introduction

How does different affective investment by students—their romantic identification with the destination or lack of it—shape their study abroad experience? How are perceptions of difference and types of learning shaped by the degree of affective investment? This chapter addresses these little-explored questions by examining two contrasting cases of American students' experiences of summer study abroad in France and Spain in 2011. It investigates the role students' affect plays in the ways they perceive difference and learn in a context where there are no (formerly) institutionalized relations of power between nations, as would be the case in (post-)colonial situations. We cannot quantify "success" and "failure" in study abroad; experiences during study abroad are multidimensional and multilayered, and give rise to multiple interpretations that may change over time. Thus, I focus here on snapshots of the students' perceptions of experience before, during, and after their study abroad experience.

Sophie (names are aliases) had studied French language and culture for ten years and had, she said, "a romantic view" of Paris, her study abroad destination. Her romanticization of France led her to consciously strive to learn a lot about France prior to and during her stay. Once there, she perceived a fundamental difference between French and American peoples and, based on her learning, sought to *become* a Parisian through detailed observation and imitation. She sought to *embody* the Cultural Other. She viewed her fellow American students negatively, as not blending in. Upon her return, however, Sophie reported disillusionment with French people. This motivated her to reflect critically on her own experience and analyze the causes of her disillusionment.

Tracy, who had studied Spanish since second grade, chose Spain as her study abroad destination but did not romanticize it or hold preconceived images and expectations of Spain. My interview during her stay revealed that she enjoyed discovering Spain, was comfortable with who she was, and appreciated the company of fellow American students, from whom she was learning about various parts of the United States. She also said her struggles with Spanish led her to empathize with the hardship English-as-a-Second-Language speakers may experience in the United States. That is, she often looked beyond the differences between Americans and Spaniards, saw diversity among her fellow American students, and recognized similarities between Americans studying abroad and immigrants in the United States. She *connected* with both those who were not so Culturally Other as one might think (Spaniards and immigrants in the United States) and those who were more Culturally Other than one might think (Americans). Without preconceptions or expectations about Spain, she embraced whatever came her way and developed a love for Spain, but critically reflected little on her experience.

The contrast between Sophie's and Tracy's cases shows how different degrees of affective investment in the destination shapes the ways they perceive cultural differences and similarities among people as well as how they learn before and during their study abroad stay. This is a little-analyzed aspect of study abroad.

This is part of my wider research on processes of "learning cultural difference" through study abroad and alternative break trips (Doerr 2012, 2013a, 2013b, 2014, 2015a, 2015b). I have discussed Sophie's and Tracy's experiences in comparison to other students' in terms of highlighting various scales of difference—global, national, regional, etc.—through their narratives (2014), diverse types of learner subject they have become (2015b), and the politics of concealing their subject positions (under review b). This chapter revisits their experiences and analyzes them with a new focus on the role of affect in their experience.

In what follows, I will discuss the existing literature on affect and its relation to notions of difference and learning, introduce the context of Sophie's and Tracy's study abroad and of the fieldwork process, describe and analyze their experiences, and compare their perceptions of difference and learning.

On Affect

Several anthropological works have critiqued the earlier study of emotion as culturally mediated and historically constructed (Geertz 1963; Rosaldo 1984), claiming that this approach often equates culture, ethnicity, and language and treats them as static and internally homogeneous. More recent anthropological studies of affect investigate how affect is mobilized in various contexts (Boellstorff and Lindquist 2004). Affect is increasingly viewed as a useful analytical tool for understanding how individuals experience political violence, the ambiguities of various industrial settings, and the effects of hegemonic race, gender, and class ideologies (Good 2004).

Subjects of analysis have included the commodification of emotion (Hochschild 1983); the expression of affect—emotionally charged renditions of desirability, belonging, and commercial viability—in terms of race, sexuality, and gender (Ramos-Zayas 2009); the production of subjects by mobilizing affect in the economic transformation toward neoliberalism (Richard and Rudnyckyj 2009); and the bonding of subjects through the economy of fear (Ahmed 2004). Drawing on the Foucauldian concept of "conduct of conduct," which Dean described as "practices that try to shape, sculpt, mobilize, and work through the choices, desires, aspirations, needs, wants and lifestyles of individuals and groups" (1999: 12), Richard and Rudnyckyj (2009) argue that particular affects, such as feelings of shame, shape others' actions while also shaping oneself as subject (for more discussion, see the chapter by Doerr and Taïeb in this volume). This chapter examines how affect shapes the perception of difference and notions of learning in the context of study abroad.

Difference and Affect

Difference and affect have been discussed mainly in the context of relations of power between the West and its Others. Exoticism, a framework of spectatorship, renders particular individuals as objects of fantasies, fears, and desires, often resulting in the display of the exoticized, as discussed in Chapter 1 of this volume (Doerr and Taïeb). In the context of colonialism, people from the "non-West" were displayed in zoos, museums, and circuses, a practice that reached its height in the nineteenth century, yet its legacy continues in "cultural performances" by ethnic minorities (Fusco 1995). The framework of the spectacle both assumes and perpetuates an asymmetrical relationship between the displayed and the spectators: the spectacle distances and normalizes the spectators, while articulating the anomalous status of the displayed (Berger 1980; Stewart 1984).

Focusing on academic and other literature, Edward Said (1978) analyzes Western conceptions and exoticizing treatment of the Other through the notion of Orientalism: a style of thought based upon a distinction made between the "Orient" and the "West," which is then used as a starting point to elaborate observations, make statements about the Orient, authorize views of it, and teach it. Based on an assumption that the Orient cannot represent itself, the West gained authority over the Orient while also defining itself in contrast to the Orient. Orientalism is about a will to understand, control, or incorporate what is different: it is how cultural domination operates (Said 1978).

In colonial literature, especially that about settler colonies, settlers relate to indigenous peoples with "fear and temptation": indigenes simultaneously embody both the demonic violence of the fiendish warrior (which settlers fear becoming) and sexual temptation liberated from the chains of civilization (which settlers fear they cannot achieve or will overachieve). So even as settlers incorporate the Other through superficial appropriation of their "culture," they reject the Others' existence in order to claim that the arrival of white settlers is the dawn of the country (Goldie 1989).

Though the existing literature offers much discussion of exoticism and its affective aspects in colonial relations, little research has addressed how individuals affectively invest when there are no clear-cut relations of power between the groups concerned. This chapter begins to fill this gap by investigating perceptions of difference developed by two American students who studied abroad in France and Spain. Although webs of relations of power do exist between the United States, France, and Spain, the official or institutionalized power relations found under colonialism are absent.

Learning and Affect

Processes of learning can be influenced by students' affect. I investigate this influence from two angles. First, I examine how the degree of affective investment influences the ways study abroad students learn, in light of the discourse of immersion. This discourse, prevalent in study abroad research, promotional materials, and guidebooks, posits immersion—living like a "local," interacting with people and the environment in the host society—as a highly valuable way of learning that sets study abroad apart from other learning experiences. Students "immerse themselves in a 'living laboratory' that forces them to become actively involved in the learning process on every level—intellectual, psychological, and emotional. This holistic dimension is what makes education abroad uniquely suited to promoting an appreciation for cultural differences in today's interdependent global community" (Laubscher 1994: xiv). Drawing on Vygotsky's theory that social interaction is crucial to learning, Che, Spearman, and Manizade (2009) argue that study abroad students learn by interacting with others whose experience differs from theirs. Moreover, researchers argue, cognitive dissonance and opportunities to figure out how things work in the new surroundings, developing an "ability to fail," learning to navigate unknown environments, and confronting one's personal limitations are all important learning experiences conducive to self-confidence, increased adaptability, persistence, risk-taking, empathy toward others, and the ability to interpret ideas from different perspectives (Brockington and Wiedenhoeft 2009; Currier, Lucas, and Arnault 2009; Cushner 2009). As for the students' point of view, Gutel (2007: 184) argues, based on a survey of study abroad students, that they tend to "perceive cultural immersion, gained from a home stay experience, as being necessary for a study abroad experience to be considered a 'successful learning experience.'"

The discourse of immersion deals with students' affect mainly in terms of their anxiety about leaving their comfort zone. For example, study abroad guidebooks state:

> Connecting with other American students can be great fun, but there are pros and cons ... It is comforting to know others who speak our native language ... It can help to ease culture shock and help us adjust. However, it can also be detrimental. Spending too much time with other Americans may keep us from leaving our comfort zone ... Students who spend most of their time socializing with other American students may miss out on terrific foreign cultural events and meeting new international friends. (Oxford 2005: 114)

> Let go of daily interactions with home. You will need to find other sources of comfort while you are overseas if you truly want to become immersed. This does not mean that you will love or appreciate your

family and friends at home less; it simply means that you will expand your network to include your host country friends. (Loflin 2007: 134)

In this chapter, I focus on a different aspect—affective investment in the host society—and how the degree of affective investment influences the ways students immerse themselves and relate to fellow American students.

I have argued elsewhere (2013b) that one of the effects of the discourse of immersion is the highlighting of the supposedly fundamental difference between home and host societies, each constructed as internally homogeneous. This chapter modifies that argument by showing that this effect is mediated by the degree of affective investment in the destination: Sophie, with a high degree of affective investment, highlighted difference by carefully observing and copying Parisians, whereas Tracy, with a low degree of affective investment, instead connected with the people in the destination, playing down the difference.

The discourse of immersion discourages spending time with fellow American students, regarding it as a kind of lingering in the comfort zone that prevents students from going out to immerse themselves in the host society (Deardorff 2009; Hovey and Weinberg 2009; Loflin 2007; Oxford 2005). Here, fellow American students are perceived as homogeneous and offering nothing to learn (for details of this critique, see Doerr 2013b). Michael Woolf (2007: 498–99) also critiques this tendency, pointing out that "significant learning operates within the group [of American students] through discussion, social interaction, intellectual exchange, and so on" (also see Vande Berg, Paige, and Lou 2012). This chapter shows how a high or low degree of affective investment pushes students to associate with fellow American students respectively less or more.

Second, I show how different *types* of learning occurred depending on the degree of affective investment. Researchers have argued that the amount of actual learning depends on the degree of reflection on one's immersion experience. Suggesting that more critical, intensive reflection stimulates more learning, researchers recommend reflective techniques like ethnographic projects, journal writing, mentoring, targeted interventions in the learning process, and so on (Bringle and Hatcher 2011; Brustein 2009; Chen 2002; Jurasek, Lamson, and O'Maley 1996; Ogden 2006; Vande Berg, Paige, and Lou 2012). This chapter shifts the gear of this line of reasoning by focusing on the role of affect: the greater affective investment leads to more prior study about the destination, more careful observation of the life and people in the destination during the stay, and more critical reflection on one's experience upon disillusion-ment with the destination, which is more likely to occur when the des-tination is romanticized. Meanwhile, less affective investment results in less prior study about the destination, more open-ended learning from both local people and fellow American students during the stay, and lower likelihood of disillusionment and therefore less critical reflection on the experience. In short, this chapter's focus on the degree of affec-tive investment offers a more nuanced understanding of diverse ways students learn through their study abroad.

Fieldwork

Sophie and Tracy are two of four Cape College students I followed in summer 2011. I chose them because of the contrast in their respective af-fective investment in their host societies and relations with fellow Ameri-can students during their stay. Cape College is a public liberal arts college in the northeastern United States with an enrollment of approximately six thousand. I followed four Cape College students participating in summer study abroad programs offered by external study abroad providers, ac-cessed via Cape College's Study Abroad Center. Two of the four students attended the same university in Bilbao, Spain; one was in Paris, France; and one was in London, United Kingdom. These students responded to a call to participate in this research that the director of the Study Abroad Center sent out via e-mail to twenty-five students on my behalf.

I interviewed all four of the students before their departure, during their stay, and after their return to the United States. During their study abroad stay, I visited all of them, spending four to six hours with each doing standardized interviews, visiting the hostel they were staying in or meeting with their host family, walking around the city, and having a meal together. They allowed me to see their daily routines. I visited two classes they were taking and interviewed two of their teachers and five local program providers. I also carried out participant observation at their orientation meeting in May 2011 and at a welcome-back potluck dinner that September, where students shared experiences and slides from their stay. Both these gatherings were organized by the Study Abroad Center of Cape College.

I used an ethnographic method that allows me to understand the students' experience in context. In-depth, open-ended interviews pro-vide information about the students' personal backgrounds, expectations, and perceptions of experience. Participant observation allows interview results to be situated in context and also offers opportunities to understand aspects of students' experiences that they themselves did not notice or did not discuss. Producing multiple layers of information, this ethnographic method gives us a window through which to understand nuanced, complex experiences of students situated in particular sociocultural contexts.

Anthropological studies has not been focusing on study abroad until recently, as its mainly short-term programs, lasting sometimes for a semester but increasingly for only weeks (Chieffo and Griffiths 2009), fall outside the conventional notion of ethnographic fieldwork based on "intensive dwelling" in a single place and "extended co-residence" with the people one is studying (Clifford 1997: 71). However, this idea of what counts as legitimate ethnographic work has been critiqued as grounded in the history of marking anthropology as a legitimate academic discipline, as opposed to travel/journalistic writing (Clifford 1997) and in the colonialist assumption that non-Western research objects are rooted in a particular place (Appadurai 1988).

This study is thus an unconventional ethnography. But although the study abroad trip itself was short, this study is situated as part of four years of ethnographic fieldwork on experiential learning at Cape College since March 2011. I conducted this fieldwork during six study abroad trips (participating in the entire two-week duration of two of these trips; see Doerr 2014, 2015b, 2016a, 2016b); one three-day and four week-long alternative break trips, all of which I participated in throughout their entire duration (Doerr 2015a, 2016c); and service-learning and experiential learning as part of class assignments.

As to my positionality, having taught as an adjunct professor at Cape College for over five years not only familiarized me with the sociocultural environment of the participating students' home college but also positioned me in a professor-student power relation with participating students. During the research, however, our relations were more equal than in regular classroom practices because they knew I was not grading them. Neither Sophie or Tracy had taken my classes.

Sophie: Romancing Paris

Before her study abroad trip, Sophie had finished her junior year at Cape College, majoring in literature with a concentration in creative writing and minoring in French. Her summer study abroad in Paris, France, for three weeks from 29 June to 23 July 2011 was organized by an external program provider that offers American college students classes taught by its own faculty members, optional excursion trips, and accommodations in a hostel room with a roommate from the same program. Sophie took French language classes.

In her pre-trip interview, Sophie identified herself as Caucasian. She had studied French for ten years at school. She had always wanted to go to France: "I'm really ... fascinated to have an experience of things that I've heard so much about." What excited her about going to Paris was: "improving my French and trying to talk with natives ... experiencing new culture and ... everything ... the food, the clothing, like their manners ... Making new friends." As to her prior knowledge, she explained: "I know a lot about the country obviously because I've been studying for a long time, so, I think I like kind of know the differences in there, like the little daily life that is different from others, things that they do ... I read French newspapers online, too. So, I learn about what's going on there."

I visited her in Paris on 12 July 2011, toward the end of her second week there. I interviewed the resident director and another staff member in the morning while Sophie was in class. From Monday to Friday, Sophie had classes from 9:30 A.M. to 12:30 P.M., after which she was free. After lunch, Sophie met with me and took me to her hostel, which was two metro lines away. After showing me her room, she took me to a nearby café to do our interview. Then, I accompanied her as she did her grocery shopping, walked around the area, and returned to the hostel, where I met her roommate. While showing me around, Sophie appeared very comfortable and well adapted to life in Paris.

During the interview, we sipped soft drinks at a café—which, she told me, is what Parisians often do for hours. I asked her when she felt she was "really in Paris." She responded that she felt that when she sat "on the bridge and feel like there is like thousand monuments within ten feet from me in every direction." I asked her how she was enjoying herself so far. "I like it," she answered. "It's good ... I love the city and it wasn't hard to make friends at all." I also asked what she had told her family about her stay. Besides how much she loved it, she had told them "odd things that happened like just cultural difference." She then raised some examples, such as that people do not smile at strangers "because it means flirting with them," a practice she found hard to emulate: "I can literally feel like my face is trying to smile and I'm like [she demonstrates trying to keep a straight face and then laughs]." She also mentioned that

French people say "Bonjour" to strangers and do not get coffee to go because they would rather stay in a café for hours, and that the sun was out later than in her home in the United States due to its higher latitude.

She responded in detail to the question of what she was enjoying most:

> Sophie: I like walking around on my own ... because I feel like a sense of independence ... Sometimes people ... ask me directions when I'm on my own, so. 'Cause ... I guess I don't always look a tourist ... They might ask me for directions cause I look like I live here ... I had one woman who's like "Do you live here?" So I'm like "Kind of" [laughs].
>
> Neriko: Do other people have that kind of experience? ...
>
> Sophie: I don't know ... the main people I'm friends with, they look pretty American ... You can tell who is American usually, like I try to dress French ... because it doesn't make you stand out as much.
>
> Neriko: How do you dress like French?
>
> Sophie: [laughs] Always flats for women. I always wear flats ... nobody will wear sneakers or anything. That's always the marker of American tourists ... wearing sneakers with shorts ... people [here] rarely wear shorts. Ever ... And they always wear like darker jeans, skinny jeans with a blazer or a coat ... Guys would always wear like skinnier jeans and like thinner looking shirts ... They don't wear baggy jeans ... You never see people wear sweatpants ever, no ... At home all I do during the school is wear sweats ... So that's another thing. I can't wear sweatpants or anything ...
>
> Neriko: But the students, American students, a lot of them wear these clothes, American clothes?
>
> Sohpie: Some of them ... Like the people I hang out with, would wear sneakers and shorts. And I just feel kind of awkward with them 'cause then I kind of can't blend in like when I'm on my own, dressed in my own way ... If I don't talk, usually people don't know, so. Once I start talking, I do have an American accent when I speak French. Then they'd know immediately somehow.

What she learned the most, she said, was how to act French:

> I also noticed that the way French women walk is different and I started walking like that ... They walk very upright and ... swing their arms a lot when they walk ... They kind of strut almost ... Americans they walk slouched over or like people tend to have not good posture ... when I'm on my own going somewhere ... I feel like I can blend in and people might think I'm French. That's kind of cool. That's cool [laughs].

When I asked her what she least enjoyed, the question seemed to shock her as irrelevant. After a silence, she said: "I mean I like it a lot here ... I guess you mean what I enjoy the least about the country and the people and that type of things and what I miss the most, right?" I said yes, and she thought about it some more. Then, she told me something that surprised me:

> Americans are really loud and boisterous ... We talk really loud or very expressive and you always know when Americans are coming because they are screaming at each other basically ... If I wanna blend in, I'm not gonna do that and try to speak quietly in the metro ... But after a while it's like, "Why can't I just like be a loud boisterous person?" But it's like what we are. But I feel like that's kind of weird and kind of annoying ... I don't wanna be looked down upon because I'm American. So I try to act in a French way, like talk quietly, that type of thing. But it's frustrating cause like I don't wanna be looked down upon for being an American. That's what sucks the most.

I asked her what she felt she would miss from Paris, and she responded:

> The culture ... all the things you do here. You know I love walking around the city and just going into the shops and the stores and like the cafes and like it's so beautiful here ... I love being able to interact in another language, too ... It's really cool to walk around the roads that have been there for thousand years basically ... I'm gonna miss that because there is so much more history and so many cool things happened here ... When you are walking around and you hear fire siren, like a bomb siren that would go off. It goes off the first Wednesday of every month just to test the siren to make sure it's working ... I stopped and thought that's probably like the same siren that's been going off since the World War II like. That's fascinating to me ... I maybe hearing the same thing that's somebody else had heard during that time period, like that's really, that's interesting to me.

When asked whether her view of France had changed, she answered yes:

> I always had a very romantic view of it because I ... learned so much about it and I kind of had a love for it ... It becomes less romantic and more normal when I'm here ... It's just a city like just any other cities and you know you see people on the subway from the suburbs going home from work and they live in suburbs ... Instead of having this like glorified view of it, it kind of gets normalized being here and doing everyday things.

Almost three weeks after her return home from Paris, I interviewed her again on 11 August 2011. Now that she was back home, I asked, how she sensed difference or similarity between France and the United States. She replied: "Not that much similarity comes to my notice. I mean people in large touristic cities don't like tourists … I think that's a universal thing, but a lot of it was much more different than I thought it would be the same."

I asked her how she had learned culture there, and she said:

I learned from watching people. So within like the first week I kind of gotten certain sort of mannerism down that made me not look like a tourist … We had an orientation session and they like told us about cultural differences and like how to act when you go to restaurant, that kind of thing. So they kind of prepared us for a little bit of it. So once they mentioned it, things I didn't know, I started noticing a lot more, so … Like the way French women walk is different, like that type of thing … They told us that like the smiling thing and how to greet people in stores and how to greet people … They told us about the metro system, public transportation and the like how the classes were structured.

When I asked her about her romantic view of Paris, she explained:

… after about two weeks or so, I started to really get homesick and I kind of wanted to go home right after it … I didn't like the people as much … I didn't feel like I could … open up to them … People here [in the United States] are really, really open and friendly … I think I had like one or two experiences [in Paris] where I am pretty sure I was speaking correct French but … I think they pretended that they couldn't under-stand because they knew I was American. I think that 'cause I am pretty sure I said things correctly and they were like "I don't understand" and I was like "I don't know other ways to say it."

Responding to the question of how her views about the United States had changed, she said: "I think this trip definitely showed me how … friendly we are … We are very loud, boisterous and like expressive of emotion. And I think you know French people are so quiet. But … to-wards the end of the trip … I … wanted to be loud and smile all the time. And I was just like 'Why can't I be loud and enthusiastic about some-thing?' [laughs]." I asked what would happen if she "acted American." She answered: "Some people would stare at us, like if we were in the subway or if we were in the restaurant … That's usually the most area that it happens the most."

When I asked her what advice she would give to future students, she said:

> I would encourage people to try to not act American and try to blend into the culture 'cause it helps you learn more about it ... I really enjoyed that kind of really imitating everyone else and trying to like see what that felt like and like see how people treated you ... You learn a lot about culture from just their body language. And you know their clothing they wear just says a lot about them ... If you hang out with your American friends and you act loud and American all the time and ... go to all these tourist sites, like you're never gonna really get into the culture. You'd always be like experiencing on the surface.

Sophie said she now wanted to travel more, but two weeks was her limit in one place. She really liked Paris, but by the third week she was sick of it and wanted to go home. If she could study abroad again, she said, she would go to Germany because she was "a little German" and the Czech Republic because a friend said it was a beautiful place.

Learning to Become French Out of Love

Sophie was very excited about visiting France, which she had learned so much about. She experienced fascination, excitement, and a romantic feeling toward the destination. Reflecting this sentiment, she invested much in France, studying the language and learning about its political issues and daily life. During her study abroad stay, this attraction to France found expression in mundane activities like sitting in cafés, speaking French, and strolling through the city, as well as in sensing the deep history behind things in Paris.

This attraction led to particular activities: observing carefully and mimicking how French people presented themselves and acted. Sophie loved appearing Parisian and having her success at doing so confirmed when people mistook her for a Parisienne. Besides becoming what she romanticized, Sophie had other reasons to mimic Parisians: to avoid misunderstandings like seeming to flirt (by smiling at strangers) or be rude (by not saying "Bonjour" to strangers), and not to stand out as an American. In Sophie's mind, being American had negative connotations in Paris: it suggested not blending in with the local scene, disturbing people and eliciting annoyance (e.g., by speaking loudly in subways and restaurants, where other people talk quietly), and not being fashionable (e.g., prioritizing comfort by wearing sweats, flip-flops, and shorts). Later, she also framed her mimicking as a way to learn about another culture.

Mimicking the Parisians meant hiding her Americanness. This had two effects. First, she developed negative views of fellow American students in terms of their not blending in. Thus she preferred to stroll through Paris on her own, distancing herself from her American friends. Second, she sometimes felt frustrated about having to hide her Americanness (see Doerr under review b for analysis of this), which became more apparent later in her stay.

Eventually her romantic view of France receded. Paris became more "normal" as another city where people go home to suburbs. Also, there was the disappointment of rejection—despite trying hard to be like the French, she had felt rejected on a couple of occasions. This led to a negative view of French people as not friendly or open. She summarized her view of France as more different from than similar to the United States. Though still in love with Paris's history and city life, Sophie was glad to be home and had little desire to go back any time soon.

Tracy: A Blank Slate to Be Filled (with Passion)

Tracy, a psychology and education major, had completed her sophomore year before going on this study abroad trip. In the predeparture interview, Tracy identified herself as "Caucasian." Prior to her visit, she had studied Spanish for thirteen years at school. Tracy attended a one-month program offered by a university in Bilbao, Spain, from 27 June to 28 July 2011.

Tracy said she wanted to study abroad in order to "learn another culture and perfect the language." She was excited about "meeting new people and learning culture, improving language, living with family." She opted to stay with a host family because she felt a home stay would give her more chances to speak Spanish and because she liked a family environment. What she wanted most to do was "interact with different people; independence—to be on my own." When asked what she knew about Bilbao, she replied: "I know that the university is really nice there and it's by the Guggenheim ... I know that it's really warm. They have nice beaches and that's really beautiful there."

I visited Bilbao from 13 July to 16 July 2011. I spent my first day there talking with the program staff at the hosting university and interviewed Tracy on 14 July, two and a half weeks after her arrival in Spain. I also visited two classes and interviewed their teachers. There were fifteen Cape College students there, and I was also visiting another Cape College student.

On the second day of my stay, I met up with Tracy at the university around noon. We walked by the river for a while, talking, and sat on a bench in a park for the interview. During the interview, I asked her what she had felt when she first arrived. She said she was excited when she arrived in Madrid, where everyone in the program met and went sightseeing for three days. Once she had moved to Bilbao, however, she was intimidated "because all of a sudden I had to only speak Spanish to my host mom. She doesn't speak any English. And kind of get used to a new living style ... It is an actual apartment and like I kind of had to get used to that living style and you know her expectations of living in a house, living respectfully and you know learning different customs and everything, so. That was a bit of an adjustment, but it's comfortable now. I really like my host mom, so." She said it had taken her four or five days to adjust.

During her stay, she took one 300-level course in Spanish grammar and one Spanish literature course. She dropped the latter in her first week because of the workload but felt she was still learning a lot: "I feel like it's worth more than a class just to be living with ... a host mom and speaking Spanish all the time. It's total immersion as opposed to, you know, whatever you'd do in an hour of class, so."

When asked how she was enjoying her stay, she responded: "I love it. Yeah, I'm having a great time. Learning a lot. I mean language and culture obviously but also about like things in general, just how to be independent and still kind of ... balance things ... It's a good experience." I asked what she had told her family about her stay, and she said: "I also said I loved it. But ... it's difficult just to adjust and to learn the different customs ... To talk in Spanish all the time. Sometimes it's really exhausting ... especially when I don't know how to say it in Spanish." Then she added:

> But it's kind of cool because you can see how like people in the US or people in other countries who don't speak English ... have to learn it ... It's more difficult for them 'cause I'm only here for a month and I know a bunch of other people who speak English, but you know people in the US might be in the US for years and years and not have other people to communicate with, so.

About her daily routine, she said: "I'm always kind of like experiencing things, learning things ... If we go for a walk like you are surrounded by the language and you're immersed in it and you know, everything is experience. You get lost in the metro, you get off the wrong stop ... It's kind of like all learning experience." The language, she said, is "hard to, like, when you don't know the language that well, to like get to know new people, like completely new people, in Spanish ... The entire time in class, we are speaking Spanish ... When I'm at my apartment, I can only speak Spanish 'cause she [her host mother] doesn't understand if I speak English."

When I asked her what was unexpected, she responded: "I tried to come here ... not really having any expectations. So however it shapes up to be, then I can just accept that. Most unexpected thing. I guess trying to balance between so many things." I asked her what she enjoyed the most. She said: "Being able to see everything ... I wanna go to Barcelona and see that, you know I can ... I like that I could have friends in different states when I go home. I like how varied the group is and how they bring different stuff to the table and just like everything." Before going home, she told me, she planned to "just explore as much as I can I guess ... Get closer with the [American] people I met here so that you know if I wanna visit, you know, Chicago, or DC, or anything in the future, I can and I'll have a tour guide [laughs] ... I've already ... made plans." To my question about whether she had expected that, she said: "I kind of hoped that I would [make American friends], but I didn't know if I would. But I'm glad that I did." Regarding whether her view of Spain had been changed by going there, she said: "Bilbao isn't really one of those touristy places, so I didn't really know what to expect ... Madrid, it was kind of what I expected. I didn't really know what to expect of Bilbao, so I'm really not sure if my expectation was met or not because I just didn't really know what Bilbao is like at all."

I asked Tracy whether she tried not to look American, and she answered:

> It's pretty friendly and pretty safe here, but it's funny 'cause we can stick out as tourists, especially traveling in a big group. And you know having backpacks and cameras and everything kind of makes us obvious tourists. But I've never found it like unsafe ... But sometimes it's awkward, like knowing that people see me speaking English ... and know I'm American. But it's not really that uncomfortable.

To my question whether people misunderstood her because she was American, she responded:

> Sometimes I feel like they don't like, like when people are at the restaurant or something, they might think that we are certain way because we are American. Or a lot of people, even that I met within the [study

abroad student] group, when I say I'm from New Jersey, they just think we are all like people from the [TV show] *Jersey Shore*. So, I guess we are more misunderstood by the people within my group from the US than I am by [Spaniards].

I asked when she felt a similarity between American and Spanish culture, and she replied:

It's cheesy but smiling is the same in every language. Although I'm surprised how many people don't smile back when you smile at them. It's really weird. So, I tried to smile at everyone ... but they stare at you ... It's awkward. But I mean it still means the same ... They speak a different language, they may have different culture, but at the core ... they have lives and still have preferences and family and friends and things like that. So you know at the core we are all the same.

After the interview, we had lunch at a restaurant and went to her host family's home, a ten-minute walk from the university. Her host family consisted of a host mother who lived alone, as her two grown sons were living elsewhere in Spain. Tracy explained that her host mother was a teacher and made Tracy speak Spanish a lot, which Tracy liked because it improved her Spanish. Tracy said she had a two-hour lunch with her host mother every day, talking in Spanish the entire time. "That's the biggest impact in this stay," she said. At the host home we enjoyed a cup of coffee, some sweets, a fruit salad called Macedonia, and talk. The host mother spoke only Spanish and I only spoke English, so we conversed via Tracy.

Tracy returned to the United States on 29 July 2011, and I interviewed her on 12 September 2011, when the new semester had begun. I asked her when she had felt she was home, and she said she still did not feel she was home. She had told her family upon her return that "I had an amazing experience and I want to go back." I asked if she was relieved to be back in the United States. "No," she said, "I want to go back." When asked again whether she had tried not to look American, she responded: "I look kind of Spanish, so it wasn't really an issue for me. The only issue was when they thought I was [Spanish] and when I didn't speak as well ... They were like 'Oh,' and that was the only time." This, she said, was because of her "skin tone." When they were surprised that she did not speak Spanish well, she just told them, "I'm from the United States." It was not really a big issue, she said.

Regarding what she had learned the most through the study abroad experience, she responded: "It's cheesy, but even though you don't speak the same language, you can connect with people, like my host mom." When I asked what part of the trip she had liked best, she said: "I liked connecting with people. Like different areas they live [in the United States]." The only Spaniard she had gotten to know well, she said, was her host mother. I asked what she thought was the same in Spain and the United States, and she answered: "When people interact, it's the same, you know. You meet up, you wanna go here and you know with friends and family and things like that. You know they go to school ..." When I asked if her view of Spain had changed, she said: "I really didn't have any views before I went. So nothing has really changed. But I mean I definitely connected with it." She affirmed that she wanted to study abroad again, but when asked where, she was unsure: "I don't really know. Maybe England or Italy or something."

Connecting with the Place/People

Tracy did not have a strong affective investment in the host society, Spain. Although she had studied Spanish since second grade, she framed her study abroad as learning about "another culture" rather than Spain specifically. This may have been because Spanish, as it is learned in the US context, is not necessarily linked to Spain but to various Spanish-speaking countries. Tracy's lack of much knowledge about Spain prior to her stay, in contrast to Sophie's knowledge of French politics and society, suggests her low degree of affective investment.

Upon her arrival, Tracy was excited but also intimidated. She reported difficulty adjusting, especially to the use of Spanish all the time with her host mother and to a daily schedule that differed from that in the United States. Tracy emphasized several times that she had had few expectations about Spain. This seemed to have worked to open her mind: she "accepted whatever" without preconceived views about what life in Spain should be like. Probably also aided by her previous lack of knowledge, Tracy appeared to be absorbing all things around her, learning various things all the time.

Another influence on Tracy's learning was her lack of fascination with Spaniards. In contrast to Sophie, Tracy did not talk about observing or mimicking local people. She also cared less about not looking American; that is, she did not try to hide her Americanness but rather was comfortable with who she was. This was probably also due to the ways Spaniards accepted Americans, compared to the ways French did. Moreover, she "looked" Spanish, though it was not a big issue when

Spaniards found out she was not. (However, Spanish-English bilingual American students of Guatemalan and Colombian backgrounds reported otherwise: Spaniards' attitudes became colder upon hearing of their Latin American backgrounds; see Doerr under review a).

Tracy considered the best part of her study abroad experience to have been connecting with people, both Spaniards and Americans. Probably aided by not fearing to look American and not feeling embarrassed about being American, she enjoyed making American friends from various parts of the United States, creating long-lasting connections. Her relation to her host mother also had a large place in her study abroad experience also.

In contrast to Sophie, who found little similarity between the French and Americans, Tracy saw much similarity between Spaniards and Americans. I argue that this does not reflect French people's greater difference from Americans so much as differences in perception and focus between Sophie and Tracy. For example, both learned that people in France and Spain, respectively, do not react to smiling as Americans do. But whereas Sophie took this as a sign of difference, Tracy talked about similarity "at the core." Tracy also gained new empathy for those in the United States who speak little English.

Through her study abroad experience, Tracy forged a strong connection to Spain and wanted to return to Spain. Notwithstanding her initial lack of affective investment, Tracy developed a strong emotional attachment to Spain—not to specific items in Spain, such as history represented by buildings, but rather to her experience and the connections to people that she developed during her stay. Nonetheless, though she wanted to go back to Spain, the next place she would study abroad could be England or Italy—there was no strong attachment to Spain as a country.

Contrasting Affective Investments and Their Effects

Sophie's and Tracy's experiences show a strong contrast in affective investment in the destination. Sophie had "love for" France, whereas Tracy had no such feeling for Spain, which was just "another culture" for her. This seemed to have diverse effects.

Sophie's affective investment resulted in disillusionment, especially regarding French people. It was not only the normalization of French life and people that put her off, but also the rejection of her being/acting

French, which she perceived as a lack of openness. Tracy's lack of affective investment spared her from such disillusionment because she had no expectations. It helped her appreciate whatever happened. This gave her a strong liking for Spain, which left her wanting to go back.

An important factor was how people in France and Spain received American students. Whether certain "American" behavior was close enough to local behavior, how the United States was viewed in general, how foreigners/tourists were viewed, how annoyance about others was expressed, and so on, would all affect Sophie's and Tracy's experiences. However, only some such factors are considered here, since my focus is on student affective investment. In the following two subsections, I compare the experiences of Sophie and Tracy specifically in terms of how their *perceptions of difference* and *learning* related to their affective investment in the host societies.

Affective Investment and Perception of Difference

Sophie's and Tracy's different experiences highlight the relationship between affective investment and the notion of difference. Sophie's affective investment in Paris was based on the perception that Paris is different from the United States: more fashionable, and more historical from an Anglocentric viewpoint (i.e., ignoring the pre-European contact history of Native Americans). This reflects the wider love-hate relationships between the United States and France, where France is considered favorably through stereotypes of being literary, artistic, gourmet, sophisticated, and savvy in enjoying goodness in life, seen in movies like *Midnight in Paris* (2011) and *Julia and Julia* (2009). That perception she developed in this backdrop encouraged her to learn—to observe differences in detail. She tried to *embody* the difference herself by *becoming* Parisian herself. The perception of success in this border crossing paradoxically highlighted the difference between French and American, because being recognized as French depended on her not looking American.

This sense of absolute difference extended to Sophie's relationships with fellow American students. While trying to be like the French, Sophie felt somewhat embarrassed about fellow American students who were unapologetic about being openly American. This had to do with Sophie's understanding that French people looked down on Americans or the "American behavior of being loud and boisterous" and would stare at them. This reflects wider US-France relations, in which the French are said to consider Americans vulgar mainly because of US status in world politics—a relative newcomer in relation to European former colonial powers yet surpassing them politically and economically. As this historical backdrop mobilized these particular affective stereotypes of each other between France and the United States influencing Sophie's perceptions, she came to distance herself from her American friends (although, she reported, they became close toward the end), preferring to explore Paris on her own.

In contrast, Tracy did not have preconceived notions of difference between Spaniards and Americans and especially did not romanticize that difference. She learned about Spaniards—mainly her host mother— by *connecting* with them. It was to do with the relationships between Spain and the United States, where there was little antagonism or rivalry; what was apparent was English's status as a global language, which affected the Spaniard's willingness to speak English in order to "practice" it and thus more accepting of American students (Doerr 2015b). Tracy did not highlight differences and borders to cross. She saw more similarity and no clear Spaniard/American binary. Compared to Sophie, Tracy cared less about looking like a local or looking American. She did not seem to pay much attention to differences between Spanish and American mannerisms or behavior. Also, she befriended her fellow American students and enjoyed their company openly, finding diversity among them. Tracy also developed empathy for Cultural Others (i.e., those whose first language is not English) within the United States, blurring a boundary. For Tracy, Spaniards and immigrants in the United States were not so Cultural Others, and Americans were more Cultural Others than one would think. I maintain that this perception is linked to the lack of affective investment, attraction, and romanticizing of the destination.

In short, I argue, Sophie's romanticization resulted in the highlighting of a fundamental difference that could be overcome by *becoming* French yet left the difference to be bridged intact. Meanwhile, Tracy's lack of affective investment blurred boundaries of difference, so that her *connecting* with people placed little emphasis on difference or boundaries. Their affective investment was backgrounded by the wider relationships between the United States and the destinations developed historically. Unlike the exoticism in colonialist power relations, the encounter with difference in this more subtle and complex relations of power created diverse views of difference influenced by the degree of affective investment.

Affective Investment and Learning

Sophie's and Tracy's cases also reveal different types of learning and perception, encouraged by different kinds of affective investment. Sophie's heavy affective investment provided her with not only much prior knowledge about the destination but also a will to observe the posture, behavior, and clothing of French people with an eye to blending in and becoming one. Sophie developed a sharply observant eye, noticing small details of difference between French and American people. Through mimicking, she learned what it is like to be French and how others reacted to it. She did not see fellow American students as potential sources of learning. Toward the end of her stay, she felt profound disillusionment with France, given her original romanticization of the country. This led her to critical reflection and examination of her study abroad experience.

Tracy's lack of affective investment was evident in her paucity of prior knowledge about the destination; however, it made her open to things that came her way. She learned by absorbing whatever came along. Thus, it was not just from/about Spaniards that she learned; rather, she reported also learning from/about the other American students, who came from various parts of the United States. However, in developing a love for Spain, she did not come to critically examine and reflect on her study abroad experience as Sophie did.

Both Sophie and Tracy "immersed" themselves in the host societies, Sophie through imitating locals and trying to behave like them, and Tracy through living with a host mother. However, the difference in their affective investment led to different types of learning through immersion: Sophie embodied difference, whereas Tracy connected with a Spaniard without highlighting the difference. They also differed in terms of their association with fellow American students. Sophie avoided them, as encouraged by the discourse of immersion, whereas Tracy developed friendships with them and gained extra learning experience from those connections.

This is not to devalue either student's learning experience. Rather, I am pointing out various ways students learn, depending on their affective investment.

Conclusion and Departure

Students' aspirations to study abroad arise from the notion of adventure and attraction to the destination (see Doerr 2012; Zemach-Bersin 2009).

Affect is an important part of the motivation to go abroad for schooling. The aim of this chapter is not to condemn such affective attraction and romanticization of study abroad destinations. Rather, it is to urge awareness of the power of affect and understand as researchers, practitioners, and study abroad students how it influences students' actions, perceptions, and learning.

The cases of Sophie and Tracy showed that strong affective investment (Sophie) led to highlighting difference, acquiring prior knowledge, detailed observation during the stay, and critical reflection about the experience. Weaker affective investment (Tracy) led to blurred boundaries among people, an emphasis on connections, and open-ended learning from various sources, but little critical reflection on the experience.

Although affect in encounters with Cultural Other has been analyzed much in (neo-)colonial relations of power (Fusco 1995; Goldie 1989; also, see Rink this volume), such affect in the encounters with Cultural Others in less explicit relations of power, such as American students studying abroad in Europe, has been little examined. This chapter sought to investigate how affect influences their perception of difference as well as ways of learning by focusing on different degrees of affective investment in the destination.

We may fall in love or out of love with a destination by studying abroad. We may emphasize differences or downplay them, depending on our affective investment. We may learn and reflect more—or less—because of our degree of affective investment. Understanding diverse study abroad experiences therefore requires investigation of affective investment. It is time we examine our fascination.

Neriko Musha Doerr received a Ph.D. in cultural anthropology from Cornell University. Her research interests include politics of difference, language and power, and study abroad and alternative break experiences. Her publications include *Meaningful Inconsistencies: Bicultural Nationhood, Free Market, and Schooling in Aotearoa/New Zealand* (Berghahn Books), *The Native Speaker Concept* (Mouton de Gruyter), and *Constructing the Heritage Language Learner* (Mouton de Gruyter), and articles in *Anthropological Forum, Compare, Critical Discourse Studies, Discourse: Studies in the Cultural Politics of Education, Identities: Global Studies in Culture and Power,* and *Journal of Cultural Geography.* She currently teaches at Ramapo College in New Jersey, US.

Note

I am grateful to those who participated in this research from Cape College and the study abroad providers, the director of the Cape College's International Education Center that allowed me to carry out this research, Karen Rodriguez and Hannah Taïeb for their insightful comments on the earlier draft, Jaime Taber for copyediting the drafts, and the anonymous reviewers of Berghahn Books for critical and constructive comments. The text's deficiencies are wholly my responsibility.

References

Ahmed, Sara. 2004. "Affective Economies." *Social Text* 22: 121–39.

Appadurai, Arjun. 1988. "Putting Hierarchy in Its Place." *Cultural Anthropology* 3(1): 36–49.

Berger, John. 1980. *About Looking*. New York: Pantheon Books.

Boellstorff, Tom, and Johan Lindquist. 2004. "Bodies of Emotion: Rethinking Culture and Emotion through Southeast Asia." *Ethnos* 69(4): 437–44.

Bringle, Robert G., and Julie A Hatcher. 2011. "International Service Learning." In Robert G. Bringle, Julie A. Hatcher, and Steven G. Jones (eds), *International Service Learning: Conceptual Frameworks and Research*. Sterling, VA: Stylus, pp. 3–28.

Brockington, Joseph L., and Margaret D. Wiedenhoeft. 2009. "The Liberal Arts and Global Citizenship: Fostering Intercultural Engagement Through Integrative Experiences and Structured Reflection." In Ross Lewin (ed.), *The Handbook of Practice and Research in Study Abroad: Higher Education and the Quest for Global Citizenship*. New York: Routledge, pp. 117–32.

Brustein, William. 2009. "It Takes an Entire Institution: A Blueprint for the Global University." In Ross Lewin (ed.), *The Handbook of Practice and Research in Study Abroad: Higher Education and the Quest for Global Citizenship*. New York: Routledge, pp. 249–65.

Che, S. Megan, Mindy Spearman, and Agida Manizade. 2009. "Constructive Disequilibrium: Cognitive and Emotional Development through Dissonant Experiences in Less Familiar Destinations." In Ross Lewin (ed.), *The Handbook of Practice and Research in Study Abroad: Higher Education and the Quest for Global Citizenship*. New York: Routledge, pp. 99–116.

Chen, Leeann. 2002. "Writing to Host Nationals as Cross-Cultural Collaborative Learning in Study Abroad." *Frontiers: The Interdisciplinary Journal of Study Abroad* 8(4): 143–64.

Chieffo, Lisa, and Lesa Griffiths. 2009. "Here to Stay: Increasing Acceptance of Short-Term Study Abroad Programs." In Ross Lewin (ed.), *The Handbook of Practice and Research in Study Abroad: Higher Education and the Quest for Global Citizenship*. New York: Routledge, pp. 365–80.

Clifford, James. 1997. *Routes: Travel and Translation in the Late Twentieth Century*. Cambridge, MA: Harvard University Press.

Currier, Connie, James Lucas, and Denise Saint Arnault. 2009. "Study Abroad and Nursing: From Cultural to Global Competence." In Ross Lewin (ed.), *The Handbook of Practice and Research in Study Abroad: Higher Education and the Quest for Global Citizenship*. New York: Routledge, pp. 133–50.

Cushner, Kenneth. 2009. "The Role of Study Abroad in Preparing Globally Responsible Teachers." In Ross Lewin (ed.), *The Handbook of Practice and Research in Study Abroad: Higher Education and the Quest for Global Citizenship*. New York: Routledge, pp. 151–69.

Dean, Mitchell. 1999. *Governmentality: Power and Rule in Modern Society*. London: Sage.

Deardorff, Darla. 2009. "Understanding the Challenges of Assessing Global Citizenship." In Ross Lewin (ed.), *The Handbook of Practice and Research in Study Abroad: Higher Education and the Quest for Global Citizenship*. New York: Routledge, pp. 346–64.

Doerr, Neriko Musha. 2012. "Study Abroad as 'Adventure': Construction of Imaginings of Social Space and Subjectivities." *Critical Discourse Studies* 9(3): 257–68.

———. 2013a. "Damp Rooms and Saying 'Please': Mimesis and Alterity in Host Family Space in Study-Abroad Experience." *Anthropological Forum* 23(1): 58–78.

———. 2013b. "Do 'Global Citizens' Need the Parochial Cultural Other? Discourses of Study Abroad and Learning by Doing." *Compare* 43(2): 224–43.

———. 2014. "Desired Learning, Disavowed Learning: Scale-Making Practices and Subverting the Hierarchy of Study Abroad Experiences." *Geoforum* 54(July): 70–79.

———. 2015a. "'Double Subject Positions' and Reproduction of Difference: Paradox of Learning about a 'Different Culture' and Pedagogy of the Privileged." *Review of Education, Pedagogy, & Cultural Studies* 37(1): 71–89.

———. 2015b. "Learner Subjects in Study Abroad: Discourse of Immersion, Hierarchy of Experience, and Their Subversion through Situated Learning." *Discourse: Studies in the Cultural Politics of Education* 36(3): 369–82.

———. 2016a. "Chronotopes of Study Abroad: The Cultural Other, Immersion, and Compartmentalized Space-Time." *Journal of Cultural Geography* 33(1): 80–99.

———. 2016b. "Learning as Othering: Narratives of Learning, Construction of Difference, and the Discourse of Immersion in Study Abroad." *Intercultural Education* 27(6).

———. 2016c. "Space of Pedagogic Imaginary: Interstice of Teacher's Intent and Students' Learning in Experiential Learning of Different Cultures." *Education and Society* 34(1): 23–37.

———. under review a. "'Global Competence' of Minority Immigrant Students: Hierarchy of Experience and Ideology of Global Competence in Study Abroad."

———. under review b. "Hiding and Construction of 'True Self': Regime of Truth and Politics of Hiding in Study Abroad." In Neriko Musha Doerr and Haeng-ja Sachiko Chung (eds.), *Politics of Hiding: Productive Suspension of "Truth" and the Pleasure/Menace of Secrecy*.

Fusco, Coco. 1995. *English Is Broken Here: Notes on the Cultural Fusion in the Americas*. New York: New Press.

Geertz, Clifford. 1963. *The Interpretation of Cultures*. London: Fontana.

Goldie, Terry. 1989. *Fear and Temptation: The Image of the Indigene in Canadian, Australian, and New Zealand Literatures*. Montreal: McGill-Queen's University Press.

Good, Byron. 2004. "Rethinking 'Emotions' in Southeast Asia." *Ethnos* 69(4): 529–33.

Gutel, Heather. 2007. "The Home Stay: A Gendered Perspective." *Frontiers: The Interdisciplinary Journal of Study Abroad* 15: 173–88.

Hochschild, Arlie Russell. 1983. *The Managed Heart: Commercialization of Human Feelings*. Berkeley: University of California Press.

Hovey, Rebecca, and Adam Weinberg. 2009. "Global Learning and the Making of Citizen Diplomats." In Ross Lewin (ed.), *The Handbook of Practice and Research in Study Abroad: Higher Education and the Quest for Global Citizenship*. New York: Routledge, pp. 33–48.

Jurasek, Richard, Howard Lamson, and Patricia O'Maley. 1996. "Ethnographic Learning While Studying Abroad." *Frontiers: The Interdisciplinary Journal of Study Abroad* 2.

Laubscher, Michael R. 1994. *Encounters with Difference: Student Perceptions of the Role of Out-of-Class Experiences in Education Abroad*. Westport, CT: Greenwood.

Loflin, Stephen E. 2007. *Adventures Abroad: The Student's Guide to Studying Overseas*. New York: Kaplan.

Ogden, Anthony C. 2006. "Ethnographic Inquiry: Reframing the Learning Core of Education Abroad." *Frontiers: The Interdisciplinary Journal of Study Abroad* 8: 87–112.

Oxford, Stephanie M. 2005. *Study Abroad: Travel Vacation in College*. Friant: Where In the World.

Ramos-Zayas, Ana Y. 2009. "Urban Erotics and Racial Affect in a Neoliberal 'Racial Democracy': Brazilian and Puerto Rican Youth in Newark, New Jersey." *Identities: Global Studies in Culture and Power* 16(5): 513–47.

Richard, Analiese, and Daromir Rudnyckyj. 2009. "Economies of Affect." *Journal of the Royal Anthropological Institute* 15(1): 57–77.

Rosaldo, Michelle Z. 1984. "Toward an Anthropology of Self and Feeling." In Richard A. Sweer and Robert A LeVine (eds), *Culture Theory: Essays on Mind, Self, and Emotion*. Cambridge: Cambridge University Press, pp. 137–57.

Said, Edward. 1978. *Orientalism*. New York: Vintage Books.

Stewart, Susan. 1984. *On Longing: Narratives of the Miniature, the Gigantic, the Souvenir, the Collection*. Baltimore, MD: Johns Hopkins University Press.

Vande Berg, Michael, R. Michael Paige, and Kris Hemming Lou. 2012. *Student Learning Abroad: What Our Students Are Learning, What They Are Not, and What We Can Do About It*. Sterling, VA: Stylus.

Woolf, Michael. 2007. "Impossible Things Before Breakfast: Myths in Education Abroad." *Journal of Studies in International Education* 11(3/4): 496–509.

Zemach-Bersin, Talya. 2009. "Selling the World: Study Abroad Marketing and the Privatization of Global Citizenship." In Ross Lewin (ed.), *The Handbook of Practice and Research in Study Abroad: Higher Education and the Quest for Global Citizenship*. New York: Routledge, pp. 303–20.

CHAPTER 7

Learning Japanese/Japan in a Year Abroad in Kyoto
Discourse of Study Abroad, Emotions, and Construction of Self

Yuri Kumagai

I have been drawn to Japan ever since I can remember. Some of my earliest memories are of walking through a Japanese garden with my mother, of paging through one of my parents' beautifully illustrated books on Japanese temples or the tea ceremony, and of my father teaching me to say "Hai! [Yes!]" whenever he would ask "Wakarimasu ka? [Do you understand?]," which remains one of the few Japanese phrases he knows ... Now, I was enthralled by the elegant geisha in their beautiful kimono, and fascinated with Shinto rituals and beliefs ... (Julia, personal statement, the study abroad application)

Since a young age I had always had a fascination with Japanese ... I grew up listening to my grandmother sing me Japanese lullabies and telling me stories about Japan—the country where she met and married my grandfather. Visiting my grandmother, who is an antique dealer specializing in Asian antiquity, I would tread carefully around her house while admiring wedding kimonos, porcelains, and elaborate scrolls, all displayed carefully around her home ... (Paige, personal statement, the study abroad application)

The role some emotions play in language learning has long attracted much interest in the field of second language acquisition. Research shows that there is a significant link between affect and achievement (Bown and White 2010a, 2010b; Gardner and MacIntyre 1993). Scovel (2001: 40) goes so far as to say "[emotions] could very well end up being the most influential force in language acquisition." However, to date, research into affect in language learning has tended to focus on a single (and usually negative) emotion, anxiety (e.g., "affective filter" hypothesized by Krashen 1981) (Dewaele 2007; Horwitz, Horwitz and Cope 1986; Horwitz 2001), and other emotions such as enjoyment, hope, pride, satisfaction, relief, anger, boredom, and shame have largely been overlooked (Bown and White 2010a, 2010b). In this study, I examine how different emotions are managed by students in order to accomplish various tasks that they face in living and studying a year abroad.

In the field of second language acquisition and foreign language education, it is often believed that immersing oneself in the target language community through participating in a study abroad program is the best way to learn the language and to gain intercultural communicative competence (Freed 1995; Gore 2005; Modern Language Association 2007). Encouraged by such a premise, many students of Japanese language participate every year in study abroad programs in Japan, hoping to become fluent in the language and to learn its cultures. Julia and Paige are such students who participated in a college-approved, year-long, language intensive study abroad program in Kyoto (the Kyoto Program).[1]

As shown in the opening quotes, both Julia and Paige, since a young age, have nurtured a romantic view—geishas, kimonos, Shinto shrines, the tea ceremony, etc.—towards Japan. In order to pursue their passions of learning Japanese language and cultures, they embarked on the study abroad. Yet, their lives in Japan during the year abroad presented vastly different pictures: Julia, often feeling powerless and anxiety about the unfamiliar situations, devoted herself to academic work, limiting her personal activities within a circle of her fellow American students in the Kyoto Program; whereas Paige, feeling joy and fulfillment in experiencing various "cultural" activities, took every opportunity to learn how to wear kimono to perform tea ceremony, making academic work somewhat secondary. While Julia has, in the end, painfully recognized and felt disheartened about the insurmountable barrier between Japanese people and foreigners in Japan, Paige was thrilled and proud of being/feeling accepted as a member of a tea ceremony group, which led her to develop a deeper appreciation for Japanese cultures.

Using interviews as primary data source, I compare and contrast two students' experiences during the year abroad in Kyoto, considering in particular the role of emotions. The study asks: What were the key emotions each student experienced, in what contexts? How did that emotion interact or further bring out other types of emotion? In what way have the emotions students felt influenced whether they partici- pated in various social networks? How have such (non-)participations facilitated their learning/using of Japanese language? What sense of self have they constructed as a result of the choices they made? By answer- ing these questions, I illuminate how students' conflicting emotions and subjectivities interact in a complex way, impacting their own under- standing of their study-abroad experiences.

In what follows, I briefly lay out relevant theoretical constructs; de- scribe the study; introduce Julia and Paige; analyze their experiences in Kyoto, Japan, paying attention to their emotions; discuss the findings in relation to the discourse of immersion; and present conclusions and future directions.

Discourse of Immersion, Emotions, and Subjectivities

The most prevalent discourse that encourages language learners to par- ticipate in a study abroad program is the discourse of immersion—i.e., learning the language by *immersing* oneself in the target language com- munity. Doerr (2013, 2014), based on the text analysis of several study abroad guidebooks, highlights three aspects that are often regarded as critical for immersion: living as locals do, making "native friends," and floating around in the environment. Studying the language abroad is of- ten portrayed as "inherently superior" to the learning in classroom settings (Schneider 2001). What could be characterized as "inherently superior" about the language learning in the study abroad context is various com- municative settings it offers where learners need to interact with expert language users (i.e., "native speakers" other than their language teachers) for authentic, real life purposes. Such a categorical assertion has been critiqued for promoting a myth that being abroad *automatically* and *nat- urally* facilitates language learning, thus making learners passive, and for falsely portraying classroom learning as inferior and unimportant (Ryan and Mercer 2011; Kinginger and Farrell Whitworth 2005).

While there is no denying that studying and living abroad can po- tentially present limitless learning opportunities, in order to take utmost advantage of life abroad, it is strongly encouraged that learners need to step out of their "comfort zone" and seek and join communities of practice of their interests (e.g., extracurricular activities, interest groups, etc.). The concept of community of practice defines learning as a social process: learning occurs through the process of legitimate participation in a given community, moving from peripheral to full participation (Lave and Wenger 1991; Wenger 1998). Learning in such contexts means a gradual socialization into a new community of practice (Kinginger 2009; Ochs 2002).

Many language learners, hoping to become a better language user by immersing themselves in the target language and cultural community, participate in study abroad programs. However, research shows that there are great degrees of individual differences not only in terms of outcomes of the learning (e.g., acquisition of linguistic and pragmatic abilities), but also overall quality of life experiences, which has facilitating or debilitating effects on their learning and views of the host cultures and of themselves (Goldoni 2013; Kumagai and Sato 2009; Trentman 2013). Why are some students driven to take full advantage of seeking and gaining a new social network (Milroy 1987) while others do not? Doerr (Chapter 8, this volume) discusses the different degree of emotional "investment" (Peirce 1995) as a factor that influences students' varying involvement in and embodiment of "cultural practices" of the host community. In my study, however, both students at the start of the study abroad had a very similar passion and desire for the life in Japan, yet various competing factors impacted the ways they sought and focused on different types of learning as a way to manage different emotions.

In this study, I use the term *emotion* roughly equating it with the term *affect*. Bown and White (2010a: 433) explain that emotions are tools "by which we appraise experiences and prepare to act on situations (Cole, Martin, and Dennis 2004): emotions facilitate decision making (Damasio 1994; Isen 2000; Isen, Daubman, and Nowicki 1987), promote learning (Stein, Trabasso, and Liwag 2000), and alert individuals to mismatches between their goals and the environment (Schwarz and Clore 1983)." As discussed by Doerr and Taïeb (see Chapter 1, this volume), in contrast to earlier approaches that view emotion as culturally mediated or as individual psychological state, emotion here is viewed as something to be managed in order to self-regulate learner's decision making, especially in relation to the dominant discourse of study abroad: immersion.

How do one's conscious and unconscious decisions, in turn, construct and are constructed by the idea of self or subjectivity? Chris Weedon (1997: 32), a feminist poststructuralist, defines subjectivity as "the conscious and unconscious thoughts and emotions of the individual, her sense of herself and her ways of understanding her relation in the world." She proposes, in contrast to the humanist view of identity, "a subjectivity which is precarious, contradictory and in process, constantly reconstituted in discourse each time we think or speak." In this view, "the individual is always the site of conflicting forms of subjectivity" (Weedon 1997: 32). By looking at learners as having a complex social history and multiple desires, we can begin to make sense of why they make certain decisions that may appear to be in conflict with their interest.

The Study

The Kyoto Program[2]

Kyoto, the former imperial capital in Japan, is often described as the oldest and most beautiful city in Japan. Richie (1986: 32) describes the city as "the home of traditional culture ... [f]illed with temples and shrines, palaces and gardens." Kyoto is, at the same time, the country's seventh largest and modern city with a population of 1.4 million people.

The Kyoto Program is one of the oldest study abroad programs in Japan, and is housed in a university located in the heart of Kyoto. The program is sponsored by a consortium of fifteen American colleges and universities, and its mission is described as being "committed to maintain high academic standards and dedication to a sound liberal arts education." In other words, the Kyoto Program is structured based on the American educational system, particularly as it takes shape in liberal arts colleges. Thus, even though it is located in Japan, the participating students do not have access to "regular" Japanese university courses.

The Kyoto Program is a year-long, language intensive, so-called junior-year study abroad program. In the program, students are placed in one of five intensive language courses depending on their proficiency (levels 1 to 5, 5 being the highest). The students take a Japanese language course for 90 minutes every morning, one language practicum course (e.g., Learning Japanese through Songs, Cooking, Calligraphy), and two elective courses (e.g., Japanese religions, Japanese poetry, Japanese linguistics) of two hours each for a week, taught in English by professors mainly from the consortium colleges. Numerous field trips to various parts of Japan are highlighted as important features of the program. Also, the homestay is stressed as an integral part of the program and all students are required to live with a host family. As argued by Brecht et al. (1997), homestay arrangements are believed to be among the most significant aspects of study abroad programs, offering students an access to the everyday practices of the host community and daily contacts with willing participants in meaningful communication.

Stanton College, where I teach Japanese language, is a competitive women's college located in the East Coast of the United States. The college sends higher numbers of students to the Kyoto Program every year; in the particular year on which this study is based, six students (among the total of 26 participants in the entire program) participated in the Kyoto Program.

The Method

As a Japanese language instructor who is interested in finding out types of learning opportunities students can have through participating in study abroad programs, I conducted in-depth, semistructured interviews with all six students who participated in the Kyoto Program during the academic year of 2010–2011. The interviews took place in the Fall semester after they came back from a year abroad in Japan. All of the students have taken my intensive Japanese language courses for at least one year prior to going to Japan (some for two years). I was, therefore, familiar with their academic standings, particularly with their Japanese language proficiency, their personalities and demeanors, and so on. Through day-to-day interactions for an extended period in the past, I have established a trusting relationship and friendly rapport with these students. My knowledge about these students would help me understand their experiences in Kyoto. I also use the students' study abroad application essay, as well as written reports on their language evaluations from their Japanese instructors in Japan as supplemental data.

For the current study, I have chosen two students, Julia and Paige, as case studies because I was surprised to learn that their experiences were strikingly contrastive despite their somewhat similar backgrounds (i.e., gender, ethnicity self-identified as "Caucasian," the same study abroad program, the same US home college) and passions. Their recounts of their experience in fact were much different from what I had expected based on my prior knowledge about them; this motivated me to analyze and make sense of their experiences from the perspective of emotion.

The aim of this study is not to assess the learning outcomes of study abroad. By comparing and contrasting the different experiences students have had, I attempt to shed some light on how their emotions and their adherence to different ways of learning—school work (Julia) and extracurricular activities (Paige)—shape their differential access to learning opportunities (Kinginger 2009). The analysis in this study is limited to the students' perspectives. They are the stories that the students decided to share with me based on their subjective realities. Thus, like any other stories, there are other sides to it. However, it is important to understand students' experiences (and their memories of them) as they themselves perceived and felt. Their very perceptions, feelings, and desires have impacted the way they lived their lives while studying abroad.

In order to understand the spectrum of emotions Julia and Paige have felt and its impact on accessing different learning opportunities and social networks, I describe and analyze their experiences in three different settings following Kinginger's (2009) categorization: (1) educational institutions and classrooms (School Life); (2) places of residence (Life with Host Family); and (3) service encounters and other informal contact with expert speakers (Other Social Contexts).

Julia

Julia is a European American who grew up in a Midwestern state in the United States. As her quote at the opening of this chapter illustrates, she relates her feeling about and image of Japan to her fond childhood memories with her parents. She began her studying of Japanese language when she was in the eighth grade by participating in a Japanese summer camp, and formally started to learn Japanese language in high school. Upon entering the college, Julia was placed at the second-year level, and took two years of Japanese language courses before participating in the Kyoto Program. Prior to the year abroad in Kyoto, she had visited Japan twice. In Japanese language courses at Stanton, Julia was a confident and outspoken student who often assumed a leadership role. In the Kyoto Program, she was placed in level 4 (the second from the highest level). Her major were psychology and Japanese.

School Life: "It Was a Lot of Work."

Julia described her school experience at the Kyoto Program as being "very similar to Stanton." She depicted her daily school life in the following manner:

> It was very busy, busier than I expected to be, ... with work! We were really working hard. The commuting in the morning takes about 45 minutes to an hour and then the whole morning was Japanese class ... and had lunch, go to classes, and usually hang out in the student lounge until they close at 4, ... and then go home, get home at 5, 5:30,

and had a little time to do homework, we had dinner, and I have a little more time to do homework after that … I was like really surprised because … we had tons of reading all the time … I liked the class a lot, but I felt kind of bad because it was a lot of work … I would have liked to do more clubs and stuff but I was like "I can't do it."

She described her weekend as:

On Saturday, sometimes I do some stuff with my friends [from the program], … but a lot of time I would stay home and do work, or relax or hang out downstairs with my host family. And Sunday was a big homework day, too. So we did a lot of homework.

For Julia, what comes to her mind recalling her school life in the Kyoto Program was "reading books" and "doing homework." Even though she felt bad about working too hard on schoolwork and wanted to do "more clubs and stuff," she was overwhelmed by her academic workload and thus felt: "I can't." Despite the fact that she was living in the Japanese language and cultural environment where she could be exposed and gain valuable and authentic experience (Block 2007; Du-Fon and Churchill 2006; Kinginger 2008, 2009), she did not take advantage of the resources "out there," and spent her school life in a similar manner as she would in the United States. Her descriptions about her daily routines suggest that they were tightly structured. This may be an indication that she preferred or felt more comfortable having a structure in organizing and managing school life. It also seems that she was not able to free herself from her ideal of a "good college student" subject position while in Japan.

Life with the Host Family: "I Would Have Liked to Spend More Time with Them."

Julia described her host family as "the best I can possibly hope for." Her host family consisted of host mother and host father, both of whom were in their late forties or early fifties, and three host sisters of which two still lived at home. Both the host father and mother worked outside the home. In response to my question "Did you do a lot of stuff with your host family?" she replied:

I didn't do that much though… That was one of the things it was interesting because they were so friendly but we really didn't do a lot. Because my host sister had, one of them worked full time somewhere and the other one, younger one, had like three part-time jobs. So they were always gone. I would have liked to spend more time with them. That was one of my biggest regret not spending more time with them, but they were just gone all the time. So ... they were always really friendly but I never really got to know them until the end.

She found it "interesting" that they "didn't do much" even though the family was "always really friendly." She reasoned that it was the family's busy schedules that prevented them from "spending more time together." Here, we could sense her ambivalent feeling about her life with the host family: she described them as "the best host family," but she made a point that "they were just gone all the time."

When I asked her about her high points living in Japan, she mentioned two family moments:

> Julia: One of the last couple of days I was there, I went to Kobe with one of my host sisters, the middle one. She was the coolest person ever. We spoke a lot together and it was kind of sad that it was one of my last days there, because I felt like we really got to know each other then. And I also went to my oldest sister's apartment at one time with my family and we ate delicious food and we played Wii with my host dad, my host sister's husband, that was really, really fun. We played mahjong, too. I never played it before so my host dad was trying to teach me, and I started doing really well.
>
> Yuri: So like the family moments.
>
> Julia: Yeah, my middle two sisters spoke pretty good English, but older one and her husband and my host parents didn't speak any English, so.
>
> Yuri: Did you speak Japanese all the time?
>
> Julia: When I was with the host family, I used Japanese all the time.

Julia enjoyed and appreciated ordinary moments such as watching TV or playing games with the host family as the most important and memorable aspect of her year in Kyoto. The fact that her host family (except for two sisters) did not speak English pushed Julia to speak only in Japanese. Thus, such family moments were also gratifying *language moments* for Julia, providing her with a sense of accomplishment as they were the only occasions when she spoke Japanese all the time.

Other Social Contexts: "I Wish I'd Have Spoken More [Japanese] While I Was There."

Julia mostly "hung out" with her American peers from the program. She said that they spoke only English with occasional use of some "Japanese words and little phrases." She regrets that she did not speak much Japanese while living in Kyoto:

> I do wish I'd have spoken more while I was there, I spoke with my host family, but I think being a little bit self-conscious did hold me back ... One of my friends, she would just talk to random people, like at the river [when] we were there, then they would come over and talk with us. I wish I could have started more of that ...

She did not undertake any extracurricular activities:

> I didn't [do any clubs]. I mean, some of my friends did clubs, then later in the year when they started like going out for a dinner and stuff, I went with them. That was really nice. But I can't do sports. I know some people did a track circle and the stuff, and some people did dancing but I have really a bad knee, I hurt it pretty bad so I couldn't do any sports, I couldn't even go dancing, and then someone did *kyuudoo* (Japanese archery), but I have weird shoulders, I mean weird elbows, so I couldn't even do that. Then I was like what's left ...?

She again regrets that she didn't participate in extracurricular activities or make more Japanese friends:

> I would have liked to join some clubs or try to make more Japanese friends because I felt like ... but it's hard though, I know a lot of people who joined clubs and put themselves out there, but you just lost touch with Japanese friends because they have a different school schedule,[3] we get there half way through their semester and the club is already going on and they [the program staff] try to give you a lot of access to it, but it is still hard ...

Julia's main contact to any social networks was her peers from the Kyoto Program. It was only when "one of her friends" decided to talk with random Japanese people or when her friends who joined the club invited her along to "a dinner and stuff" that she gained access to communicative contexts where she spoke Japanese. What prevented her from being more active in speaking Japanese was her anxiety ("self-consciousness") about making mistakes. Her desire to take up the position of a competent Japanese speaker who speaks perfect Japanese without mistakes paralyzed her from seeking opportunities to use the language.

Feeling of Powerlessness, Anxiety, and Disheartenment

One emotion that runs through Julia's story is her sense of powerlessness—not being able to control how to shape the trajectory of her life.

Whenever she talked about aspects of her life in Kyoto that she regret-
ted or wished otherwise, she gave external factors as reasons for her
inability to undertake the tasks. She wanted to spend more time with
her host family and to get to know them better, but "they were gone all
the time," and so it was impossible. As we saw in the section of School
Life, "tons of reading" and "a lot of homework" made it impossible ("I
can't.") to take up any club activities. However, shown in the section
of Other Social Contexts, while mentioning that "some of her friends"
participated in club activities, she gave her reasons for not joining clubs
as "bad knee" and "weird elbows." Even though there are many extracurricular activities that do not require physical fitness, she did not seek
such options. She also explained that "a lot of people who joined clubs"
could not keep in touch with Japanese friends due to "a different school
schedule": scheduling conflicts made it impossible to make Japanese
friends.

Julia talked about her feeling of self-consciousness, and gave that
as a reason for shying away from seeking and exploring contexts where
she needed to speak Japanese. Her anxiety about making mistakes
(being self-conscious), however, is only apparent in Other Social Contexts. She did not demonstrate the feeling of anxiety in either school or
homestay contexts. This may indicate her fear about unfamiliar social
contexts. Her sense of powerlessness and fear about the unfamiliar may
have been derived from her feeling of exclusion caused by a "deep barrier" that she felt existed between "in-group" (Japanese) and "out-group"
(foreigners):

> ... because I'm clearly not Japanese, I feel like there was a barrier there,
> which was kind of hard because you kind of clustered together with
> the Kyoto Program people, then you've got to push yourself and get
> out and interact and break through that barrier, but ...

> I think you know living here, especially at Stanton, there are so much
> diversity and just like all the stuff going on all the time, then Japan is
> kind of like, there really is that in-group and out-group thing and ...
> So I think that was interesting to really live there and still feel kind of
> the outsider in the end. I don't mean to make it sound like "Oh, I was
> outside all the time," but to live there so long and get this sense ... I'm
> always being kind of outside.

Julia painfully felt that there was a barrier between herself and the
Japanese people. From the above comments, we could sense her feeling of entrapment ("clustered together with the Kyoto Program people"),

which she found it very difficult to "break through," even though she felt that she "has got to push [her]self and get out and interact" with Japanese people. By comparing her life at Stanton College, without making a clear assertion, she hinted that the Japanese society made her feel stifled due to lack of "diversity" and not having "all the stuff going on all the time."

Although she did not mention her feeling of exclusion ("being an outsider/a foreigner") when talking about her life with her host family, this could be the reason why she felt "interesting" that they were "really friendly" but at the same time "didn't do much together." She might have felt that she was treated in a way that was "friendly," but never accepted as a part of the family, thus being positioned as an "outsider," a long-term guest.

Her feeling of exclusion seems to have gradually developed through accumulating "little things"—experiences of small incidents and behaviors of Japanese people that she came into contact with day-to-day. In response to my question about whether she had any bad experiences while in Japan, she said:

> I think the worst ever happened to me in Japan was on the train people talk about me in Japanese next to me, and I was like, "Ah, ah. I understand what you are saying." They are like "How old do you think she is?" Little kids would stare at me, and I was like "Ooookaaaay." I would ask for a direction maybe in Japanese, and "No, I don't speak English." I was like "No, it's ok. You don't have to. I speak Japanese." Then they would be like "No, I don't speak English," then, just walked away. I was like "Ooookaaaay." So just little things, you know. I'm clearly a foreigner.

Similar incidents of discrimination, of being treated as the "Other," and of being the target of curiosity are well documented and discussed in scholarly as well as in popular articles about Japan (Miller 1982). The Japanese ideology of "*uchi* (insider) vs. *soto* (outsider)" is also a well-known topic that all students of Japanese learn in college. Julia too learned it in class prior to going to Japan. When students actually experienced these incidents, however, each of them reacted and dealt with the situations differently. Some enjoy the special attention or take advantage of the situations to their benefit while others feel disappointed and end up disliking Japan (Kumagai and Sato 2009). In the case of Julia, her feeling of disheartenment is clear; yet she seems to be blaming herself by saying "I'm clearly a foreigner" as if to show an understanding about the ways Japanese people treated her. This way of thinking may be her way to cope with and manage her emotion: It is not *her* as an individual person, but rather her *status* as a foreigner that caused exclusion and rejection.

Loss of Passions: Feeling Disappointed, Needing to Restore a Sense of Normality

Describing her mundane experience such as going to a grocery store, Julia indicated a little bit of annoyance, which was a result of her feeling of disorientation. She said:

> When you walk into a grocery store, it's just like totally different. It's not totally different but they packaged a little bit differently, there are different foods, and I just want like regular food, you know, "regular"! So I would buy my own peanut butter. Then I would have that in the morning.

Different packaging and different food in the grocery store reminded her that she was in a "foreign" country, away from a "regular" home environment. In an attempt to restore a sense of normality or to have a charade of "regular" life, she "[bought] her own peanut butter and [had] that in the morning."

Now that she is back from a year in Japan, she seems to have lost her passions—even though it may be temporary—toward Japan:

> Nearly at the end of the program, right when I came back, I was like, "I'm done with this for a while. I will take a little break." I was not like done forever, but I really need a break from Japanese right now. I just wanna speak bunch of English, read some English books ...

She wants to take a break from Japan and Japanese, and to "speak" and "read English"—i.e., to live a "regular" and normal life. After she came back from the year in Japan, she decided to stop studying Japanese language as she said she needed "a break."

Her needing to take a break from Japanese is a result of her frustration and disappointment of her experience living in Japan. The dominant discourse of study abroad that emphasizes the importance of immersion—being "out there" to experience the language and culture by meeting, interacting, and becoming a friend with "natives"—made her feel that she was somewhat a "failure." Even though she had successfully completed her academic year with fine grades, lived with the host family without any problems, and developed a keen awareness for the deeply rooted *uchi* vs. *soto* ideology, such learning is not highly valued in the discourse of immersion.

Paige

Paige was born and grew up in Switzerland. Her mother is a European American who married a Swiss man and later moved to Switzerland. As her maternal grandparents live in California, Paige has traveled to the United States every summer. She went to a boarding high school in the United States prior to coming to Stanton. Paige cited an emotional connection to Japan through her familial background, particularly with her maternal grandmother, who lived in Japan as a military nurse for three years after the World War II and then became an antique dealer specializing in Asian antiquities. When Paige's mother was young, she hosted a Japanese exchange student whom Paige calls "my aunt."

She had never studied Japanese prior to coming to Stanton. However, as is often the case for Europeans, Paige grew up learning multiple languages: German and English were the languages of her schooling, and she also learned to speak Italian, Russian, French, Hungarian, and Hebrew. When I asked her why she decided to study Japanese, she told me that she wanted to learn something different that she could "learn from scratch." She also said that she has a personal interest in Japanese because she can use it with people she knows (i.e., her "aunt" and "God-father" who is a Japanese friend of her mother). Paige was a comparative literature major focusing on English and German literatures.

Paige is a self-declared "auditory learner." She described her reason for participating in the Kyoto Program as follows:

> I learn mostly being immersed in culture. I felt like I hit a wall in my Japanese study, at least I wasn't getting past it, and just based on my prior knowledge about how I learn the language I knew that dropping myself in the culture completely where I hear it all the time would be the best way for me to continue learning.

As for her goals in participating in the program, she said:

> I think I had clear set of hopes in my mind, and those probably mostly revolved around going over that mental block I found, because I was really enjoying Japanese but I was disheartened. I could communicate but my written and recognition was very weak so I was hoping to go there and find that I was able to survive in Japanese, like be able to

communicate and express myself, and I really just wanted to get to know Japanese people and the culture ... especially the traditional Japan, like kimono and tea ceremony.

It is clear from her comments above that Paige embodied the discourse of immersion. True to her own assessment of her weakness in "written and recognition" of Japanese, prior to going to Japan, she has had a hard time grasping the basic sentence structures and reading and writing of *Kanji* (Chinese characters) while she was very communicative in speaking. She was not afraid of making mistakes and was always eager to say what she wanted to say even with her limited command of Japanese. In the Kyoto Program, Paige was placed in the level 2 (the second level from the bottom).

School Life: "We Were in Japan to Be in Japan."

Paige evaluated her school life in the Kyoto Program more positively than Julia:

I think the school experience academically was not as hard as Stanton. But I found it very good because that helped solidify my knowledge about Japanese ... My favorite course was probably the one taught by Professor James because it incorporated field trips every week to temples so I feel like I really got to know Kyoto ... My Japanese classes were very intensive and I learned a lot in them. But I think I learned more from my host parents because of daily conversation ...

Paige did not think the academic workload was as heavy as that at Stanton. Instead of recalling the "textbook reading" as in the case of Julia, she highlighted the course that integrated the city of Kyoto as a learning text (i.e., the course taught by Professor James). The workload students carry varies depending on the course they enroll in: some are more demanding than others; some take advantage of and integrate the local context (i.e., Kyoto) into the curriculum better than others. It also depends on how much effort students put into the course as they try to balance the academic and social in their daily life. In comparison to Julia, Paige focused on and valued more her life outside of school as a learning environment. Focusing on outside of school was her conscious decision; however, it did not come without consequences. Referring to her low points while in Japan, she said:

I think my low points were usually academically related 'cause even though the courses weren't as hard, sometimes the teachers didn't seem to understand that we were in Japan to be in Japan and they assigned a mountain of work suddenly and it would take away time I wanted to spend with my host parents or what I was doing extra-curricularly. And sometimes that would hurt my academics quite a bit because I would choose to do those experiences over the academic work because I was learning more from them even though it wasn't reflected on the grade. And sometimes that was really frustrating.

As the above comment clearly shows, Paige "was in Japan to be in Japan," not to be only in the classroom. For her, spending time with her host family and learning from "out there" was much more important and educational than getting better grades in courses at the program.[4] Being forced to make such choices, as she said, was clearly a source of frustration.

Life with the Host Family: "Always Looking Out for Me to Have the Best Experience."

Paige described her host family as "I had the best host family imaginable!" and highlighted the life with them as one of the most valuable and important aspects of her life in Japan. Her host parents were in their early sixties, and have two daughters who live in a nearby city with their husbands and children. The host father had just retired from his work a year prior to the arrival of Paige, and the host mother was a stay-at-home wife.

Paige described the daily activities that she had with her host family:

I would go on day excursions with them, mostly with just my host mother ... She would take me out for shopping for all the articles that I need for my kimono class... Or when it was a *hanami* time (viewing of cherry blossom), she would take me to different temples just to see the *sakura*, or to see changing fall leaves. She always says like "What are you doing right now? Have you done your homework? Let's go out!" She was just genuinely sweet and always looking out for me to have the best experience.

Her host mother seems to have taken Paige under her wing in order to give her the best experiences possible by assuming the role of a "cultural guide" seriously. She also played an important role for providing Paige with a main access—at least, initially—to the social life outside of the school. Unlike Julia's host family, Paige's host family put their time and effort in order to provide Paige a path to various social networks and communities of practice, which I describe next.

Other Social Contexts: "We Wanted to Do Whatever Culturally They Said Was Japanese."

Two weeks after arriving in Kyoto, Paige began taking a lesson of *sadoo*, or tea ceremony, once a week and continued until she left Kyoto a year later. She also took kimono lessons (i.e., to learn how to wear kimono). She found both the *sadoo* and the kimono teachers through her host mother's social connection. Her kimono teacher also taught Paige ikebana (flower arrangement), and *invited* her to participate in calligraphy lessons.

Paige also joined a salsa dance club[5] that she found online. It gave her access to a whole new social life besides the program and the host family. She met and became a good friend with a Japanese male college student through the salsa club. He then invited her to a group of his friends.

> Paige: I made quite a few Japanese friends. And that occurred mostly when I started going to salsa every Friday night. I found a small salsa club in Kyoto online. I became really good friends with a student who went to Kyoto University. He was a med. student there, and he became a good friend because he studied in England for a year, which is where he met salsa, so his English was really good …
>
> Yuri: What made you so active? I know some really didn't go out of their comfort zone but you seem like you really explored a lot.
>
> Paige: I guess I just missed dancing, and I wanted salsa. I didn't find a lot of things in common with other students in the Kyoto Program. It seems like a lot of them were like just excited about really going out to *izakaya* (a Japanese-style drinking place) and, not even going to *izakaya* but British pubs, which doesn't interest me. So I guess I went out my way to sort of find things that I can fit in …

One of the drives that might have pushed her to go outside of the Kyoto Program circle was her feeling of not fitting in the group. She separated herself from her American peers and sought other people that she could relate to. She told me that there was a male student from the Czech Republic who was the only student she hung out with from the Kyoto Program. She described their affinity as: "We only wanted to speak Japanese and wanted to learn Japanese. And we wanted to do whatever culturally they said was Japanese."

Paige was determined to "find that [she] was able to survive in Japanese, like be able to communicate and express [her]self, and [she] really just wanted to get to know Japanese people and the culture" as she said was her goal of studying abroad in Japan. She devoted her time to learning and experiencing "traditional Japan" through tea ceremony, kimono, calligraphy, and flower arrangements. At the same time, she did not limit herself to "traditional Japan," but also wanted to continue what she liked to do: the salsa dancing. This suggests that she was open to various kinds of cultural difference and mixing. Through that, she created her own new social networks, and made Japanese friends on her own. As we can see, she took a full advantage of study abroad and completely immersed herself by being adventurous and exploring the environment, embodying the dominant discourse of immersion.

Lack of Anxiety, Feeling Accepted, and Falling in Love

Paige has a high tolerance for ambiguity, which was well captured in the following comments:

> A lot of other students in the Kyoto Program were shocked by not hearing any English [while in Japan]. But that actually didn't shock me as much because I'm used to being in a country where I don't necessarily understand things, even in my own country with four national languages. So I'm really used to a situation where I have no idea what they are saying.

Unlike Julia who had a strong anxiety about making mistakes and felt fear about unfamiliar environments, Paige lacks such anxiety and was able to accept and dealt with the situations as they were.

When I asked her what she has learned from all the experiences she had in Japan, she said:

> I think I learned a lot of patience, which I hadn't had up until that point. Sitting *seiza* (lit., "proper sitting," the traditional, formal way of sitting), and watching, you know, not being able to ask questions, not just because I couldn't necessarily do in Japanese early on, but because you do not interrupt in tea ceremony. It's silent. So that took a lot of training … I also think that I learned different appreciation for Japanese culture, which you can't just get from watching once or twice but being really accepted into the circle … And as long as you are trying to do that and making attempt to learn it even though you are coming from a different cultural background, they are willing to accept you as long as they see you are taking what they are doing seriously, and wanting to learn honestly.

"Being patient," "just watching," "not asking," "being silent," and "not interrupt[ing]" are what Paige learned from, and in order to learn, Japanese traditional arts. She also thinks that having "sincerity," "internal reverence," "taking seriously," and "wanting to learn honestly" are what is necessary in order to be accepted as a member of the community—becoming a legitimate peripheral participant. Having such dispositions overcomes and transcends cultural differences, Paige believes. We can sense her confidence and pride she gained from these experiences in her words above. Unlike Julia who felt the insurmountable barrier that existed between Japanese and foreigners and thus felt excluded, Paige felt that she was accepted to the community of practice because she "really stuck it out" and "really fell in love with it."

Passions Continue: Sense of Fulfillment and Satisfaction

Paige seems to have developed lasting relationships with her host family and her kimono teacher. Her host family invited Paige to stay with them after the program was over; and both her host family and kimono teacher opened up their homes to have Paige's parents stay while they were visiting Japan. Paige described her high points in Japan as the connection she developed with her host family "because it's almost like indescribable."

Responding to my question as to whether or not all her expectations were met, she said:

> I'm not so sure if they were all met, but I can say that the Kyoto Program experience really was more than I could imagine. Really, it probably fulfilled things I was not necessarily looking for, just with the connection I made with my host family and the things I was able to learn and people I was able to meet.

Her comments suggest that she was satisfied with her experience in a year in Kyoto, particularly what she was able to do outside of the program. In terms of her language development, she said:

> I'm sure my writing and reading skills have improved but it's definitely not improved as much as I would have liked. But that also says something about me, 'cause I focus much more on my verbal; I always focus on communication. And I really felt by the time I left I could understand and communicate and I didn't have to figure out how to say what I wanted, and not saying other things because I didn't know how to. I always felt I could say what I wanted.

She feels that:

> I've achieved something and I don't want to lose it. ... I know I'm gonna see them [her host parents] some point, I'm sure. I will return to Japan. When? I don't know yet, but I know I will.

Her desire for communicating with Japanese people is even stronger now because of the personal connections she developed while she was living in Japan. She treasures the relationships and determines to maintain them. After she came back from Japan, she did not enroll in the Japanese course; however, she audited my advanced-level course, sitting in every class throughout the semester because she did not want to "lose it." By developing strong connections with her host parents, being accepted to the *sadoo* community, and making close Japanese friends, Paige seems to have developed a sense of a confident, capable "Japanese" self.

Discussion

Living and studying abroad is a dynamic, complicated process where a multitude of factors interact with each other, creating a complex, unique environment of learning for each student (Kinginger 2009). Julia's and Paige's experiences in Kyoto present stark differences as shown above. On the one hand, Julia approached school life in Japan in a very similar manner as she would in the United States by making herself busy with homework, which consequently prevented her from participating in any extracurricular activities—or so she felt. Being a good college student—i.e., completing all the homework and getting good grades—was somehow in conflict with fulfilling the expectation of studying abroad— i.e., being immersed in the language/culture. This made Julia feel completely overwhelmed with multiple tasks and desires. As a result, Julia drew on a discourse of "being a good college student" in order to manage her anxiety and fear of an unfamiliar environment. On the other hand, Paige decided that she was "in Japan to be in Japan" by spending time with her host family and engaging in various activities outside of the school context, which resulted in unfavorable academic grades. Even though her learning was not reflected in grades, she has a sense of accomplishment and satisfaction for what she has achieved in the year in Kyoto drawing on the discourse of immersion.

Both Julia and Paige enjoyed life with their host family, but the quality and quantity of access to social networks each family could provide differed greatly. Both families were equally experienced host families, hosting students for six or seven years at that time. However, being older, socially well connected, and having more time to spare, Paige's host family was able to pay more attention to and accommodate her personal wants and desires. Her host parents were retired people with more free time and inclination not only to spend time with her but also to introduce her to Japanese "traditional" arts and rituals. Julia's host family was younger and busier with their own daily schedule and routines; that is not necessarily a negative quality because Julia was able to experience "normal" life in Japan instead of being a focus of "special attention." Yet, it nonetheless provided differing (i.e., limited) access to various social networks.

Due to their differing access to social networks and their differing senses of self-efficacies (i.e., sense of their ability to carry on a task), Julia's and Paige's lives outside of the school context differed greatly. Julia felt she "can't do clubs" while Paige was driven to "find places to fit in." Consequently, Julia had limited chances to use Japanese whereas Paige found and created various opportunities to communicate in Japanese in diverse settings with a variety of people.

Both Julia and Paige had a desire to become fluent in Japanese and to understand Japanese cultures, and the year in Kyoto was the perfect opportunity to do just that. Then, why did they choose to spend their time in Kyoto so differently? On the one hand, anxiety played a major role shaping Julia's decision making for her life: Julia was shying away from being more active and outgoing because she was "self-conscious about speaking Japanese" and gets "paranoid about making mistakes." Her ideal self-image of a perfect Japanese speaker paralyzed her, making it hard for her to become adventurous and to test the limits of what she can do with Japanese language. As Pellegrino Aveni (2005: 4) explains, "the language learner wishes to create and maintain an ideal sense of self in the second language, yet the very act of language use threatens that image."

On the other hand, Paige's lack of anxiety facilitated her resilience and tenacity in seeking and creating new social networks. DuFon and Churchill (2006: 20) discuss that whether one can successfully build a social network is related to the learner's personal traits such as "openness, ability to make oneself socially salient, persistence in working to gain access, and tolerance for and attention to unmodified input." They further claim that "the last trait is related not only to personality, but also to the learner's level of proficiency" (2006: 20). While DuFon and Churchill give one's personality and language proficiency as reasons for his/her "tolerance for unmodified input," I would also argue that one's socio-historical background in past language socialization is a particularly significant factor. In the case of Julia and Paige, in fact, Paige's language proficiency (in an academic sense) is much weaker than Julia's. Yet, as we saw in the previous section, Paige's lack of anxiety and tolerance for ambiguity in a foreign context were a result of her Swiss background. While many American students, like Julia, tend to have less exposure to different languages and to different cultural practices, for students from Europe (especially Switzerland), multilingualism is a part of their "natural habitat" (Murphy-Lejeune 2002).

If we draw on the dominant discourse of "immersion," then we may end up concluding that Paige's study abroad experience was a success story while Julia's a "failure." But is it really the case? Certainly, learning about so-called traditional cultures, being adventurous, and making "native" friends—i.e., being "immersed" in the language and culture—as Paige has done has an important value. However, at the same time, experiencing a regular life of one Japanese family by living family moments such as chatting in a family room and watching TV too have a great educational value: students may realize that the daily life of a middle-class family in a modern city in Japan and in the United States (or other countries) may not be so different. Emphasizing only what is different (or exotic) and spectacular promotes stereotypes and romanticism.

One can argue that Paige's romantic images about Japan were never challenged, and thus she did not get a chance to critically reflect on her own "stereotypical" ideas about Japan; she went to Kyoto with images of kimono and scrolls, and came back to the United States with renewed, stronger passions for traditional arts. In contrast, even though Julia went to Japan with similar passions, she came back recognizing that Japan may not be so fantastic after all. Though it might not have been a pleasant experience, she was able to deeply reflect on the social exclusion that many foreign residents may in fact face in Japan. Julia has learned something significant that only a long-time stay in the country can provide.

It is clear that various types of emotions, or affect, have played a significant role in shaping how Paige and Julia organized their lives. They decided to spend their time the way they did in order to manage and to make sense of their emotions they felt in various settings. Those decisions, consequently, impacted greatly the types of learning that they were able to access while living in Japan.

Conclusions

In this chapter, I illustrated two students' experiences for a year in Kyoto, paying attention to the various emotions evoked in different settings. I attempted to show how students' subjective desires and emotions have shaped their access to social networks—i.e., various learning opportunities—which subsequently impacted their construction of their subjectivities in relation to the discourse of immersion. This study is no way to make a judgment about who had successful or unsuccessful study abroad experiences; it is to provide a nuanced account for each student's experiences in relation to her emotions in order to understand why she chose to live the way she did. Whether or not a student can gain access to social networks, and thus get a foot into a community of practice, is not simply a matter of his/her investment alone. Often conflicting emotions, students' shifting subjectivities, and their perceptions about the social environment in which they are situated interact in a complex way, shaping their ideas about what is possible, necessary, and desirable.

What do we expect of students in living and studying abroad? From the point of view of language learning, we hope that they experience various types of communicative settings and become able to interact with people at ease. We hope that they find a community—no matter how small that may be—where they feel a part and want to become a legitimate member. We want them to take up and inhabit the subject position of a capable, confident "language user," not of a powerless "language learner." We also want them to develop a deeper understanding that great diversity exists in any group and their earlier expectations may have been essentialized depictions of the people and country.

What is equally important is we recognize that great diversity exists among study abroad participants and that even with similar passions and desires, and with similar preparation and aspirations, the ways they perceive situations, react emotionally, and come to decide how to organize their lives differ significantly. To recognize and value the students' diverse experiences in study abroad, and not to make some feel a false sense of "failure," we need to begin creating alternative discourses of study abroad that do not overemphasize the importance of "immersion."

Yuri Kumagai received her Ed.D. in the Language, Literacy, and Culture program from the University of Massachusetts Amherst and is Senior Lecturer of Japanese at Smith College. Her specializations are critical literacy and multiliteracies in world language education. She has published numerous journal articles and book chapters in English and Japanese. Her most recent publications include: *The Routledge Intermediate to Advanced Japanese Reader: A Genre-Based Approach to Reading as a Social Practice* (Routledge 2015) and *Multiliteracies in World Language Education* (Routledge 2016).

Notes

I would like to express my gratitude to anonymous reviewers and the editors of this volume, Neriko Musha Doerr and Hannah Davis Taïeb, for their constructive feedback on earlier versions of the chapter.

1. The name of the college, the study abroad program, and the students are all pseudonyms.
2. Although the Kyoto Program is college approved and recommended, students are free to choose any other study abroad program depending on their choice of the geographical location as well as of the kinds of elective courses that a program offers. I am not affiliated with any of the study abroad programs.
3. In Japan, unlike the United States, the academic year starts in April. This makes it difficult for students participating in study abroad programs that follow the US academic calendar to join clubs as they recruit new members at the beginning of their school year.
4. The grades students receive from the study abroad programs do not affect their GPA at Stanton College.
5. Salsa, though it is not a "tradition" in Japan, has become very popular in Japan to the extent that Japanese salsa dancers have won the championships in the world contest in recent years.

References

Block, David. 2007. *Second Language Identities*. New York: Continuum.
Bown, Jennifer, and Cynthia J. White. 2010a. "Affect in a Self-Regulatory Framework for Language Learning." *System* 38: 432–43.

——. 2010b. "A Social and Cognitive Approach to Affect in SLA." *IRAL-International Review of Applied Linguistics in Language Teaching* 48: 331–53.

Brecht, Richard D., Victor Frank, J. Ward Keesling, F. O'Mara, and A. R. Walton. 1997. *A Guide for Evaluating Foreign Language Immersion Training*. Washington, DC: Defense Language Institute.

Cole, Pamela M., Sarah E. Martin, and Tracy A. Dennis. 2004. "Emotion Regulation as a Scientific Construct: Methodological Challenges and Directions for Child Development Research." *Child Development* 75: 317–33.

Damasio, Antonio R. 1994. *Descartes' Error: Emotion, Reason and the Human Brain*. New York: Avon.

Dewaele, Jean-Marc. 2007. "The Effect of Multilingualism, Sociobiographical, and Situational Factors on Communicative Anxiety and Foreign Language Anxiety of Mature Language Learners." *International Journal of Bilingualism* 11(4): 391–409.

Doerr, Neriko Musha. 2013. "Do 'Global Citizens' Need the Parochial Cultural Other? Discourse of Immersion in Study Abroad and Learning-by-Doing." *Compare: A Journal of Comparative and International Education* 43: 224–43.

——. 2014. "Desired Learning, Disavowed Learning: Scale-Making Practices and Subverting the Hierarchy of Study Abroad Experiences." *Geoforum* 54: 70–79.

DuFon, Margaret A., and Eton Churchill (eds). 2006. *Language Learners in Study Abroad Contexts*. Clevedon, UK: Multilingual Matters.

Freed, Barbara F. (ed). 1995. *Second Language Acquisition in a Study Abroad Context*. Philadelphia: John Benjamins.

Gardner, Robert C., and Peter D. MacIntyre. 1993. "A Student's Contributions to Second-Language Learning. Part II: Affective Variables." *Language Teaching* 26: 1–11.

Goldoni, Federica. 2013. "Students' Immersion Experiences in Study Abroad." *Foreign Language Annals* 46: 359–76.

Gore, Joan Elias. 2005. *Dominant Beliefs and Alternative Voices: Discourse, Belief, and Gender in American Study Abroad*. New York: Routledge.

Horwitz, Elaine. 2001. "Language anxiety and achievement." *Annual Review of Applied Linguistics* 21: 112–126.

Horwitz, Elaine K., Michael B. Horwitz, and Joann Cope. 1986. "Foreign language classroom anxiety." *The Modern Language Journal* 70: 125–32.

Isen, Alice M. 2000. "Positive Affect and Decision-Making." In M. Lewis, J. M. Haviland-Jones, and L. Feldman Barrett (eds), *Handbook of Emotions*. New York: Guilford, pp. 417–35.

Isen, Alice M., Kimberly A. Daubman, and Gary P. Nowicki. 1987. "Positive Affect Facilitates Creative Problem-Solving." *Journal of Personality and Social Psychology* 47: 1206–17.

Kinginger, Celeste. 2008. "Language Learning in Study Abroad: Case Studies of Americans in France." *Modern Language Journal* 92: 1–124.

——. 2009. *Language Learning and Study Abroad.* Basingstoke, UK: Palgrave Macmillan.

Kinginger, Celeste, and Kathleen Farrell Whitworth. 2005. *Gender and Emotional Investment in Language Learning during Study Abroad* (Vol. 2, pp. 1–12). CALPER Working Papers Series. University Park: Pennsylvania State University.

Krashen, Stephen D. 1981. "Bilingual Education and Second Language Acquisition Theory." *Schooling and Language Minority Students: A Theoretical Framework* 51–79.

Kumagai, Yuri, and Shinji Sato. 2009. "'Ignorance' as a Rhetorical Strategy: How Japanese Language Learners Living in Japan Maneuver Their Subject Positions to Shift Power Dynamics." *Critical Studies in Education* 50: 309–21.

Lave, Jean, and Etienne Wenger. 1991. *Situated Learning: Legitimate Peripheral Participation.* Cambridge: Cambridge University Press.

Miller, Roy Andrew. 1982. *Japan's Modern Myth: The Language and Beyond.* New York: Weatherhill.

Milroy, Lesley. 1987. *Observing and Analysing Natural Language: A Critical Account of Sociolinguistic Method.* Oxford: Blackwell.

Modern Language Association, Ad Hoc Committee on Foreign Languages. 2007. "Foreign Languages and Higher Education: New Structures for a Changed World." New York: Modern Language Association.

Murphy-Lejeune, Elizabeth. 2002. *Student Mobility and Narrative in Europe: The New Strangers.* London: Routledge.

Peirce, Bonny Norton. 1995. "Social Identity, Investment, and Language Learning." *TESOL Quarterly* 29: 9–31.

Ochs, Elinor. 2002. "Becoming a Speaker of Culture." In Claire Kramsch (ed), *Language Acquisition and Language Socialization: Ecological Perspective.* London: Continuum: pp. 99–120.

Pellegrino Aveni, Valerie A. 2005. *Study Abroad and Second Language Use.* Cambridge: Cambridge University Press.

Richie, Donald. 1986. *Introducing Japan,* rev ed. Tokyo: Kodansha International.

Ryan, Stephen, and Sarah Mercer. 2011. "Natural Talent, Natural Acquisition and Abroad: Learner Attributions of Agency in Language Learning." *Identity, Motivation and Autonomy in Language Learning* 160–76.

Schneider, Alison. 2001. "A University Plans to Promote Languages by Killing Its Languages Department." *Chronicle of Higher Education,* 9 March.

Schwarz, Norbert, and Gerald L. Clore. 1983. "Mood, Misattribution, and Judgments of Well-Being: Informative and Directive Functions of Affective States." *Journal of Personality and Social Psychology* 45: 513.

Scovel, Tom. 2001. *Learning New Languages: A Guide to Second Language Acquisition.* Boston: Heinle & Heinle.

Stein, Nancy L., Tom Trabasso, and Maria D. Liwag. 2000. "A Goal Appraisal Theory of Emotional Understanding: Implications for Development and Learning." In Michael Lewis and Jeannette M. Haviland-Jones (eds), *Handbook of Emotions,* 2nd ed. New York: Guilford, pp. 436–57.

Trentman, Emma. 2013. "Imagined Communities and Language Learning during Study Abroad: Arabic Learners in Egypt." *Foreign Language Annals* 46: 545–64.

Weedon, Chris. 1997. *Feminist Practice and Poststructuralist Theory,* 2nd ed. New York: Blackwell.

Wenger, Etienne. 1998. *Communities of Practice: Learning, Meaning, and Identity.* Cambridge: Cambridge University Press.

PART III

Serving with Passion

Romantic Images of Self and Other in Volunteering Abroad

CHAPTER 8

One Smile, One Hug

Romanticizing "Making a Difference" to Oneself and Others through English-Language Voluntourism

Cori Jakubiak

Introduction

> The bourgeois is obsessed with whatever it is that "he" hasn't got,
> whether a suntan or a sense of community. And while the former is
> buyable, the latter, despite the movements of the property market, is
> not. Yet it is a premise of capitalism that everything can be exchanged.
> —Williams cited in Conran, 2006

The above quote, cited in an article about volunteer tourism (Conran 2006), illustrates the way in which the phenomenon engages with emotional intimacy—or, the promise of it—as a way to compel people to volunteer abroad. Alternately referred to as international voluntary service (Sherraden et al. 2006), volunteer tourism has drawn increasing amounts of public and academic attention over the last decade. Defined by Stephen Wearing (2001: 1) as "volunteer[ing] in an organized way to undertake holidays that might involve aiding or alleviating the material poverty of some groups in society," volunteer tourism has been widely featured in US public media outlets ranging from the *New York Times* (Higgins 2011) to CNN (Scott 2011). In these media representations, volunteer tourism is cast as an ideal way for well-meaning, socially conscious people to "leave their mark on the world" (Global Volunteers 2011) and "make a difference" (Cross-Cultural Solutions n.d.) to poor, distant others while on vacation by combining travel with service. Further, the lure of a possible emotional connection with distant others in part motivates the volunteer tourism market (Conran 2011).

Generally moving unidirectionally in a Global North–Global South flow, volunteer tourism can be deep (3–6 months) or shallow (1–2 weeks) (Callanan and Thomas 2005). The service projects in which volunteer tourists engage while abroad include, among others, nature trail maintenance, building construction, childcare, and classroom teaching. English language teaching, specifically, is a common volunteer tourism option (Collins, DeZerega, and Heckscher 2002). Many of the nongovernmental organizations (NGOs) and private corporations that sponsor volunteer tourism offer English language teaching programs that are temporally shallow and require neither professional educator credentials nor prior teaching experience. An interrogation of what I call *English-language voluntourism,* or English language teaching in the volunteer tourism context, both raises numerous questions and provides unique insights on the current historical moment. This chapter examines three interrelated research questions vis-à-vis English-language voluntourism. First, what are the romantic discourses and discourses of emotion evoked in sponsoring organizations' promotional literature and in the talk of current and former volunteers? Second, how are the purposes of English-language voluntourism defined in these same contexts, and how are romantic and emotional motivations drawn upon or transformed in these discourses? Third, what broader discourses are indexed and/or reappropriated in discussions of English-language voluntourism's purposes? In answering these three questions, I suggest that English-language voluntourism's simplified, romantic portrayal of short-term, English language teaching in the Global South as humanitarian aid not only reflects and expands neoliberal prerogatives, but also constructs Global South people as exotic, distant others who are simultaneously needy and compelling. Before developing these arguments further, I first situate English language voluntourism within a body of related research.

Volunteer Tourism: Helping, Hindering, or Something Else Entirely?

Academic literature on volunteer tourism has been expanding rapidly over the last decade, particularly since the mid-2000s. Early work on volunteer tourism (Callanan and Thomas 2005; Stoddart and Rodgerson 2004; Wearing 2001) suggests that volunteer tourism represents an ideal form of new, or alternative, tourism (Poon 1993), a decommodified form of travel that disrupts power imbalances between and among hosts and guests. More so than traditional, international mass tourism, new tourism is argued to be ecologically sound (Mowforth and Munt 2006; Swarbrooke et al. 2003) and allow travelers the chance to interact with local people in authentic, meaningful ways—to go "backstage" in Dean MacCannell's (1976/1999) sense of the term (McIntosh and Zahra 2007).

Research on contemporary tourism more generally notes the ways in which a search for authenticity dominates the practice (Mowforth and Munt 2006; Munt 1994; Tucker 1997). According to MacCannell (1999/1976), the Western desire to experience the "authentic" is an outcome of capitalist alienation. MacCannell explains, following Marxist theories of political economy, that in a fast-paced world of industrial consumption, "Modern Man is losing his attachments to the work bench, the neighborhood, the town, the family ... at the same time, he is developing an interest in the 'real life' of others" (91). Thus it is theorized why, over the last few decades, many view travel in the Global South as a way to get in touch with "the real." It is offered that people living in basic conditions are authentic in a way that middle-class people living in the Global North are not. Global South people, travel industry literature suggests, interact more with their environments, find personal engagement in their work, and are not alienated from the labor process. To visit and interact with these "authentic" people and their communities is argued to serve as a balm to the alienation that many people in the West experience in their day-to-day lives (Clifford 1997).

While the Marxist theory of alienation offers one reason as to why people in the Global North may seek authenticity through practices such as volunteer tourism, theories on recent sociopolitical economic trends offer another explanation. As anxiety about an ever-expanding McWorld (Ritzer 2004) increases, many people are seeking new and differentiated travel experiences to escape the predictability, standardization, and commodification of quotidian life. As Martin Mowforth and Ian Munt (2006: 71–73) put it, "The laments of the fake [under rapid processes of globalization], for example, can be seen to reflect the suggestion that we are moving towards an undifferentiated global culture and the accelerating desire to experience real cultures through travel." Real culture, in the context of globalization, is that which is less touched by the market. The exotic, distant other—i.e., people who wear traditional clothing, live in primitive housing, or drive horse-carts—are held up in the Western imagination as "authentic," outside the sphere of globalization's rampant commodification processes (Tucker 1997). Yet, Westerners' desires to "consume" authenticity through travel and contact with a Global South Other commodifies that very other. "Otherness and authenticity are united in a desire to ensure that culture and ethnicity are preserved and aestheticized," Mowforth and Munt (2006: 74) write. "It is the promotion of primitiveness within which authenticity becomes the principal commodity." New tourism's romantic propensity to uphold contact with other, so-called primitive, cultures as a way to experience authenticity thus commodifies the very processes from which it purports to provide an escape (see Fletcher 2014 for a thorough discussion of this tension).

Other research on volunteer tourism offers that the phenomenon is indicative of postmodernity. Pekka Mustonen (2005; 2007) as well as Jim Butcher and Peter Smith (2010) (following Giddens) posit that travelers' desires to engage in civic action through socially conscious consumption (in this case, the purchase of a volunteer vacation) represents a form of life politics. Life politics involves a distancing from grand political narratives and tacit acceptance of a social milieu in which civic action is wrought through individual acts of consumption rather than through collective channels. Other observers claim that volunteer tourism represents global civil society in action and the positive influence of NGOs (Keese 2011; McBride and Sherraden 2007; Sherraden et al. 2006). Finally, an existent body of work on volunteer tourism argues that Global North volunteers can accrue multiple benefits by participating in such programs. Reported positive outcomes include not only sustained civic engagement over time (McGehee and Santos 2005), but also personal catharsis (Zahra and McIntosh 2007) and a deeper sense of self (Wearing, 2001). These latter two outcomes suggest that some participants in volunteer tourism programs receive emotional returns on their time and capital investments; the consumption of a volunteer vacation may yield affective outcomes in a way that other consumer experiences do not (see Butcher and Smith 2015 for more on volunteer tourism as therapeutic for service participants).

A divergent body of research on volunteer tourism, however, has taken a more critical turn. Kate Simpson's (2004; 2005) examinations of volunteer tourism within the context of the European gap year, for example, suggest that short-term, international volunteering often affirms rather than challenges participants' pre-held stereotypes of poverty and constructs a "geography of need" (2004: 686). Other research offers that "cross-cultural understanding," "genuine exchange between hosts and guests," and similar, oft-quoted "natural" outcomes of volunteer tourism (Wearing 2001; McMillon, Cutchins, and Geissinger 2003) are not so natural after all. Rather, sponsoring organizations must be strategic, intentional, and directly facilitative if they wish to see volunteer tourism program participants achieve (or at least voice) such outcomes (Palacios 2010; Raymond and Hall 2008). Even among the recipients of volunteer tourists' efforts—the "voluntoured"—research indicates that education levels are correlated to a more critical stance on volunteer tourism and its effects (McGehee and Andereck 2009). Such findings corroborate research on domestic service-learning, which also suggests that participants in service-learning programs need carefully scaffolded, well-designed, pre-, during-, and postservice education in order to deconstruct their own privilege and see their personal roles in structural inequality. Without such critical education and reflection, participants in service-learning programs risk viewing their work as simple charity and may neglect to interrogate the broader reasons as to why voluntary service is required in society at all (Endres and Gould 2009; Nenga 2011).

Relatedly, critical studies in volunteer tourism aver that the phenomenon may actually be perpetuating the very problems it purports to solve (Butcher and Smith 2010; Conran 2011; Heath 2007; Jakubiak 2012; Sin 2010; Vrasti 2013). Mary Conran's (2011: 1461) work on volunteer tourism in Thailand, for example, demonstrates that participants' use of intimacy as the framing feature of their volunteer service—i.e., smiling, connecting, and "feeling [one anothers'] heartbeats"—depoliticizes development work. Intimacy, she asserts,

> overshadows the structural inequalities on which the [volunteer tourism] encounter is based and reframes the question of structural inequality as a question of individual morality. This reframing contributes to a cultural politics, which normalizes the privatization of social services and economic development by NGOs ... in effect support[ing] the continued expansion of neoliberal cultural ideologies and economic policies. (2011: 1455)

Numerous scholars have noted the ways in which neoliberal social, political, and economic formations contribute to widespread vulnerability among people in the Global South (Davis 2006; Harvey 2005). In the volunteer tourism context, intimate encounters with distant others—an experience marketed by NGOs as a way to recruit participants into volunteer tourism programs (Keese 2011)—may foreclose other, more pivotal discussions of resource distribution and reify neoliberal prerogatives. Relatedly, as I argue elsewhere (Jakubiak 2012), the discourses surrounding English-language voluntourism, or short-term English language teaching and learning in the Global South, rely on and recreate what Peter Dicken (2003) calls *hyperglobalism*. Hyperglobalism suggests that Western-driven economic globalization is total, natural, and not worth challenging. English-language voluntourism's insistence on the appropriateness of English language learning and use as the way to mitigate the effects of hyperglobalism concurrently reinforces hyperglobalism, thus helping to bring about the very globalization process that is treated as a referent. Volunteer tourism's claims, then, to being a sustainable form of development (Wearing 2001; WorldTeach n.d.) or "pro-poor" form of tourism (Keese 2011) find dissent in the academic literature.

Academic critique of the phenomenon notwithstanding, volunteer tourism in general and English-language voluntourism specifically continue to attract broad public support, both as socially just forms of new tourism (Andereck et al. 2012) and as a means of international development (Rieffel and Zalud 2006). Although scholars have begun to interrogate the links between language education and development—particularly English language education and development (Pennycook 1999; Williams and Cooke 2002)—little attention yet has been paid to the effects of English language teaching through volunteer tourism. The findings presented in this chapter, then, provide insight on the links among English language teaching, development work, and volunteer tourism. Moreover, in paying attention to individual volunteers' affect, this chapter reveals some of the power relations inherent in English-language voluntourism. Before turning to an explication of these findings, however, I first present my investigative methods.

Study Methods

This study was part of a larger, multisited ethnographic study (Marcus 1995) that spanned the course of two and a half years. In June and July of 2007, I conducted participant observation in Costa Rica as a volunteer English language teacher under the auspices of an NGO-sponsored volunteer tourism program. In June and July of 2008, I worked as volunteer program assistant in the Northeastern US home offices of the same NGO. Established in 1986, the NGO is approximately twenty years old has a loose affiliation with a private university, from among whose faculty it draws its board of directors. In 2008, the NGO sponsored a total of 15 programs in 11 countries; 6 of these programs were summer long and 9 were a year in length. I worked alongside full-time NGO employees (all alumni of the NGO's programs, either short or long term) with the goal of understanding how English-language voluntourism programs are designed, supported, and monitored from a US base.

Data for this particular study consist of field notes from participant observation in two sites, 34 interview transcripts, and 20 English-language voluntourism sponsors' promotional websites. While volunteering in Costa Rica, I conducted 16 open-ended, semistructured interviews with 14 other members of my 21-person volunteer cohort (two participants were interviewed twice; I combined their respective interviews each into two single, separate documents). Interviews were conducted primarily during the NGO-sponsored one-week orientation session (prior to volunteers' teaching) or during the two-day, NGO-sponsored, midservice conference (at which point volunteers had been teaching for approximately four weeks). Participants were selected using a process of convenience sampling (Patton 2002); if and when a fellow volunteer and I happened to be simultaneously free from other obligations, I asked if we could sit down and talk. Interview questions in the Costa Rican context were drawn from a preestablished protocol that sought to explore participants' motivations for having volunteered, their perceptions of the purposes of English teaching and learning in the host country and/or the local community, and their understandings of the significance and role of English-language voluntourism programs in Costa Rica and the world more broadly. All interviews in Costa Rica lasted between 30 and 45 minutes, and most were conducted at either the open-air restaurant compound that comprised the orientation site or at the youth hostel in which the program cohort stayed during the midservice conference. All interviews were audio-recorded and later transcribed for analysis.

The other twenty interviews that provided transcripts for this study were conducted with former volunteer program participants in January 2009. Questions for these interviews were taken from a protocol similar to that used in Costa Rica: I asked participants to speak to their motivations for having volunteered, their perceptions of the purposes of English language teaching/learning in their former host community, and their understandings of the significance and role of English-language voluntourism programs in general. Overall, the retrospective interviews were longer than those conducted in Costa Rica (suggestive of how busy and preoccupied many in-service program participants were), and they lasted between 30 and 75 minutes each. A process of purposeful sampling (Patton 2002) was used to recruit interview participants for this portion of the study. I used the NGO's alumni databases as well as the assistance of the NGO's director of admissions and recruitment to contact summer program alumni who had volunteered in the last two years and who currently resided in the Northeastern US city where the NGO is located. All retrospective interviews were conducted in coffee shops near the NGO offices, in the NGO offices themselves, or on the campus of the private university with which the NGO is affiliated. As in Costa Rica, all interviews were audio-recorded and later transcribed for analysis.

In both settings (Costa Rica and the Northeastern US city), interview participants' identity categories were consistent with research in international volunteering at large. This body of work suggests that participants in volunteer tourism are likely to be female, under thirty, and of middle- to upper-middle-class backgrounds (TRAM 2008). Out of 31 total participants (3 of my interview participants were interviewed in both 2007 and 2009), 19 (61%) identified as female; all but 1 were under age thirty; and at least 20 (65%)—to judge from the private, prestigious universities they attended—possessed markers of middle- to upper-middle-class cultural capital (Bourdieu 1979/1984). Many of my interview participants, moreover, had received full or partial financial support from their home universities for their volunteer efforts; fewer than half of them had paid full program fees (which can run up to $5000 for an eight-week program). Most of my participants identified as White (22 of 31); others identified as Asian-American (3 of 31); Indian-American (3 of 31); Latina-American (1), Ecuadorian (1), and African-American (1), respectively.

Twenty English-language voluntourism sponsors' promotional websites were also used as data for this study. A process of purposeful sampling (Patton 2002) was used to identify English-language voluntourism sponsors that are based in the United States or United Kingdom, offer English language teaching programs that are temporally shallow, and do not require that participants possess teaching credentials or prior teaching experiences.

Interview transcripts, field notes, and sponsoring organizations' websites were analyzed using a constructivist grounded theory approach (following Charmaz 2006). In contrast to an objectivist approach to grounded theory, which "attends to data as real in and of themselves and does not attend to the processes of their production" (Charmaz 2006: 131), a constructivist grounded theory approach seeks to interpret the social world. Thus, the findings presented here are (by theoretical design) partial.

Following a recursive process that involved initial, or open, coding, writing analytical memos, and focused coding (Emerson, Fretz, and Shaw 1995), I ultimately generated four superordinate categories that expressed the different ways in which participants talked about English-language voluntourism. Superordinate categories were generated inductively (based on ideas in interviewees' talk) and deductively (based on ideas implicit in the interview questions or present in academic literature). Verbatim quotes in the text below serve either as typical examples (or exceptions to) conceptual codes, and they were selected based on how well they communicated the central idea of a conceptual category. I named the four superordinate categories *romanticizing English-language voluntourism at large*; *romanticizing English-language voluntourism's impact on the voluntoured*; *romanticizing English-language voluntourism's impact on the self*; and *romanticizing the Other*.

Romanticizing English-Language Voluntourism at Large

A discourse that I call *romanticizing English-language voluntourism at large* circulates around and within English-language voluntourism. Promotional literature and the talk of in-service and former volunteers frequently characterizes English-language voluntourism as more "real" than other forms of travel and more authentic than mass tourism or studying abroad. English-language voluntourism is not only argued to provide cultural experiences that are unavailable outside of volunteer tourism, but is also suggested to fulfill one's long-held dream of "really" experiencing the distant other. In illustration, i to i Volunteering, an English-language voluntourism sponsor, issues the following call to prospective volunteers:

> Take one of our volunteering trips and you'll work on locally run projects that benefit local communities and the environments in which they live. You'll become part of the local community and have the kind of authentic cultural experiences that backpackers and package tourists daren't even dream about. (i to i: n.d.)

Even though some of i to i's English-language voluntourism programs can be as short as one week (i to i: n.d.), it is offered that visiting volunteers will become full, participating members of their host communities nevertheless. The organization's use of competitive language, moreover ("You'll … have the kind of cultural experiences that backpackers and package tourists daren't even dream about") indexes how new tourism practices in general (and volunteer tourism specifically) are manifestations of late modernity. Under conditions of late capitalism (Harvey 1989) in which the construction of self-identity proceeds largely through personal consumption or lifestyle choices, participating in English-language voluntourism has become a form of symbolic capital, a way for individuals to differentiate themselves from others through the commodification of unique experiences (Heath 2007; Tucker 1997). i to i's nod to peoples' need to engage in such differentiation suggests the preeminence of this desire among English-language voluntourism program participants and in the societies from which they hail.

In-service and former English-language voluntourists also voiced sentiments that reflected *romanticizing English-language voluntourism at large*. Their words suggest a preconceived notion not only of what development work is, but also the confident belief that visiting volunteers are part and parcel of such work. Lauren, a White, twentysomething, former volunteer from the US Northeast majoring in social work, exemplified *romanticizing English-language voluntourism at large* in a discussion of why she had volunteered in South Africa. She said:

> I always knew [development work] … was within me. I always knew that, you know—I'd always saw myself in a white T-shirt and jeans and working in a small village. … Ever since I was little, we had *National Geographic* come in the mail, and it was just looking through those pictures and just kind of seeing a *completely* different life that lacks so many things that we have here. So I think it was just seeing the bare minimum—just, you know, seeing pictures of the people there. So, I kind of grew up that way. (29 January 2009, emphasis in original)

Development work, in Lauren's estimation, is something done *by* people in the Global North *to* Global South people—people, as she puts it, who possess the "bare minimum," or have " a *completely* different life that lacks so many things that we have here." This idea of an Us/Them binary divided along Global North–Global South lines not only flattens out differences within these respective areas (e.g., erasing Global North poverty and Global South wealth) but also mutes questions as to why the world is perceptually divided along Global North–Global South lines in the first place. Lauren's stated desire, however, to experience the Global South through vaguely imagined "development work" reflects what Mowforth and Munt (2006: 67) describe as new tourism's fetishization of poverty. Within new tourism practices, "inequality, poverty and political instability ... are ... called upon both to titillate and legitimate travel, to help distinguish these experiences from mere mass tourism." Lauren's suggestion that development work consists of "wearing a white T-shirt and jeans" and "working in a small village" reflects not only a fetishized view of poverty, but also a romanticized notion of what development work is and looks like. Of note is that Lauren's idea of development work has little to nothing to do with *teaching*, even though school teaching was what she went to South Africa to do.

Mike, a white, nineteen-year-old economics major from the US Northeast and an in-service program participant, also voiced comments reflective of *romanticizing English-language voluntourism at large*. His description of what he imagined to be the unique role of English-language voluntourism in Costa Rica reflects the romantic tenets of new tourism. Mike characterizes English-language voluntourism as distinct from mass tourism in that, like Lauren, he sees it as offering an authentic, true experience that is unavailable to general tourists. In Mike's words,

> [W]e are trying, to, like, become part of Costa Rica ... whereas the tourists are, are still going to distance themselves. They're here as Americans in Costa Rica. And while I'm here as an American in Costa Rica, I'm an American who's going to try, and, for two months, to become part of Costa Rica. ... I feel like we're almost going to see real Costa Rica, you know... [V]olunteering for an extended period of time—it can be more difficult, because ... you'll actually have to face real Costa Rica, and at some ... points it's not going to be easy. (9 June 2007)

Mike's assertion that facing what he terms "the real Costa Rica" will pose challenges or be difficult at times reflects not only the idea that English-language voluntourism is "authentic" in MacCannell's (1976/1999) sense, but also a presumed dichotomy between life in the United States and life in Costa Rica. Mike attributes hardship to the "real" Costa Rica; implied is that life in the United States, by contrast, is not hard. Such a statement indexes the privileged position of most English-language voluntourists (TRAM 2008) and suggests a lack of understanding of poverty and inequality within the Global North. The discourse of *romanticizing English language-voluntourism at large,* then, not only glosses over inequity within regions, but also fails to interrogate why such divisions are perpetuated in the first place.

Romanticizing English-Language Voluntourism's Impact on the Voluntoured

In addition to romanticizing the phenomenon at large, discourse surrounding and promoting English-language voluntourism frames the practice's impact through rose-colored lenses. What I call *romanticizing English-language voluntourism's impact on the voluntoured* discourse describes the phenomenon as generating uniform change in host communities regardless of the length of a volunteer's teaching stint, the efficacy or credentials of the visiting volunteer, or the needs or current status of the host community. Per Cross-Cultural Solutions, a well-known English-language voluntourism sponsor, "You can make a difference. One smile. One hug. One conversation. *That's all it takes*" (Cross-Cultural Solutions, n.d., emphasis in original). Implied here is that physical contact and smiles between volunteers and their hosts can alleviate the effects of widespread structural inequality. Similarly, i to i, the English-language voluntourism sponsor mentioned above, tells prospective volunteers that "Volunteer teaching abroad will leave you feeling fulfilled in the knowledge that you're making a tremendous impact on the future lives of underprivileged children—it really is a win, win situation!" (n.d.). In this depiction, the difference made or "tremendous impact" English-language voluntourism supposedly has is either unquantifiable or not quantifiable until the future. The impact of English-language voluntourism programs cannot be empirically accounted for in the present. Instead, "feeling fulfilled"—or, in the case of Cross-Cultural Solutions' aforementioned description, smiling and hugging—counts as development work. Left unaccounted for is whether the lives of the recipients of smiles or hugs have been materially or socially improved.

The discourse of *romanticizing English-language voluntourism's impact on the voluntoured* was also reflected in the talk of in-service and former program participants. Many English-language voluntourists imagined that their personal impact on a host community would be long-lasting and life-changing for the recipients of their efforts. Jim, an

Asian-American in his midtwenties taking a corporate leave to serve in Costa Rica, reflected this position, stating that "it would be nice if, if, I would be talked about, like, five or ten years down the road by the same people that I ... taught and that I met with" (9 June 2007). Despite the brevity of his volunteer teaching stint (approximately six weeks), Jim imagined that his host community members would be so transformed by his presence and work there that they would recall him a decade later. While some volunteers do, indeed, have a long-lasting impact on the recipients of their service efforts, research suggests that this impact is often mediated by their monetary or material gifts to local community members (Sinervo 2011).

Josie, a twenty-year-old, White, female biology major and former program participant from the US Midwest, also expressed *romanticizing English-language voluntourism's impact on the voluntoured.* She viewed her volunteer role in Ecuador as having administered love and care; doing these things, she offered, constituted the help or aid she was there to deliver. In her words,

> Imagine you're a little girl growing up in [a small Ecuadorian village]. And ... there's an American coming to be with you ... to pay attention to you and who cares about what you have to say. ... I am most proud that I was able to go there and demonstrate to the people I met that there ... is someone in the U.S. who cares about them. (30 January 2009)

Josie's identification of caring, not teaching, as the key component of English-language voluntourism is consistent with research in volunteer tourism at large, which suggests that volunteer tourism operates within a moral economy. In voluntourist-staffed after school centers in Cusco, Peru, for example, Aviva Sinervo (2011: 2) notes that there exists an "uneasy intersection of affectivity and economy that provides opportunities for connection between tourists and children. ... Foreigners rely on particular constructs of childhood and poverty to justify their interventions in aid projects." In the context of English-language voluntourism, the moral economy of care still predominates; volunteer teachers seek opportunities to exchange care and affection with seemingly downtrodden students in the classroom context. For English-language voluntourists like Josie, whether students learn any English through a volunteer's instructional efforts is less important than whether they feel loved or cared about—particularly by a visiting American.

Romanticizing English-Language Voluntourism's Impact on the Self

What I call *romanticizing English-language voluntourism's impact on the self* discourse marks another way in which romantic discourses operate on and through the practice. In promotional literature and in the talk of in-service and former volunteers, it is offered that participating in an English-language voluntourism program will bring a volunteer new revelations, more focused life direction, and increased appreciation for one's current life and standards of living. Related research suggests that volunteer tourists often cite the opportunity to learn more about themselves as a primary motivation for engaging in the practice (Coghlan and Gooch: 2011); similar explanations were also offered by participants in this study. However, rather than voicing commentary to the effect that *teaching* (in and of itself) might constitute a unique way to learn about themselves, most in-service and former English-language voluntourism program participants spoke solely of experiencing the Global North–Global South divide. Suzanne, a Midwestern, White, 18-year-old in-service program participant in Costa Rica majoring in biology, gave word to this idea explicitly by stating:

> I'd like some guidance [from this experience] ... I want to ... at least try to remember that I have opportunities that not only do people in America not have, I have opportunities that people in Costa Rica could never dream of—and that I should be very grateful. I hope to be a little more grateful after this trip. ... I want to realize that I have it so good. (5 June, 2007)

Suzanne's romantic commitment to the idea that participating in English-language voluntourism could contribute to meaningful self-change was such that she was willing to undergo strain in the short term. She followed up the previous statement by admitting that

> Here, I frankly don't expect it to be fun most of the time. I expect to get pretty depressed and pretty lonely, and I'll probably think, "Oh, man— why didn't I just stay at home and, you know, work and sit by the pool?' I—but I'm going to come out of it, hopefully, as a more understanding, patient, world-wise person. (5 June, 2007)

The *romanticizing English-language voluntourism's impact on the self* discourse evidenced in Suzanne's talk reflects critical work in new tourism studies, which observes that under conditions of late modernity, experiencing moderate danger, having brushes with exotic illnesses, or participating in physically challenging activities index culturally "authentic" experiences (Butcher 2003; Fletcher, 2014; Swarbrooke et al. 2003). Classroom teaching, by contrast, offers less of an authentic rite of passage. Furthermore, Suzanne's tacit acceptance of her English-language voluntourism experience as being more about personal self-growth than community development or language instruction reflects the extent to which romanticized discourses of self-improvement through "struggle" adhere to English-language voluntourism. Development through English-language voluntourism may be more about the development of visiting volunteers than the (economic or social) development of the host community (see also Simpson 2005 for work in this vein).

Other in-service and former program participants also deployed the discourse of *romanticizing English-language voluntourism's impact on the self.* For example, Catherine, a White, female, twentysomething in-service program participant from the US Northwest majoring in the liberal arts, explained that the NGO orientation week in Costa Rica had quickly altered her former priorities. She explained: "[I]t's already sort of changed who I am. ... Back home, I'm like, 'Oh, I can't be seen wearing the same things twice in one week—that's horrible.' And here, no! No one cares" (4 June 2007). In a similar vein, Lauren, introduced above, claimed that "[Since volunteering] I personally buy a lot less. Personally. I have, like, three pairs of pants and I set a deadline where I'm going to wear [only] white T-shirts. ... So, my goal is just to wear jeans and white T-shirts, to kind of just get away from this materialistic thing" (29 January 2009).

While some research posits that long-term, personal change can be an outcome of participation in volunteer tourism (McGehee and Santos, 2005; Wearing 2001; Zahra and McIntosh 2007), comments from participants in this study suggest that the personal change facilitated by English-language voluntourism is most often not that which leads to critical reflection on and/or action to combat the structural causes of inequity. Instead, the personal change facilitated by participation in English-language voluntourism programs may be a codification of one's identity as a savvy, caring global traveler who packs lightly. While self- or personal change alone may not be an altogether negative outcome of English-language voluntourism, the fact that many stakeholders claim that its positive effects are two-way—i.e., both volunteer teachers and their students are affected equally—creates a tension between English-language voluntourism as *development of the self* and as *de-*

velopment for the Global South (see Jakubiak 2016 for more on English-language voluntourism as development). Affective development of the self becomes the exclusive priority of volunteers, people who already possesses material resources; by contrast, Global South individuals must "develop" on behalf of their economic futures and communities.

Romanticizing the Other

Another way in which romanticizing discourses circulate in and through English-language voluntourism is in its construction of the Other. What I call *romanticizing the Other* discourse permeates English-language voluntourism promotional literature as well as the talk of in-service and former program participants, who often revered people in the Global South for their basic, "authentic" ways of living. In illustration, Josie, introduced above, expressed a lament that the Ecuadorian village in which she had volunteered seemed to be altering materially and socially. She stated:

> [T]he area where I was, is, like, such on the cusp of, of change. And I mean, I, think about their way of life, and, like, some of the aspects I don't want to change. Like, you know, going out in the morning to, to milk the cow every morning. And then, you know, the moms— you know, the neighborhood moms—come and, you know, get their share and, you know, you socialize and stuff. ... It just seemed ... fun. ... [T]hose chores are fun. (30 January 2009)

A rich body of literature has documented the ways in which poverty, basic standards of living, and humble lifestyles in the Global South are consumed and fetishized in new tourism practices (Conran, 2006; Mowforth and Munt 2006; Munt 1994; Sinervo and Hill 2011; Tucker 1997). Butcher (2003), in particular, argues that what he terms New Moral Tourism actively strives to constrain development in the Global South in the names of cultural preservation, authenticity, and eco-friendliness. Josie's commentary, above, illustrates both a romantic view of her host community and the idea that technological change should not occur there. Chores like hand-milking cows (while time consuming for people in the Global North) are to be preserved and lauded in the Global South as iconic of local culture and authenticity.

The talk of Joe, introduced above, also reflected a wistful sense that people in the Global South, though poor, live more authentically and closer to the bone than do people in the Global North. Discursively linking poverty to culture, he suggested that economic security is not the key to peoples' present or future happiness. Rather, he used *romanticizing the Other* discourse to suggest that being materially deprived offers benefits not widely available to those living in the Global North:

> [I]n a culture like this [in Costa Rica], when you see how happy people are and how united their families are, it kind of goes to show that, you know, money really isn't the key to happiness. Sometimes it can be more of a distraction than a benefit, I guess. ... [E]ven though [a] family doesn't have hot water, and even though they have to walk half an hour uphill to get to work, and they have that hot sun on their tin roof, you know, they can still enjoy life better than a lot of people in developed countries. (9 June 2007)

Although Joe's observation that happiness and money are not directly correlated has indeed been empirically suggested (Hamilton 2004), it coheres with research suggesting that many participants in volunteer tourism programs emerge grateful for their personal privilege rather than critical of a structurally unequal world (Simpson 2005). However, Joe's overall dismissal of economic considerations in a quality of life calculus reflects a romanticized view of poverty. His employment of *romanticizing the Other* discourse reflects what numerous volunteer tourism researchers have termed the "poor but happy" trope (Sin 2010) in which material privation is conflated with a rich cultural life (see also Vrasti 2013).

Amanda, a White, female, Latin American studies major and former program participant from the US West Coast, also used language that reflected *romanticizing the Other* discourse. She shared that while volunteering in Costa Rica, she had been romantically involved with a young man in her host community. The relationship ended when her volunteer service time was completed, however, due in large part to what she termed "cultural differences." Amanda offered that Global South poverty is akin to a cultural barrier between Global North and Global South people; ergo, a relationship between two people from these different social spaces faces insurmountable challenges. In Amanda's words,

> I had a Tico *novio* [boyfriend]. ... So, me coming back to this world [the United States] was so different, because I had, like, left a piece of my heart not only in my community ... I actually, like, did kind of properly fall in love with this guy in my community. Where I just thought—you know, at the time when I was there, I didn't think past leaving. And I was like, "Oh, it's so nice here. You know, it's very relaxing. Everybody's

so warm. I love being here." But coming back, and ... realizing ... the [American] people are more focused on themselves and kind of more selfish and, and ambitious, you know what I mean? ... And then just realizing ... you can't do, like, a long-distance third world thing because even if you have cultural empathy or, or some amount of cultural empathy for what it's like to live in Costa Rica; there's just not going to be a reciprocal effect. (29 January 2009)

Amanda's commentary reflects *romanticizing the Other* discourse in numerous ways. For one, it reflects an understanding of English-language voluntourism (and travel in the Global South more generally) as a period of liminality. Tourism scholarship has long noted travel's role as a liminal space; travel is often a period of time in which guests try on new identities and behaviors with (seemingly) minimal consequences for life back home (Hutnyk 1996). Amanda characterizes her relationship with a Costa Rican man as having occurred in a liminal space; throughout the course of the relationship's duration, she "didn't think past leaving." Upon returning to the United States, however, Amanda saw cultural difference as prohibiting any continuation of the relationship. It was a product of a liminal time, and as the volunteer vacation is over, so, too, is the romance. However, her claim that she did "properly" fall in love in Costa Rica suggests (that to her surprise), she felt feelings that transcended the liminal space of travel—something for which she hadn't bargained.

Apologists for volunteer tourism as a development strategy suggest that participation in these programs can lead to long-lasting social and personal change for volunteers (McBride and Sherraden 2007; McMillon, Cutchins, and Geissinger 2003). Given that many participants view volunteer tourism as a liminal time, however, it may be unreasonable to expect English-language voluntourism to facilitate long-term or far-reaching outcomes. As Arthur Asa Berger (2004: 37) writes, "the foreign travels of ... college students [from the United States] are ... ritual activities tied to their liminality that mark the period in which their childhood is ending and young adulthood is dawning. After their travel, these students will be reintegrated into their communities." Amanda's current attitude toward her Costa Rican relationship suggests this same idea.

Amanda viewed her return to the United States as a time of reintegration into existent social and cultural norms rather a time to challenge those norms. Thus, English-language voluntourism reified rather than challenged Amanda's ideas of what it means to be a middle-class American. She declared that being from the Global South prohibits one from ever truly understanding the selfishness and ambition that define life in the Global North. This gap renders moot the possibility of a working, romantic relationship between herself and a Costa Rican boyfriend. Despite claims that participation in volunteer tourism, then, leads to broadened horizons (Wearing 2001), participation English-language voluntourism, for some, codifies difference and naturalizes economic disparity as "culture" (see also Vrasi 2013).

Falling Out of Love with English-Language Voluntourism: Deromanticized Discourse

Despite the preponderance of data in this study suggesting that romanticized discourses of help, self-change, and the Other circulate widely within English-language voluntourism, discrepant data emerged as well. A small number of in-service and former program participants voiced concern and incredulity over what they felt were the numerous, naïve assumptions underpinning English-language voluntourism and similar, short-term humanitarian efforts. Peg, a former program participant in Namibia, for example, expressed cynicism at the idea that English-language voluntourism is an altruistic endeavor aimed at Global South development. A White, twentysomething African studies major who had worked with Somalian refugees in her Midwestern hometown prior to commencing university studies, Peg was particularly offended by the comments of others in her volunteer cohort. In her view, many volunteers possessed severely limited understandings of Africa as well as classroom teaching, which severely affected the credibility of English-language voluntourism. She explained:

> I think [international volunteer programs are] really fashionable. That was the impression that I got from a lot of the other volunteers who came who were from, like, totally random paths of life. They had never done teaching before, some of them ... there were two students from NYU who were like, music business majors, and they were like, "I just wanted to go to Africa." And I was like [pause]—because Africa, to me, is an ideologically charged word and, you know, and it represents 53 countries, you know, 2,000 languages. It means a lot of different things, different little pieces to me, whereas to them it was like this one, big continent.... I think there are a lot of volunteer programs that are very fashionable because you can go to a developing country and—whatever that means—or, a "third world" country—it cracks me up when people say that. Like, "the third world"—what's? You know. Anyway,

whatever. Or, like, "Africa" … these words that are sort of glamorous, and everybody will say, "Good luck on your trip to Africa. Good luck on your trip to the third world," whatever that means. So, it's associated with, like, a lot of prestige. (29 January 2009)

Peg's sentiments resonate with critical, empirical work on volunteer tourism that suggests that short-term, volunteer service projects not only treat the symptoms rather than causes of wide-scale social problems, but also risk furthering the ideological formations that generate inequity in the first place (Conran 2011; Jakubiak 2012; Simpson 2004; 2005; Sin 2009; 2010; Vrasti 2013). Peg's dismay, for example, that many participants in her English-language voluntourism program cohort possessed no prior teaching experience finds support among critical educational researchers, who also note that a global trend in education is for the most vulnerable students to have the least experienced, least credentialed people as their teachers (Darling-Hammond 2010). Such is one way that broader structural inequity is perpetuated.

Peg's bemusement, moreover, with what she views as others' garnering prestige by going to Africa (or the Global South more broadly) reflects an implicit understanding of the ways in which English-language voluntourism operates within what Sue Heath (2007) terms an economy of experience. Within this economy, unique or compelling travel experiences are collected as forms of symbolic capital, which can then be later parlayed into economic or social resources (see also Rink, this volume). Discussing why the gap year—time during which young people take time off from school to travel and volunteer—is becoming increasingly popular in Great Britain, Heath (91–92) writes that

recent trends in education policy, linked to broader changes in the labor market, have triggered a process of middle-class retrenchment. This has resulted in students having to find new ways of gaining distinction in a world where educational qualifications are no longer sufficient in themselves to guarantee success.

The prestige, then, that Peg observes in her peer group earned by "going to Africa" finds root in a wider formation that reflects the current political economy. Ironically, the very social problems for which English-language voluntourism is the supposed remedy create the pragmatic need for volunteers to engage in these programs in the first place (Vrasti 2013). Peg's observations are astute in that she while she notes the futility of English-language voluntourism as a development intervention, she recognizes the practicality of participating in English-language voluntourism as a way to collect symbolic capital—capital increasingly important in a time of economic austerity.

Conclusion

Many current debates on volunteer tourism center on whether the practice is truly a decommodified form of travel or an exemplary practice of new tourism (Wearing, McDonald, and Ponting 2005). Other discussions focus on the power distribution between and among hosts and guests (Sinervo 2011; Sin 2009; 2010), while still other works explore the role of NGOs in volunteer tourism (Keese 2011) and ways to expand the practice (Andereck et al. 2012). In the study presented here, I sought to widen the scope of discussion by focusing on one kind of volunteer tourism, English-language voluntourism, and examining how the romantic discourses that surround the practice are largely taken up by volunteer participants.

The findings of this study suggest that romanticizing discourses of English-language voluntourism's power, its ostensible impact on the self and others, and its construction of an exotic Other circulate widely within and around the practice. Romantic, simplified views of help, caring, and Global South people find purchase in the talk of in-service and former English-language voluntourists as well as in promotional literature. This finding corroborates research on volunteer tourism more broadly, which avers that volunteers' focus on individual affect prohibits broader discussions of and corrections to the ideological foundations on which short-term development interventions are based. As Conran writes,

> intimacy is a core aspect of the volunteer tourism experience … [which] overshadows the structural inequality that volunteer tourism seeks to address and reframes it as a question of individual morality. By reframing the experience in this way, volunteer tourism participants inadvertently contribute to the continued expansion of the cultural logic and economic policies of global capitalism. Hence, without more radical structural change, the sustainability of the accomplishments of NGOs, which take advantage of international volunteers' time, money and labor, remains tenuous. (2011: 1467)

By casting time, effort, and experiences in romantic ways, English-language voluntourism may be, in Butcher and Smith's (2010: 34) words, little more than "simple, commendable charity."

Yet, by focusing *on* the romantic, affective discourses that circulate within and around English-language voluntourism—as I have done in this chapter—the structural issues and ideological foundations on which English-language voluntourism is based become increasingly apparent. Reading the romance of English-language voluntourism allows for a fine-grained look at how, similar to domestic educational initiatives such as Teach for America in the United States, volunteer tourism relies on and re-creates privilege (for some) through noblesse oblige, short-term encounters with difference, and the deprofessionalization of teaching (Darling-Hammond 2010). In that sense, taking seriously the romantic discourses that adhere to English-language voluntourism is a step toward politicizing the practice.

Cori Jakubiak is an assistant professor of education at Grinnell College, where she teaches courses in educational foundations, linguistics, and place-based education. Her research program uses a critical applied linguistics lens to examine English-language voluntourism, or English language teaching through volunteer tourism.

References

Andereck, K., N.G. McGehee, S. Lee, and D. Clemmons. 2012. "Experience Expectations of Prospective Volunteer Tourists." *Journal of Travel Research* 51(2): 130–41.

Berger, A.A. 2004. *Deconstructing Travel: Cultural Perspectives on Tourism.* Walnut Creek, CA: AltaMira.

Bourdieu, P. 1984. *Distinction: A Social Critique of the Judgment of Taste,* trans. R. Nice. Cambridge, MA: Harvard University Press. (Original work published 1979.)

Butcher, J. 2003. *The Moralization of Tourism: Sun, Sand … and Saving the World?* London: Routledge.

Butcher, J., and P. Smith. 2010. "'Making a Difference': Volunteer Tourism and Development." *Recreation Research* 35(1): 27–36.

———. 2015. *Volunteer tourism: The lifestyle politics of international development.* London: Routledge.

Callanan, M., and S. Thomas. 2005. "Volunteering Tourism: Deconstructing Volunteer Activities within a Dynamic Environment." In M. Novelli (ed.), *Niche Tourism: Contemporary Issues, Trends, and Cases.* Oxford: Butterworth-Heinemann, pp. 183–200.

Charmaz, K. 2006. *Constructing Grounded Theory: A Practical Guide through Qualitative Analysis.* London: Sage.

Clifford, J. 1997. *Routes: Travel and Translation in the Late Twentieth Century.* Cambridge, MA: Harvard University Press.

Coghlan, A., and M. Gooch. 2011. "Applying a Transformative Learning Framework to Volunteer Tourism." *Journal of Sustainable Tourism* 19(6): 713–28.

Collins, J., S. DeZerega, and Z. Heckscher. 2002. *How to Live your Dream of Volunteering Overseas.* New York: Penguin.

Conran, M. 2006. "Beyond Authenticity: Exploring Intimacy in the Touristic Encounter in Thailand." *Tourism Geographies* 8(3): 274–85.

———. 2011. "They Really Love Me! Intimacy in Volunteer Tourism." *Annals of Tourism Research* 38(4): 1454–73.

Cross-Cultural Solutions. Retrieved 16 May 2012 from http://www.crosscultur alsolutions.org/.

Darling-Hammond, L. 2010. *The Flat World and Education: How America's Commitment to Equity Will Determine Our Future.* New York: Teachers College Press.

Davis, M. 2006. *Planet of Slums.* London: Verso.

Dicken, P. 2003. *Global Shift: Reshaping the Global Economic Map in the 21st Century,* 4th ed. New York: Guilford.

Emerson, R.M., R.I. Fretz, and L.L. Shaw. 1995. *Writing Ethnographic Fieldnotes.* Chicago: University of Chicago Press.

Endres, D., and M. Gould. 2009. "I Am Also in the Position to Use My Whiteness to Help Them Out": The Communication of Whiteness in Service-Learning." *Western Journal of Communication* 73(4): 418–36.

Fletcher, R. 2014. *Romancing the wild: Cultural dimensions of ecotourism.* Durham: Duke University Press.

Global Volunteers. 2011. Brochure. St Paul, MN: Global Volunteers.

Hamilton, C. 2004. *Growth Fetish.* London: Pluto Press.

Harvey, D. 1989. *The Condition of Postmodernity.* Cambridge, MA: Blackwell.

———. 2005. *A Brief History of Neoliberalism.* Oxford: Oxford University Press.

Heath, S. 2007. "Widening the Gap: Pre-university Gap Years and the 'Economy of Experience'." *British Journal of Sociology of Education* 28(1): 89–103.

Higgins, S. 2011, July 13. "Budget Excursions for Volunteers." *New York Times.* Retrieved 1 October 2011 from http://travel.nytimes.com/2011/07/17/travel/ volunteer-tourism-for-travelers-on-a-budget.html.

Hutnyk, J. 1996. *The Rumor of Calcutta: Tourism, Charity and the Poverty of Representation.* London: Zed Books.

i to i. n.d. Retrieved 16 May 2012 from http://www.i-to-i.com/volunteer/.

Jakubiak, C. 2012. "'English for the Global': Discourses in/of English Language Voluntourism." *Journal of Qualitative Studies in Education* 25(4): 435–51.

———. 2016. Ambiguous aims: English-language voluntourism as development. *Journal of Language, Identity and Education* 15(4): 245–258.

Keese, J.R. 2011. "The Geography of Volunteer Tourism: Place Matters." *Tourism Geographies* 13(2): 257–79.

MacCannell, D. 1999. *The Tourist: A New Theory of the Leisure Class.* New York: Sulouken. (Original work published 1976)

Marcus, G. 1995. "Ethnography in/of the World System: The Emergence of Multi-sited Ethnography." *Annual Review of Anthropology* 24: 95–117.

McBride, A.M., and M. Sherraden. 2007. *Civic Service Worldwide: Impacts and Inquiry.* Armonk, NY: M.E. Sharpe.

McGehee, N.G.G., and K. Andereck. 2009. "Volunteer Tourism and the 'Volun-toured': The Case of Tijuana, Mexico." *Journal of Sustainable Tourism* 17(1): 39–51.

McGehee, N.G.G., and C.A. Santos. 2005. "Social Change, Discourse and Volun-teer Tourism." *Annals of Tourism Research* 32(3): 760–70.

McIntosh, A.J., and A. Zahra. 2007. "A Cultural Encounter through Volunteer Tourism: Towards the Ideals of Sustainable Tourism?" *Journal of Sustain-able Tourism* 15(5): 541–56.

McMillon, B., D. Cutchins, and A. Geissinger. 2003. *Volunteer Vacations: Short-Term Adventures That Will Benefit You and Others,* 8th ed. Chicago: Chicago Review Press.

Mowforth, M., and I. Munt. 2006. *Tourism and Sustainability: Development and New Tourism in the Third World,* 2nd ed. London: Routledge.

Munt, I. 1994. "Eco-tourism or Ego-tourism?" *Race & Class* 36(1): 49–59.

Mustonen, P. 2005. "Volunteer Tourism: Postmodern Pilgrimage?" *Journal of Tourism and Cultural Change* 3(3): 160–77.

———. 2007. "Volunteer Tourism—Altruism or Mere Tourism?" *Anatolia: An Inter-national Journal of Tourism and Hospitality Research* 18(1): 97–115.

Nenga, S.K. 2011. "Volunteering to Give Up Privilege? How Affluent Youth Vol-unteers Respond to Class Privilege." *Journal of Contemporary Ethnography* 40(3): 263–89.

Palacios, C.M. 2010. "Volunteer Tourism, Development and Education in a Post-colonial World: Conceiving Global Connections Beyond Aid." *Journal of Sustainable Tourism* 18(7): 861–78.

Patton, M.Q. 2002. *Qualitative Research and Evaluation Methods,* 3rd ed. Thou-sand Oaks, CA: Sage.

Pennycook, A. 1999. *Development, Culture, and Language: Ethical Concerns in a Postcolonial World.* Retrieved 7 March 2006 from http://www.clet.ait.ac.th/hanoi_proceedings/pennycook.htm.

Poon, A. 1993. *Tourism, Technology, and Competitive Strategies.* Wallingford, UK: CABI.

Raymond, E.M., and C.M. Hall. 2008. "The Development of Cross-cultural (Mis)understanding through Volunteer Tourism. *Journal of Sustainable Tourism* 16(5): 530–43.

Rieffel, L., and S. Zalud. 2006. *International Volunteering: Smart Power.* (Policy Brief No. 155). Washington, DC: Brookings Institution.

Ritzer, D. 2004. *The McDonaldization of Society* (Revised new century ed.). Thousand Oaks, CA: Pine Forge Press.

Scott, M. 2011. "10 Volunteer Opportunities for Free Travel." *CNN Travel,* September 12. Retrieved 10 October 2011 from http://www.cnn.com/2011/09/12/travel/vounteer-free-travel/index.html.

Sherraden, M.S., J. Stringham, S.C. Sow, and A.M. McBride. 2006. "The Forms and Structure of International Voluntary Service." *Voluntas* 17: 163–80.

Simpson, K. 2004. "'Doing Development': The Gap Year, Volunteer-Tourists and a Popular Practice of Development.' *Journal of International Development* 16: 681–92.

———. 2005. "Dropping Out or Signing Up? The Professionalization of Youth Travel." *Antipode* 37(3): 447–69.

Sin, H.L. 2009. "Volunteer Tourism—'Involve Me and I Will Learn'?" *Annals of Tourism Research* 36(3): 480–501.

———. 2010. "Who Are We Responsible to? Locals' Tales of Volunteer Tourism." *Geoforum* 41: 983–92.

Sinervo, A. 2011. "Connection and Disillusion: The Moral Economy of Volunteer Tourism in Cusco, Peru." *Childhoods Today* 5(2): 1–23.

Sinervo, A., and M.D. Hill. 2011. "The Visual Economy of Andean Childhood Poverty: Interpreting Postcards in Cusco, Peru." *Journal of Latin American and Caribbean Anthropology* 16(1): 114–42.

Stoddart, H., and C.M. Rogerson. 2004. "Volunteer Tourism: The Case of Habitat for Humanity South Africa." *GeoJournal* 60: 311–18.

Swarbrooke, J., C. Beard, S. Leckie, and G. Pomfret. 2003. *Adventure Tourism: The New Frontier.* Oxford: Butterworth Heinemann.

TRAM. 2008. *Volunteer Tourism: A Global Analysis.* New Amsterdam: Atlas.

Tucker, H. 1997. "The Ideal Village: Interactions through Tourism in Central Anatolia." In S. Abram, J. Waldren, and D.V.L. Macleod (eds.), *Tourists and Tourism: Identifying with People and Places.* Oxford: Berg, pp. 107–28.

Wearing, S. 2001. *Volunteer Tourism: Experiences That Make a Difference.* Wallingford, UK: CABI.

Wearing, S., M. McDonald, and J. Ponting. 2005. "Building a Decommmodified Research Paradigm in Tourism: The Contribution of NGOs." *Journal of Sustainable Tourism* 13(5): 424–39.

Williams, E., and J. Cooke. 2002. "Pathways and Labyrinths: Language and Education in Development." *TESOL Quarterly* 36(3): 297–322.

WorldTeach. n.d. Retrieved 13 August 2011 from www.worldteach.org.

Vrasti, W. 2013. *Volunteer Tourism in the Global South: Giving Back in Neoliberal Times.* New York: Routledge.

Zahra, A., and A.J. McIntosh. 2007. "Volunteer Tourism: Evidence of Cathartic Tourist Experiences." *Tourism Recreation Research* 32(1): 115–19.

CHAPTER 9

"People with Pants"

Self-Perceptions of WorldTeach Volunteers in the Marshall Islands

Ruochen Richard Li

"I Wish I Were a Ripelle"

In the Marshall Islands, the word *ripelle* translates as "people with pants." The term is used to refer to foreigners, whom the Marshallese originally distinguished from themselves because the foreigners covered their legs with clothing. In 2005, forty-four other *ripelles* and I arrived in the Marshall Islands. We were WorldTeach volunteer teachers, primarily from the United States. Our responsibility was to help educate the students of the Marshall Islands. I taught English to tenth grade students in the nation's largest high school. One of my first assignments to my students was to write an essay responding to the prompt—"Describe the first time you met a *ripelle*." Amy, who was the pupil of numerous previous WorldTeach volunteers, finished her essay first. In her concluding sentence, Amy wrote, "I wish I were a *ripelle*." I brought Amy's essay to a Marshallese teacher to ask for her opinion. The teacher shook her head and told me, "This is what happens when Marshallese students grow up with *ripelle* teachers. They lose themselves."

My experience with the WorldTeach program in the Marshall Islands highlights a paradox many developing nations, particularly Pacific Islands nations, encounter. These countries desire foreign aid and assistance for the purposes of development (Rutheiser 1991; Thomas and Postlethwaite 1984; Luteru and Teasdale 1993). However, many Pacific Islanders dislike that encountering powerful foreign influences compels indigenous peoples to question the value of their own societies and cultures (Thaman 1997, 2003; Hezel 1990). WorldTeach volunteers in the Marshall Islands are a manifestation of this tension. They represent the international assistance that some Marshallese believe will help foster development, and they exemplify the type of foreign influence that other Marshallese would like to remove from their nation's infrastructure and social fabric.

The purpose of this chapter is to explore romance and affect through the paradoxical roles of international aid, using WorldTeach volunteers in the Marshall Islands as a case study. For example, how did romantic sentiments motivate volunteers' actions and decision making? What types of affects were mobilized in such a contradictory environment? And how did volunteers manage their affects?

I first provide background information about the Marshall Islands and the WorldTeach program. Because the neocolonial context of the Marshall Islands is vital to this study, I then explore relevant literature about neocolonialism, particularly in the Pacific Islands. Next, I use two theoretical lenses—modernization and anticolonialism—to explain how WorldTeach volunteers in the Marshall Islands might perceive their roles in a dichotomous manner. I then describe the results provided by the volunteers during their interviews and discuss them vis-à-vis modernization and anticolonialism. Finally, I explore how this study contributes to this volume's discussion of romance and affect in study abroad and volunteer programs.

Pearls of the Pacific

Located in the central Pacific Ocean, seven degrees above the Equator and midway between Hawaii and Papua New Guinea, lie the twenty-nine coral atolls and five islands that comprise the Republic of the Marshall Islands. These "Pearls of the Pacific," as nicknamed by early explorers, are scattered throughout 750,000 square miles of ocean but have a land area roughly the same size as the District of Columbia (Economic Policy, Planning, and Statistics Office 2004). World Bank estimates (2005) placed the 2008 Marshall Islands population at roughly 53,000. Eighty percent of Marshallese live in the urban areas of Majuro Atoll and Ebeye Island on Kwajalein Atoll. The remainder live in rural "outer island" settings.

After World War II, the Marshall Islands fell under the administration of the United States as part of the Trust Territory of the Pacific (Hezel 2003). During this time, the territory gained international attention by being the site of sixty-seven nuclear weapons tests conducted by the United States, including "Castle Bravo,"[1] the largest nuclear device ever detonated (Niedenthal 2001). The Marshall Islands achieved independence in 1979, but negotiations with the United States regarding financial responsibility persisted, with compensation for the environmental and health related consequences of nuclear testing acting as an important point of contention (Hezel 2003).

In 1986, the Marshall Islands entered into the Compact of Free Association with the United States. This agreement allows the United States to use parts of Kwajalein Atoll for the operation of the Ronald Reagan Ballistic Missile Defense Site. In exchange, the Marshall Islands receives funds to care for the medical needs of nuclear testing victims, monetary assistance for the Marshallese government, and access to numerous public services, such as the United States Postal Service and Federal Emergency Management Agency (Barker 2004). Under the Compact of Free Association, citizens from both countries are allowed near unfettered access to either nation, including the rights to immigrate without visas and work indefinitely without permits.[2] The Compact of Free Association was renewed in 2003 and will expire in 2023 (Barker 2004).

Economically, the Marshall Islands is largely dependent upon foreign assistance, primarily from the United States. In 2005, nearly 70 percent of the Marshall Islands' $131 million GDP ($2,362 per capita) was from direct foreign aid, with over 80 percent of that aid originating from the United States (Asian Development Bank 2006). Marshallese education spending is high, with 20 percent of the national budget being earmarked for this purpose in 2010 (Marshall Islands Journal 2010). However, despite continuous high spending, outcomes have been relatively weak. As of 2005, less than 3 percent of the over-twenty-five population possessed a four-year college degree.[3] In 2002, 57 percent of Marshallese fourth grade students tested at the lowest levels on the Pacific Islands Literacy Levels examination in English, and 73 percent of them tested at the lowest levels in math (Asian Development Bank 2006).

In 2002, Marshall Islands representatives entered into a partnership with WorldTeach, an international volunteer teaching program based out of the United States, to improve educational achievement (WorldTeach 2010a).[4] Under this arrangement, the Marshallese government funds two permanent onsite WorldTeach staff, along with volunteer teachers who arrive annually. WorldTeach volunteers are contracted to teach a full school year in the Marshall Islands, departing their home countries in July and returning the following July. Volunteers undergo an initial month-long orientation, a one-week in-service conference during winter vacation, and a short end-of-the-year debriefing conference. Their funding includes round trip airfare, local housing, utilities, health insurance, and a stipend of $300 per month (WorldTeach 2010a).

From 2002 to 2010, WorldTeach sent 286 volunteer teachers to the Marshall Islands. Eighty-eight percent of the 239 volunteers who listed a home country were from the United States (WorldTeach 2010b). Volunteers taught primary and secondary students in both urban areas and outer islands. While the expressed purpose of WorldTeach volunteers is to teach English, many also teach other subjects. Marshallese is the commonly understood language of the Marshall Islands, but all school instruction is conducted in English.

Neocolonialism in the Pacific Islands

Decades of foreign influence have left an indelible footprint on the Pacific Islands, and achieving political sovereignty has not resulted in complete independence. This partial sovereignty has been labeled "neo-colonialism" by some scholars, defined as the domination of sovereign states, directly or indirectly, by other nation-states (Altbach and Kelly 1978; Bray 1993). Ruthesier (1991) extends this definition to include international organizations, such as the World Bank and the United States Peace Corps, as agents of neocolonialism. He then utilizes this definition to study neocolonialism in Belizean education and finds that, despite being sovereign, the foreign educational presence in Belize is very palpable. US consultants, for example, promote Western practices and the use of Western textbooks while US Peace Corps teachers instruct Belizean students in primary and secondary schools (Rutheiser 1991). In other words, while the foreign presence in Belizean education has shifted since British colonialism, it has not diminished, nor has it ceded control.

The same can be said, perhaps even more strongly, about the Pacific Islands. In a comprehensive study of postcolonial education in various Pacific Islands nations, Thomas and Postlethwaite (1984) find evidence of powerful and influential foreign presences in Ministry of Education personnel, school faculty, and teaching materials, such as books and visual aids. For example, they note, many teachers, particularly those who teach more advanced topics in secondary schools, and even some school administrators, are foreign expatriates. More recent studies of Pacific Islands education have also found that financing and curriculum design are largely controlled by external entities, if not foreign experts in the island nations themselves (Luteru and Teasdale 1993; Thaman 1993). Furthermore, almost all Pacific Islands textbooks are developed in foreign countries and are usually recommended for use by foreign educational organizations (Thomas and Postlethwaite 1984; Lane and DeBrum 2007). Similar to what Ruthesier discovered in Belizean education, the foreign presence in Pacific Islands education has shifted since colonial occupation, but it has not diminished, nor has it ceded control.

Nevertheless, simply stating that neocolonialism is present in Pacific Islands countries does not completely capture the strength of these international relationships in the region. While many countries around the world are subjected to some form of neocolonialism, the Pacific Islands countries are the most dependent upon financial assistance, and therefore the neocolonial powers that disburse that assistance. Most Pacific Islands nations, for example, derive over 20 percent of their revenue from foreign aid, by far the greatest proportion of any region in the developing world (Lal and Fortune 2000). In the more extreme cases, such as the Marshall Islands, we saw previously that over two-thirds of its GDP is from direct foreign assistance.

Dependency upon foreign aid is important to our understanding of neocolonialism because the conditions under which aid is disbursed are the vehicles through which external entities establish a neocolonial relationship with the Pacific Islands. Luteru and Teasdale (1993) write that the locus of control for these monetary exchanges rests with the donor countries, not recipient countries. The political, military, and commercial interests of donor countries often dictate when and under what conditions aid will be disbursed to Pacific Islands recipients. And because international aid represents such a large proportion of Pacific Islands nations' budgets, donor countries and aid organizations are effectively able to direct many of the operations and undertakings of Pacific Islands governments. They therefore create some of the most powerful neocolonial relationships in the world via the aid they offer (Hezel 2003; Luteru and Teasdale 1993; Barker 2004).

Fully Decolonizing Is Desired but Difficult

The strong neocolonial presence in the Pacific Islands impacts Pacific Islanders' perceptions of themselves and the legitimacy of their local knowledge (Thaman 2003). Research and journalistic accounts have both documented that indigenous languages are becoming less widely understood. Likewise, traditional knowledge such as navigational methods and oral folklore are becoming devalued and forgotten (Thomas and Postlethwaite 1984; Rudiak-Gould 2009). Thaman (2003) writes that Pacific Islanders have become conditioned to believe that European culture is at the top of a linear social development spectrum, and that Pacific Islands art, music, and history hold an inferior position. Rudiak-Gould (2009) remarks that foreign domination in the Marshall Islands has eliminated knowledge of all but one traditional dance. In order to help preserve their cultures and identities, many Pacific Islands scholars and leaders have called for a decolonization of local institutions, particularly education, in which foreign personnel, structures, and goals are replaced by indigenous forms (Thaman 1997, 2003; Hezel 1990). In the Marshall Islands, for example, the "Rethinking Education" conference of 2007 emphasized the need to merge present-day schooling with indigenous knowledge, such as by offering courses in canoe construction (Marshall Islands Ministry of Education 2008).

Nevertheless, while many Pacific Islanders are trying to end their countries' neocolonial relationships, their nations' geopolitical conditions do not allow for that to occur. Pacific Islands countries have very limited natural resources and are greatly isolated from world markets (Luteru and Teasdale 1993). However, their colonial histories have introduced a more Western way of life and now, as sovereign nations, they must import most of their goods and even food stuffs from foreign countries in order to maintain their new lifestyles (Peoples 1978). The financial resources required to achieve this lifestyle must inevitably be borrowed. In addition, high fertility rates and low education attainment levels have increased the demand for more formal schooling, also established during colonial times. This necessitates even more borrowing, including the importation of technical assistance from countries such as Japan, Australia, and the United States (Thaman 1993).

International Volunteerism and Exchange Occur in the Context of Neocolonialism

International volunteers in the Pacific Islands thus occupy a precarious position. They represent foreign domination, but also potentially useful professionals and experts. Do volunteers view themselves in these ways, and how do they navigate these identities? Much of the research that has been conducted into international volunteers in developing countries has focused upon US Peace Corps volunteers. One set of studies explores the acculturation of volunteers in their host communities (Rhoades 1978; Alverson 1977; Cohn and Wood 1985). Another body of research examines the psychological and demographic characteristics that distinguish successful volunteers from unsuccessful volunteers (Harris 1972, 1973; Hare 1966). Unfortunately, these works study volunteers as individuals in a "contextual vacuum" in that they do not discuss the volunteers' roles in the greater environment of neocolonialism. Moreover, most are rather outdated and might not properly convey the views and opinions of more recent international volunteers.

Another related body of scholarship focuses on the experiences of not only volunteers but also international students and expatriate employees. These studies analyze various cross-cultural exchanges in order to explain how individuals view themselves and develop their identities in the context of an increasingly globalized world. For instance, Williams (2005) and Carlson and Widaman (1988) find that college students who study abroad have better intercultural communication skills than their peers who did not, as well as an increased awareness of international politics. Gu (2010) and Oliver (2009) study the motivations and cultural experiences of expatriates teaching English in China and South Korea. This global citizenship literature helps us understand how individuals interact with the greater international context in which they are situated. However, this research does not view global exchange from the perspective of neocolonialism, and thus does not address issues of dominance and power.

Two Theoretical Lenses

Because of the contradictory roles of neocolonialism in the Pacific Islands, one single theoretical framework is inadequate to fully explain its presence in the Marshall Islands. Instead, in this section, I describe two theories, modernization and anticolonialism, and their alternative interpretations of neocolonialism. I then apply these theories to frame and explain the experiences of WorldTeach volunteers in the Marshall Islands.

Modernization

Modernization theorists argue that development exists on a rational and linear continuum between the traditional and the modern (Fagerlind and Saha 1989; Fuller 1991). Developing countries are simply at an earlier stage of development, at the onset of their progression toward more modern stages of development (Fagerlind and Saha 1989; Fuller 1991). Specifically, Fagerlind and Saha (1989) suggest that five national variables—institutions, behavior, society, values, and economic development—are closely related to each other and that the modernization of one leads to modernization of the others. Fuller (1991) uses this analysis to reason that many developing countries advocate for mass schooling because education represents a modern institution, one that is responsible for socializing modern behavior and values into students.

From the perspective of modernization theory, neocolonialism is viewed as the sharing of modern institutions, behavior, societies, and values between more developed nations and less developed nations. This exchange then helps the less-developed nations reach later stages of economic development. Technical assistants from a developed nation, for example, might help leaders from developing nations craft an educational system that will modernize local societies and values, and in turn stimulate economic growth.

Anticolonialism

Anticolonialism theorists argue that the relationship between the developed and the developing world is best understood as a dialectic between oppressors and oppressed (Fanon 1961, 1968; Freire 1970). Freire (1970) believes that oppressors have dehumanized the oppressed by delegitimizing their languages, cultures, and values. Fanon (1961) suggests that oppression has engendered an "inferiority complex" in colonized peoples that expresses itself as valuing the language, dress, and mores of their colonizers. Anticolonialism scholars advocate for oppressed peoples to engage in revolutionary upheaval in order to achieve humanization and liberation from colonial knowledge and processes. It is the role of education to teach students from oppressed groups about the state of their relationship with their oppressors and to prepare them to be active members of liberation. Moreover, such education must be implemented internally among the oppressed, and not externally from the oppressors to the oppressed (Freire 1970), for gestures of generosity from the oppressors to the oppressed are rooted in power disparity and only serve to perpetuate an unjust social order.

From the perspective of anticolonialism theory, neocolonialism represents the continued presence of oppressors as agents of subjugation. Their relationship with the oppressed necessarily reproduces a debilitating inferiority complex rooted in colonialism. The assistance of the international community, even for the purposes of liberation, is considered to be "false generosity" (Freire 1970) based upon social injustice, which only exacerbates the self-depreciation of oppressed peoples.

WorldTeach Volunteers

The presence of WorldTeach volunteers in the Marshall Islands would thus be explained differently by the competing narratives of modernization theory and anticolonialism theory. From the perspective of modernization theory, WorldTeach volunteers are catalysts of development whose purpose is to help the Marshall Islands modernize. From the perspective of anticolonialism theory, WorldTeach volunteers represent oppressive figures who reproduce their unjust dominance by instructing students in the colonial language and encouraging students to value colonial institutions and knowledge.

How, then, do WorldTeach volunteers view their social and professional roles in the Marshall Islands? To what extent can WorldTeach volunteers' expressed roles be understood through a lens of modernization? To what extent can they be understood through a lens of anticolonialism? How do volunteers' reported actions and behaviors reflect the interpretations of modernization and anticolonialism?

The Marshall Islands is situated at the intersection of two competing theories of modernization and anticolonialism. Foreign volunteer teachers who find themselves in this environment experience a tension with respect to how they view their roles in the Marshall Islands. Foreign volunteer teachers' roles can be interpreted differently according to the dueling narratives of anticolonialism and modernization.

Research Process

In total, 286 WorldTeach volunteers worked in the Marshall Islands from 2002 to 2010. Nineteen of the 286 volunteers underwent "early termination," a term used to designate volunteers who left the Marshall Islands before completing their one-year teaching contracts. I exclude these individuals from my population of interest because their shorter amounts of time spent in the Marshall Islands potentially altered how they view their roles and how they view the Marshall Islands. The remaining 267

WorldTeach volunteers comprise the total population of interest for my study. Some stayed in the Marshall Islands for longer than one year, but not always as WorldTeach volunteers. Their current ages range from 23 to 82. Women comprise 65 percent of all volunteers. I invited 60 potential participants, who represent the full extent of my personal relationships with returned WorldTeach Marshall Islands volunteers, via e-mail and Facebook communications to partake in my research. I also asked them to encourage other WorldTeach volunteers from the Marshall Islands to respond. No incentive to participate was provided.

Fifteen individuals, selected on a first-come first-serve basis after I sent my invitations, became the participants of this study. Table 9.1 in the appendix lists the participants and their demographic information. Pseudonyms are used in place of real names. Participants' demographic information is consistent with the population of interest.[5]

Data was collected through interviews with the fifteen participants. All interviews were conducted via Skype and were recorded. Only one interview was conducted with each participant. Each interview lasted no longer than forty-five minutes. All conversations were conducted with the aid of an interview protocol I developed based on a review of relevant literature and the results of a small pilot study.

Conflicting Roles

I found that WorldTeach volunteers in the Marshall Islands were in great agreement about numerous roles they believe they held. However, volunteers also reported that that their ability to fulfill those roles was often constrained by other identities and positions they believed they occupied. Therefore, I organize my findings according to four of these relationships that volunteers discussed: teaching but being inexperienced, improving pedagogy but not wanting to impose values, promoting cultural exchange without depreciating Marshallese culture, and being a role model without elevating the status of people from the United States. I then discuss affect that was mobilized and how it was managed.

Teaching English but Being Inexperienced

Fourteen out of fifteen participants claimed that their role, particularly their professional role, was to improve their students' English language abilities. In addition to English being part of the Marshallese educational curriculum, nine volunteers also believed that learning English was important for their students because fluency in English confers social mobility. For primary school teachers, this meant that their students could excel on the national high school examination and enroll in limited high school spaces. For high school teachers, this meant that their students would be able to pursue higher education and be more attractive to potential employers.[6] Kate O'Neal expressed a commonly held belief when she explained that her role was

> "To teach English so that the kids on the outer islands could eventually have the means necessary to find jobs on the main island and, perhaps, go to the mainland and find jobs or advanced education, etc. But the idea was to get those kids speaking English to the level where they could thrive outside of their outer island."

While teaching English is an expressed priority for WorldTeach volunteers, ten volunteers also mentioned that they felt very unequipped to actually teach. None of the participants had teaching experience prior to becoming WorldTeach volunteers. Nine had recently graduated from college and did not have full-time professional experience in any field. These volunteers reported that their lack of experience constituted a severe limitation to their capacity to be effective teachers. For example, when I asked Abigail Thomas what she wished she would have known prior to arriving in the Marshall Islands, she answered, "I did not know how to make a lesson plan. I never made one. I would have started on that way earlier … I had no idea and I think that would have been a great benefit to me." Debbie White added:

> I just don't think I was a very good teacher. I think that I lacked an understanding of how to manage a classroom, which was a huge detriment, particularly with third graders. And I think that my lack of Marshallese and my lack of understanding Marshallse culture was a challenge in trying to get certain points across.

Improving Pedagogy but Not Imposing Values

Two-thirds of the participants stated that one of their roles in the Marshall Islands was to improve the teaching methods of their schools. Volunteers questioned Marshallese pedagogy, specifically the emphasis on rote memorization techniques. Many volunteers described instruction at their schools as teachers simply writing definitions of words onto the chalkboards, and students copying the definitions into their notebooks. For instance, Thomas summarized education at her school as: "They [students] would memorize the definitions for the test which I think was just a huge waste of time. It was just pure memorizing skills with having no idea what that means, how to apply it, or anything else." In response to these circumstances, volunteers employed what they believed to be more active pedagogy into their classrooms, such as discussion-based instruction and group work. Volunteers wanted these methods to become models for teachers working at schools where they worked. Dolores Lander stated:

> It [WorldTeach] has brought new teaching methods to some of the islands, to some of the other teachers. I think that in some schools ... I know that it has provided professional development opportunities for the local teachers ... So over time that school has brought in lesson plan templates and has brought in rescheduling their day to have reading separate from writing ... Those kinds of changes have happened because of the influence of volunteer programs ...[7]

While improving pedagogy was important to volunteers, they also emphasized that they believed their role was not to impose their own personal opinions and cultural values onto their schools and communities. Josh Bennington expressed a feeling shared by many participants:

> The added problem is that you are doing that [influencing institutions] as a volunteer, as a graduate volunteer fresh out of college from a foreign country who may or may not have a grasp of the local culture, who may or may not have good grasp of how local institutions work already, and may or may not seek to impose institutions that are just familiar to them onto another country and society. I think those are all really pertinent questions about what's happening.

This sentiment caused volunteers to exercise what they thought was a certain amount of passive restraint in expressing their beliefs. For example, Matt Prescott tried to encourage his principal to adopt a stricter attendance policy. However, he encountered a conundrum in trying to do so because he did want to impose his own will in his school:

> Those were tricky conversations [about the attendance policy] ... At a very core level there was no question for me that it was an important problem to address ... At the same time I was very self-aware in those conversations and tried very hard not to, you know, [engage in] my style of arguing and all of that [because] that is totally inappropriate.

How volunteers overcame this type of predicament varied between individuals. Two mentioned that they implemented what they believed to be better practices in their own classrooms, but did not directly ask other teachers to adopt the practices for their own use. Three others were more direct and eschewed the desire not to impose their own opinions and values. Bennington, for instance, petitioned his principal when he saw a teacher physically discipline a student, a frequent occurrence in the Marshall Islands:

> There is not much I can do to control that [the other teacher's physical punishment] or to do anything about that. But I still felt that if it was in front of me, I should do it. If we see it, there is a moral obligation to do something about it, even if we know that it will go on without us.

Promoting Cross-cultural Exchange without Depreciating Marshallese Culture

Volunteers strongly believed that one of their roles was to promote cross-cultural exchange with their Marshallese communities. Helen Mann thought that the cultural exchange she brought to the Marshall Islands "enriched the lives" of the community in which she lived. Claudia Smith said that she wanted to "broaden the horizons" of her students by exposing them to a different set of social values. Perhaps unsurprisingly, volunteers also mentioned their inexperience and their role as cultural ambassadors in conjunction. Margaret Harris said:

> There wasn't a whole lot about me as a 22-year-old that made me in any sense a superior teacher to a regular Marshallese teacher. But I think the thing that I brought to the table instead was that eye-opening stranger from a strange land piece that I think was really important ... I feel like one of the big things I could bring to the classroom is this knowledge and background of being from someplace else.

Nevertheless, volunteers who wanted to promote cross-cultural exchange quickly realized that engaging in such exchange was rarely value-neutral because of their status as US nationals. Due to historical and political circumstances, such exchange has usually been unidirectional—from the "outside," primarily the United States, to the Marshall Islands (Hezel 2003). Consequently, ten volunteers spoke about the "idolization" of United States culture they observed and experienced, from food, to music, to television, to fashion. Sam Thibbert mentioned, "They [Marshallese] looked to our culture, the culture that we came from, and the educational area that we came from as an ideal ... something to strive for, where I came from." This disparity in perceived value made volunteers very uncomfortable about being cultural representatives. In this context, volunteers were worried that, by simply being Western and "exchanging" their culture with their communities, they were reinforcing a historical construct that depreciates Marshallese culture and identity. For example, eight of the nine outer island volunteers commented on being very aware of how their material possessions were prized by their Marshallese communities. Their cameras, MP3 players, and even books and magazines became the objects of envy for people around them. Charlie Newsome mentioned:

> Anything that was sort of kitschy Westernized stuff is more important than Marshallese, local, local foods and so on. So it was frustrating to see them [Marshallese] put so much value on stuff like that and I guess it's because they've either heard it through, probably through any popular culture that's made its way over there and also seeing people first hand. You know the volunteers who come over and they have lots and lots of stuff, and they want to have that stuff as well. And they think that stuff is better.

Thomas added that the discomfort volunteers experienced in this type of environment became so severe that the WorldTeach Marshall Islands office even contacted the friends and families of volunteers to ask that they stop sending so many materials and donations.

Being a Role Model without Elevating People from the United States

The roles that volunteers believe they held show that individual volunteers occupy multiple roles that disagree with each other. In other words, what one volunteer believes he/she is, or tries to be, is often incompatible with something else he/she is, or tries to be. As a final example of this conundrum, six volunteers mentioned that they believed one of their roles was to be a positive example for their students and fellow teachers. However, four of these same volunteers also spoke about embracing the previously mentioned role of not imposing cultural values and institutional structures, which seems to oppose their positions as social and professional role models.

The case of Claudia Smith illustrates this conflict well. In her interview, she mentioned that she was upset by how much she thought the children in her community consumed and idolized Western media:

> It was hard to have the little girls look up and see Lizzie McGuire and
> really see her as a role model in the sense that they felt like they needed
> to become her. Not that she was a bad influence, but she was an influ-
> ence from a different culture. So they were trying to imitate someone
> who was going to have different values, different ways of dressing ...

Nevertheless, earlier in her interview, Smith also mentioned that one of
the purposes she felt she had was to be a role model for her students,
particularly her female students. I then asked her how she reconciled
her own identity as a role model, given that she is from the same culture
as Lizzie McGuire, whom she does not think should be a role model for
her students. Smith responded:

> I think being a role model wasn't in how do you dress and what mate-
> rial things are important to you. I was trying to be more of a role model
> in how you treat people and how you respect yourself and in things
> that I think cross cultural boundaries. Just being somebody who gen-
> uinely cared about them.

She did not, however, address the fact that she still saw herself as a
Western role model for Marshallese children. Smith exhibited uncertainty
because what she wanted to be is also something she believed people in
her position should not be.

Explaining Conflict

My findings reveal that WorldTeach volunteers adopt conflicting roles
in the Marshall Islands. From the perspective of my conceptual framework, I argue in this section that volunteers' roles can be interpreted as
simultaneously modernist and anticolonial. This interpretation, however,
is limited because volunteers' reported actions often deviate from strict
understandings of both modernization and anticolonialism. Utilizing explanations from both theoretical frameworks, I suggest that how volunteers' self-perceptions can be best interpreted actually shifts. Initially, their
self-perceived roles can be best understood through the lens of modernization, but as they stay in the Marshall Islands their self-perceived roles
can be better understood through the lens of anticolonialism.

As Modernists

Many of the self-perceived roles that volunteers adopt appear to be
modernist in nature. For example, improving pedagogical practices can

be viewed from the perspective of modernization theory as changing certain institutions and structures for the purpose of development (Fagerlind and Saha 1989). Moreover, and consistent with modernization theory, volunteers also express that they believed changing values is an important responsibility for them. Such is the case when Bennington called his anti–corporal punishment petition a "moral obligation." From a modernist perspective, physical discipline is considered traditional and must be transformed for a country to achieve progress towards modernity (Fuller 1991).

However, while some of the roles that volunteers believe they held can be explained by modernization theory, not all of them can. In fact, some roles seem to contradict the premises of modernization theory. Deferring to Marshallese faculty members, for example, seems antithetical to orthodox understandings of modernization theory. If volunteers wish to change institutional and social behavior, why would some choose not to do so when given the opportunity?

Examining the participants' interviews reveals that volunteers' motivation to modernize was tempered by a desire not to be perceived as cultural imperialists. For example, volunteers were uncomfortable with how much more perceived value US goods, ideas, and culture held compared to Marshallese goods, ideas, and culture. More importantly, volunteers thought that their presence in the Marshall Islands, and the continuous flow of Americanism that they facilitated, helped reinforce the idea of the superiority of the United States and the West. They believed that the more they tried to modernize the country, the more Western materials and ideology would be brought into the Marshall Islands, and the more Marshallese culture would be depreciated. WorldTeach volunteers thus took great care in deciding how to introduce new structures, such as Prescott not wanting to be confrontational about implementing a stricter attendance policy. In this manner, volunteers fulfilled their roles as modernists, but did so in a much more cautious manner than a strict reading of modernization theory would predict.

As Anticolonialists

Volunteers' hesitancy to impose their own cultural values and opinions can be explained from the perspective of anticolonialism theory. Pursuant to this theoretical lens, volunteers recognized that their culture and their home government were in dominant positions with respect to the culture and government of the Marshall Islands. Their comments about how they observed Western goods and culture to be superior to their Marshallese counterparts indicate that they identified the existence of a power disparity. Furthermore, volunteers felt that they were regarded as expert educators despite having very little to no teaching experience. This again shows that volunteers thought that their status in Marshallese society was related to the Marshallese perception of people from the United States, rooted in the colonial history of the Marshall Islands.

Perhaps the best example of gaining this awareness is demonstrated by Margaret Harris. In her interview, Harris said that she was "surprised" and "shocked" by the "admiration or love of the US" she witnessed. In talking about her "celebrity status," she stated:

> It caused some internal stomach churning. I felt guilty. Not only was the admiration and adoration of you, as a 22-year-old who knows nothing, undeserved, but knowing the history of your country, the country you were a citizen of, the history, the hardships, the awful, awful, awful things that we put this country through, it was very guilt inducing. I think you have to realize that, okay, I don't deserve this, and my country certainly does not deserve this.

Though not explicitly using the vocabulary of anticolonialism theory, Harris certainly seems to identify the existence of what Fanon (1961) calls an "inferiority complex." The admiration or love that she perceived Marshallese to have for the United States is, in Harris's opinion, unfathomable given the history between the two nations. She bluntly said that the elevated status she believes she held was undeserved, and that she feels guilty for having received it. From the perspective of anticolonialism theory, Harris is recognizing oppression and feels great consternation due to her role as an oppressor. These kinds of thought processes no doubt contributed to volunteers' decisions to try to position themselves as more submissive agents who did not force their ideas upon people in their communities.

Although some attitudes and actions reported by volunteers can be understood through the lens of anticolonialism theory, many of their beliefs and behaviors cannot be explained by a rigid understanding of this theoretical perspective. Specifically, volunteers' ideas of how the liberation of oppressed peoples can ultimately be won do not coincide with the tenets of anticolonialism theory. According to Freire (1970), liberation can only be achieved via an internal upheaval. External assistance is considered false generosity, and only perpetuates oppression.

WorldTeach volunteers, on the other hand, appear to believe that their presence and assistance can actually empower Marshallese.

This idea is succinctly captured by Donna Johnson. In her interview, she mentioned the history of nuclear testing in the Marshall Islands and claimed that "the Marshallese were not properly dealt with in that situation." When I asked her how she felt about her own role as someone from the United States in that type of environment, she said:

> I was actually really proud to be going. I kind of felt like I could come and help them. And I did not come in with this high and mighty attitude by any means because they definitely helped me a lot, showed me, opened my eyes to a lot too. But I was glad that I could give them assistance and do whatever they asked of me and just try my best, and hopefully it would help them in some way.

Although Johnson understood the tenuous relationship between the United States and the Marshall Islands, she did not believe she exacerbated negative sociopolitical circumstances. Rather, she said she was proud to be a volunteer in the Marshall Islands, as opposed to worried about her presence. More importantly, she believed that the attitude she had in going to the Marshall Islands contrasted with the "high and mighty" attitude of previous people from her country.[8] Instead of telling Marshallese what to do, she would do "whatever they asked of me." This type of interaction and discourse, Johnson thought, would then help diminish the dominant status of people from the United States, as opposed to bolster it.[9] She could, in fact, and in contrast to what Freire argues, empower Marshallese with her external assistance.

Outer Islands Volunteers Are More Likely to be Modernists

While the conflict between volunteers' perceived roles can be explained, to a certain extent, by both modernization and anticolonialism theory, the strength of direction of that conflict seems to vary depending upon whether volunteers worked on an outer island or an urban island. Outer island volunteers' self-perceived roles can be understood more readily through the lens of modernization theory, whereas urban island volunteers' self-perceived roles can be understood more readily through the lens of anticolonialism theory. For example, the word *colonialism* is mentioned by three out of six urban island volunteers, and zero out of nine outer island volunteers. Five out of six urban island volunteers discussed the history or current sociopolitical circumstances of the Marshall Islands. Only one out of nine outer island volunteers did. Finally, feeling guilty was discussed by three out of six urban island volunteers, and only two out of nine outer island volunteers. Importantly, the two outer island volunteers who talked about guilt both stayed in the Marshall Islands after they completed their WorldTeach contracts and subsequently worked on urban islands.

From the perspective of modernization scholarship, this disparity in the perceptions volunteers is caused by different levels of exposure to modernity. As mentioned before, modernization is concerned with the development of certain country-level variables, among them institutions and economic development (Fagerlind and Saha 1989). Thus, the physical indications of modernization should be most apparent in urban areas, where government offices and financial enterprises can be found, and not rural areas. This suggestion is supported by Inkeles (1975), who finds that individuals in developing countries associate modernity with urban centers, and urbanity in general. This dichotomy is particularly clear in the Marshall Islands. The two urban atolls—Kwajalein and Majuro—both boast significant characteristics of modernity. In Kwajaelin, the Ronald Reagan Ballistic Missile Defense Site, with its Western amenities and structures, dominates the physical and social landscape. Majuro, the capitol, is home to all federal government offices and almost all of the country's industrial and commercial operations.

Volunteers working and living in these urban areas were much more exposed to and aware of modernity than volunteers in outer islands. They interacted daily with the Ministry of Education, other federal agencies, and were up-to-date regarding the current events of the Marshall Islands. Seeing the economic circumstances of the Marshall Islands and the relationships between Marshallese and United States expatriates gave urban volunteers a frame of reference vis-à-vis colonialism and neocolonialism that outer island volunteers did not have. Since understanding anticolonialism theory is predicated upon understanding history and political contexts, it thus follows that urban island volunteers were more likely to adopt this perspective. Outer island volunteers, on the other hand, experienced much more difficult living circumstances and isolation. Food and water shortages were common, since refrigeration and public water were not available. Students' education levels were lower, and teachers had weaker command of the English language. As a result, outer island volunteers were probably more motivated to develop and modernize the institutions of their immediate communities.

What is interesting, however, is that increased contact with modern influences seems to have engendered a certain amount of trepidation in volunteers' opinions about the role of modernity. Urban island volunteers, after all, self-report actions and behaviors that align more closely with anticolonialism theory, and not modernization theory. In other words, their greater familiarity with modernization did not necessarily make them greater advocates of it. Outer island volunteers, on the other hand, with less exposure to modernity, are stronger proponents of it.

Romantic Motivations, Uncomfortable Affects

As potential agents of modernization in a nontraditional, colonial destination, WorldTeach volunteers in the Marshall Islands exhibit some of the expected romantic sentiments mentioned in the introduction of this volume, such as a desire for adventure and moral fervor. These notions, however, become uncomfortably challenged as volunteers develop affects of guilt and privilege in their new communities. In this section, I examine volunteers' experiences through the lens of romance, explore how their contradictory roles mobilized their affects, and discuss how they managed their affects.

Romance Is a Two-Way Street

Conversations with WorldTeach volunteers suggest that they hold romantic views of the Marshall Islands and of their own roles in the country, likely even before they arrived. While I did not explicitly ask what motivated them to volunteer in the Marshall Islands, their comments indicate that romantic sentiments were influential. For example, Harris describes herself as an "eye-opening stranger from a strange land." She also identifies her otherness as potentially her greatest asset as an educator of Marshallese students.

This type of discourse aligns with study abroad literature, especially in nontraditional destinations. Harris evokes the theme of curiosity and speaks about her endeavor with a sense of adventure. Other volunteers imagine themselves as modernizers in an "exotic" and developing environment. For instance, O'Neal claims that her role was to help her students "find jobs and advance education in the country." This comment reflects what study abroad literature describes as a desire to help others and train local youth in global skills.

What volunteers learn after living in the Marshall Islands, however, is that they are not the only ones who hold romantic notions of foreign others and places. They discover that the Marshall Islands are not as untouched as they imagined and that the historical interactions between the Marshall Islands and the West have engendered in Marshallese people a romantic view of Westerners, particularly Americans, and the West in general. According to these romantic views, Americans are knowledgeable, powerful, and wealthy. For instance, several volunteers mentioned that their status as highly qualified educators was accepted without much hesitation, contrary to their professional experience and much to their chagrin. Association with American culture and materials is also highly coveted. Newsome and Smith further identify Marshallese romantic views of the West when they respectively explained that, "Anything that was sort of kitschy Westernized stuff is more important than Marshallese, local ..." and that Lizzie McGuire is considered a role model by some Marshallese.

WorldTeach volunteers' romantic notions of themselves become challenged when they discover that they, too, are romanticized. They realize that acting on their romantic views about themselves as modernizers might encourage the development of Marshallese romantic notions of Americans as expert and superior. Volunteers then experience several affects due to this tension. What affects emerge? How are they mobilized? And how do volunteers manage the affects they feel? These questions are explored next.

Developing and Mobilizing Affect

Given WorldTeach volunteers' contradictory roles in the Marshall Islands, the affects that emerge expectedly include guilt, privilege, and a sense of uncertainty about how to behave. Harris, for example, describes some of her experiences as "stomach churning" and "guilt inducing." Bennington, referring to the privilege he had as a Westerner, adds that he was unsure if his suggestions were simply imposing familiar institutions onto an unfamiliar environment. These volunteers are, in effect, developing affects due to personally experiencing, and perhaps also perpetuating, the power disparity discussed by anticolonial theorists.

The encounters that mobilize these affects are diverse. Bennington's discomfort seems to have arisen due to professional relationships. He recognized that, as an outsider to his community, he did not understand the status quo and the needs of his school. Nevertheless, he felt an urge to impose what was familiar to him and implies that his peers would have let him do so. His situation created feelings of insecurity and trepidation. Prescott's experiences, particularly reforming his school's attendance policy, echo those of Bennington. But not only was Prescott worried about imposing his own institutions, he was also concerned about *how* he might have done so. He characterized his method of problem resolution, which relies on argument and debate, as inappropriate for his school's environment. His feelings of uncertainty, therefore, were more ubiquitous and probably also arose in exchanges unrelated to his work.

For other volunteers, mobilizing affect primarily occurred in their interactions with their host families and immediate communities. Newsome's recognition of power disparity was related to his discovery that his "kitschy Westernized stuff" was more prized and prestigious than Marshallese goods. Similarly, Smith saw that young girls in her community considered Lizzie McGuire to be a role model for themselves. These experiences mobilized affect related to guilt and privilege. Volunteers realized that who they are and where they are from was regarded as "better" than their Marshallese counterparts. These affects are then backgrounded in the historical and current relations of power between the United States and Marshal Islands.

Mobilization of affect, however, was not distributed equally among the volunteers. Since these affects are mobilized by discourse consistent with anticolonial theory, urban island volunteers thus experience the aforementioned affects more than outer island volunteers. As mentioned previously, feeling guilty—indicating that affect related to privilege and power was mobilized—was discussed by three of six urban island volunteers and two of nine outer island volunteers, both of whom later moved to an urban island. To the extent that volunteers' romantic notions of the Marshall Islands and their own roles are challenged after being in their communities, outer island volunteers, it follows, have their romantic notions challenged less than their urban island peers do. In turn, the affects discussed here were not mobilized as readily for outer island volunteers as for urban island volunteers.

Managing Affect

After developing affect, WorldTeach volunteers had to manage their affects, both through their resulting actions and emotionally. With respect to actions, some volunteers proceeded with their original intentions, in spite of their newly developed affects. For example, Bennington, despite feeling uncertain about his powerful position, decided to still impose institutional reform when he reported the teacher who physically disciplined a student. Bennington's decision could suggest that he made a distinction between how he felt and what he did, or between his anti-colonial affect and his romantic role as a modernizer. While he feels insecure as a volunteer, he believes in his purpose at his school.

This type of affect management is also exemplified by Dolores Lander, who previously stated that she believes WorldTeach imbued more effective pedagogy into Marshallese education. While she is pleased with this achievement, at another point in our conversation she revealed that she has mixed feelings because she was modernizing her outer island students, whose educational ambitions were leading them away from their families and homes and towards urban centers. Furthermore, Lander said, "There were times when I felt really guilty about it, because I felt like here I am a part of the problem." Of course, these feelings did not stop her from showing teachers at her school new pedagogical methods and educating her own students with those methods, which might have pushed her students further away from their traditional homes and lifestyles. Like Bennington, Lander separated her feelings from her actions. The affect she experienced did not impede what she believed her role to be.

On the other hand, Prescott's comments suggest that the affect he experienced did change his actions. He implied that, in another environment, he would have been more argumentative about the need to address his school's attendance policy. In the Marshall Islands, however, he hesitated. I did not ask Prescott if he did address the policy and, if he did, how he did so. Nevertheless, it is safe to assume that, if he did, he did so later than he intended and was not as argumentative as he would have been in another context. Prescott could have addressed the attendance policy more obtusely, and that might have led to quicker reform. The kind of anticolonial affect he experienced, though, deterred him from acting, potentially to the detriment of school policy and contrary to any romantic notions he might have held about himself as a modernizer.

How volunteers emotionally managed their affect is more difficult to determine. Data collected from several volunteers suggest that they simply never reached a comfortable emotional denouement. Lander, for example, in referring to potentially pushing students away from their traditional homes, said, "I still feel mixed. I don't know the right answer.

But I do know that it is a problem." The nature of the WorldTeach program and volunteers' commitments to it may have incentivized this type of response. Volunteers, after all, only live in the Marshall Islands for one year. It is more convenient to let their uneasy emotions lie than spend time and energy on resolving any uncomfortable affects that emerged. This view is exemplified by Harris, who says, in reference to the guilt she felt, that it was "intimidating" to be so admired as a 22-year-old. But she likely echoes the exhausted feelings of many volunteers when she concluded, "Disorder is okay. It's the way things are going to be."

People with Pants

International education assistance to developing nations is intended to help nations create infrastructure and grow capital. This narrative, however, is complicated by notions of neocolonialism and dependency. Many of the countries that receive assistance were formerly colonies and many of the countries that provide assistance were formerly colonizers. As a result, relationships rooted in historical oppression are at risk of being preserved under the well-intended guise of aid.

This situation is particularly relevant with respect to the Marshall Islands. Foreign occupation technically ended in 1979 when the country gained sovereignty, but the vestiges of the nation's colonial legacy have not been eliminated. The lifestyle that Marshallese lead, from the food they consume, to the clothes that they wear, to the language they speak, all bear the indelible marks of colonialism. In order to maintain this way of life that they now covet, Marshallese must depend on foreign powers, particularly the United States, for financial and technical resources. These factors combine to jeopardize the status of Marshallese culture, customs, and values.

WorldTeach volunteers in the Marshall Islands find themselves in an unenviable situation. From the perspective of modernization theory, they are tasked with teaching young Marshallese and improving the country's institutions. Yet, from the perspective of anticolonialism theory, adopting such authoritative roles in a country with a strong history of foreign domination necessarily perpetuates an oppressive relationship. Volunteers thus assume their roles and responsibilities with great caution and care. They want to improve education, but do not want to impose their own structures. They want their students to learn about the world around them, but do not want them to envy the world around them. They want to be positive examples for their communities, but do not want their communities to view foreign individuals as role models.

WorldTeach volunteers, in a sense, are simply a part of the complicated historical relationship between the United States and the Marshall Islands. Nearly sixty years ago, the United States tested the Castle Bravo bomb on Bikini Atoll. To justify that act, people with pants told Marshallese that their islands would have to be destroyed "for the good of mankind, and to end all wars" (Niedenthal 2001). That event, and the colonial domination it represents, sent not only physical shockwaves throughout the Marshall Islands, but social, political, and economic ones as well. And while the physical clean-up necessitated by Castle Bravo is finished (though not necessarily completed), the social, political, and economic clean-up necessitated by its impact is ongoing. WorldTeach volunteers are part of that clean-up process. The challenge for volunteers, however, is discovering how to clean up effectively without creating a bigger mess. For volunteers are also people with pants, and thus must reconcile the romanticism of their role with the uncomfortable affects they experience.

Table 9.1: Research Study Participants—Returned WorldTeach Marshall Islands Volunteers and Demographic Information

Name	Gender	First time working	First Location	Second Location	Stayed in Marshall Islands after WorldTeach
Abigail Thomas	Female	Yes	Outer Island	Urban Island	Yes
Carol Hutson	Female	No	Urban Island	Not Applicable	No
Charlie Newsome	Male	Yes	Outer Island	Not Applicable	No
Claudia Smith	Female	No	Outer Island	Not Applicable	No
Debbie White	Female	Yes	Urban Island	Urban Island	Yes
Dolores Lander	Female	No	Outer Island	Urban Island	Yes
Donna Johnson	Female	Yes	Outer Island	Not Applicable	No
Helen Mann	Female	No	Outer Island	Urban Island	Yes
Josh Bennington	Male	Yes	Urban Island	Not Applicable	No
Kate O'Neal	Female	Yes	Outer Island	Urban Island	Yes
Mallory Channing	Female	Yes	Urban Island	Urban Island	Yes
Margaret Harris	Female	Yes	Urban Island	Not Applicable	No
Matt Prescott	Male	No	Urban Island	Urban Island	Yes
Sam Thibbert	Male	No	Outer Island	Not Applicable	No
Zoey Granderson	Female	Yes	Outer Island	Urban Island	Yes

Interview Protocol: Questions Listed in Order of Usage During Interviews

Opening Questions:

1) What were you doing before you became a WorldTeach volunteer?

2) Where did you serve as a WorldTeach volunteer? When? What did you teach?

Informational Questions:

1) What motivated you to participate in the WorldTeach Marshall Islands program?

2) How did you first learn about the Marshall Islands?

3) How were you received your community?
   –Describe your relationships with your Marshallese coworkers, students, people in your community, etc. What were your feelings toward them?
   –Were you respected? Why?
   –In what ways were your relationships with the people at your site different from your relationships with people in the United States?

4) What do you think your professional purpose in the Marshall Islands was?
   –What made you believe that you were achieving your purpose?
   –What made you believe that you were not achieving your purpose?

5) Describe what you think your fellow volunteers felt their professional purpose to be.

6) Describe the delivery of education services at your school.
   –What about your school do you feel was successful?
   –What about your school do you feel was unsuccessful? How did you respond?

7) Tell me about some of the formal or informal activities you participated in outside of class.
   –How did you become involved in those activities?
   –Why did you become involved in those activities?

8) Who were your closest friends in the Marshallese community?
   –How did they become your close friends?
   –How was your relationship with them different than your relationship with your friends in your home country? How was it similar?

Evaluatory Questions:

1) Compare your experiences with your initial expectations.
2) What do you think is a valid compliment about WorldTeach? And volunteers?
3) What do you think is a valid criticism of WorldTeach? And volunteers?

Hypothetical Questions:

1) If you could have done something differently while in the Marshall Islands, what would it have been?
2) What do you think future WorldTeach volunteers to the Marshall Islands should know?

Table 9.2. Participants' Interview Transcripts

Name	Definition	Example
Americana	Fascination with American culture	Students love Eminem
Being an example	Acting as a role model for teachers, students, or Americans	Considering self an ambassador
Better pedagogy	Improve teaching practices	Criticizing rote memorization
Cross-cultural exchange	Learning about different cultures	Teaching students about American culture
Guilt	Feeling undeserving, responsible for bad things	Being a celebrity despite only 22-years old
History and sociopolitics	Talking about the history of sociopolitical status quo of Marshall Islands	Talking about nuclear testing
Inexperienced	Lack of teaching experience	Not knowing how to make a lesson plan
Not imposing	Don't want to tell Marshallese what to do	Deferring to Marshallese during meetings
Social mobility	Advancing in life due to education	Leaving the country for college
Teach English	Job is English instruction	"My job was to teach English"

Ruochen Richard Li was a high school teacher and counselor in Majuro, the capitol of the Republic of the Marshall Islands, from 2005 to 2008. He has worked at educational nonprofit organizations and research institutions and operated his own consultancy. Ruochen holds an MA in international education administration and policy analysis from Stanford University and a BA in anthropology from the University of Chicago.

Notes

I wish to thank WorldTeach, my research participants, Teresa LaFromboise, Christine Min Wotipka, Magdalena Gross, and members of the class for comments on this study. Most of all, I wish to thank all the teachers and students of the Marshall Islands.

1. At 15 megatons, the output from Castle Bravo was equivalent to the collective output of one Hiroshima-sized bomb detonated every day for 60 years (Niedenthal 2001).
2. Currently almost 1/6 of the world's Marshallese population resides in the United States of America (Asian Development Bank 2006).
3. The only tertiary institution in the Marshall Islands is a two-year community college, though it has recently added a small number of four-year degrees.
4. Dartmouth College and the Japanese International Cooperation Agency also send volunteer teachers, but WorldTeach volunteers are much more numerous.
5. WorldTeach also does not ask for racial/ethnic identity information from its applicants. My experience with the WorldTeach program, and the experience of the participants of a pilot study I conducted, suggests that the overwhelming majority of WorldTeach volunteers are white/Caucasian. This information is potentially very significant with respect to how volunteers perceive themselves, and are perceived.
6. All tertiary educational institutions in the Marshall Islands use English as the medium of instruction. Marshallese students can apply as domestic residents to US colleges, and are eligible to receive financial aid.
7. It is interesting that Lander would say this, given the previous finding that volunteers are inexperienced educators. Mallory Channing did mention that, despite her inexperience, "Just by default by going through the American school system you know a certain amount about how it works and you kind of bring that knowledge with you." These data indicate that volunteers might make a distinction between experience as an educator, and knowledge as an educator.
8. Johnson did not mention if she was referring to former WorldTeach volunteers, Peace Corps volunteers, military, or just the perception of Americans in general.
9. That WorldTeach volunteers agree to one-year teaching stints in the Marshall Islands needs to be considered when evaluating how they perceive their own roles with respect to liberation and oppression. While leaving

during the school year, or early termination, has occurred, it is frowned upon. Therefore, volunteers may not have perceived leaving the country entirely, which advocates of anticolonialism theory might suggest, as a realistic course of action.

References

Altbach, Philip, and Gail Kelly. 1978. *Education and Colonialism*. New York: Longman.

Alverson, H.S. 1977. "Peace Corps Volunteers in Rural Botswana." *Human Organization* 36(3): 274–81.

Asian Development Bank. 2006. "Juummemmej: Republic of the Marshall Islands Social and Economic Report 2005." Manila, Philippines: Asian Development Bank.

Barker, Holly M. 2004. *Bravo for the Marshallese: Regaining Control in a Post-Nuclear, Post-Colonial World*. Belmont, CA: Wadsworth/Thomson.

Bray, Mark. 1993. "Education and the Vestiges of Colonialism: Self-Determination, Neocolonialism and Dependency in the South Pacific." *Comparative Education* 29(3): 333–48.

Carlson, Jerry S., and Keith F. Widaman. 1988. "The Effects of Study Abroad During College on Attitudes Toward Other Cultures." *International Journal of Intercultural Relations* 12(1): 1–17.

Cohn, Steven F., and Robert E. Wood. 1985. "Foreign Aid at the Grass Roots: The Interaction of Peace Corps Volunteers with Host Country People." *Human Organization* 44: 167–71.

Economic Policy, Planning, and Statistics Office. 2004. "Republic of the Marshall Islands Statistical Yearbook 2004." Majuro, Marshall Islands: Economic Policy, Planning, and Statistics Office.

Fagerlind, Ingemar, and Lawrence J. Saha. 1989. *Education and National Development: A Comparative Perspective*, 2nd ed. Oxford: Pergamon.

Fanon, Frantz. 1961. *The Wretched of the Earth*. New York: Grove.

———. 1968. *Black Skin, White Masks*. New York: Grove.

Freire, Paulo. 1970. *Pedagogy of the Oppressed*. New York: Herder and Herder.

Fuller, Bruce. 1991. *Growing-Up Modern: The Western State Builds Third-World Schools*. New York: Routledge.

Gu, Qing. 2010. "Variations in Beliefs and Practices: Teaching English in Cross-Cultural Contexts." *Language and Intercultural Communication* 10(1): 32–53.

Hare, A.P. 1966. "Factors Associated with Peace Corps Volunteer Success in the Philippines." *Human Organization* 25(2): 150–53.

Harris, Jesse G. 1972. "Prediction of Success on a Distant Pacific Island: Peace Corps Style." *Journal of Consulting and Clinical Psychology* 38(2): 181–90.

———. 1973. "A Science of the South Pacific: Analysis of the Character Structure of the Peace Corps Volunteer." *American Psychologist* 28(3): 232–47.

Hezel, Francis. 1990. "Recolonizing Islands and Decolonizing History." Retrieved from http://www.micsem.org/pubs/articles/historical/frames/recoldecolfr.htm.

———. 2003. *Strangers in Their Own Land: A Century of Colonial Rule in the Caroline and Marshall Islands*. Honolulu: University of Hawaii Press.

Inkeles, Alex. 1975. "Becoming Modern:" *Ethos* 3(2): 323–42.

Lal, Brij V., and Kate Fortune. 2000. *The Pacific Islands: An Encyclopedia*. Honolulu: University of Hawaii Press.

Lane, Patrick, and Sally-Ann DeBrum. 2007. *Education for All Mid-Decade Assessment*. Majuro, Marshall Islands: Marshall Islands Ministry of Education.

Luteru, P. H., and G. R. Teasdale. 1993. "Aid and Education in the South Pacific." *Comparative Education* 29(3): 293–306.

Marshall Islands Journal. 2010. "Ading's $130m Plan for New Fiscal Year." *Marshall Islands Journal*, 27 August.

Marshall Islands Ministry of Education. 2008. *Rethinking Education in the Marshall Islands Conference: Summary Report of Conference Activities & Action Plan*. Marshall Islands: National Training Council, Pacific Resources for Education and Learning and Ministry of Education.

Niedenthal, Jack. 2001. *For the Good of Mankind: A History of the People of Bikini and Their Islands*. Majuro, Marshall Islands: Bravo.

Oliver, Nicolette. 2009. "Motivations and Experiences of Expatriate Educators in South Korea." Salt Lake City: Western Governors University. Retrieved from http://eric.ed.gov/PDFS/ED505958.pdf.

Peoples, James G. 1978. "Dependence in a Micronesian Economy." *American Ethnologist* 5(3): 535–52.

Rhoades, R.E. 1978. "Peace Corps and the American Development Philosophy." *Human Organization* 37(4): 424–26.

Rudiak-Gould, Peter. 2009. *Surviving Paradise: One Year on a Disappearing Island*. New York: Union Square.

Rutheiser, Charles. 1991. "Cultural Colonization and Educational Underdevelopment: Changing Patterns of American Influence in Belizean Schooling." *Belizean Studies* 19(1): 18–30.

Thaman, Konai Helu. 1993. "Culture and the Curriculum in the South Pacific." *Comparative Education* 29(3): 249–60.

———. 1997. "Reclaiming a Place: Towards a Pacific Concept of Education for Cultural Development." *Polynesian Society* 106(2): 119–30.

———. 2003. "Decolonizing Pacific Studies: Indigenous Perspectives, Knowledge, and Wisdom in Higher Education." *The Contemporary Pacific* 15(1): 1–17.

Thomas, R. Murray, and T. Neville Postlethwaite. 1984. *Schooling in the Pacific Islands: Colonies in Transition*. Oxford: Pergamon.

Williams, Tracy Rundstrom. 2005. "Exploring the Impact of Study Abroad on Students' Intercultural Communication Skills: Adaptability and Sensitivity." *Journal of Studies in International Education* 9(4): 356–71.

World Bank. 2005. "Opportunities to Improve Social Services in the Republic of the Marshall Islands."

WorldTeach. 2010a. "WorldTeach." Retrieved from http://www.worldteach.org.

——. 2010b. "WorldTeach Volunteer Data." Obtained from WorldTeach.

Conclusion

Hannah Davis Taïeb and Neriko Musha Doerr

Each chapter in this volume focused on particular kinds of affect in particular destinations and considered in different ways how affect works in the lives of students and volunteers. From different disciplinary perspectives, these authors approach related questions: how affect motivates people to cross borders, to learn languages, to transform themselves; how affect can exoticize others, obscure political issues or suggest contradictions; how students and volunteers themselves, or educators, choose to work with and manage affect. What conclusions can we now draw?

Here, we will first discuss each of this book's chapters, reviewing our authors' conclusions. We will then look at theoretical contributions to the anthropology of affect and border-crossing, bringing in our theoretical lens as introduced in Chapter 1. We will then go on to consider how these texts can point towards new approaches and practical educative strategies for study abroad and volunteering abroad. Last, we will suggest some directions for future research.

A Review of the Chapters

In Part II of this volume, Karen Rodriguez's chapter, using a psycho-analytical approach, brings out the complexity of emotions aroused by travel and by language learning, including not just desire but also shame, self-hatred, the desire to possess the other or lose oneself in the other, to incorporate the other or to be incorporated. These emotions, for Rodriguez, are far from trivial; they are not just romantic pastiches to be discarded as the student comes into contact with "reality." Rather, they can be powerful, if sublimated, transformed into a real engagement with the alterity of another language—a language in which the learner will discover a new subjectivity.

The creativity of the process is underlined here. Just as Michael Woolf, in the preface, brings out the creative element in the stance of the romantic observer, here Rodriguez, citing Kristeva, suggests the transformative potential involved in coming into one's own in a new language. The learner does not adapt to new rules and ways, rather, as she[1] finds her voice in the new language, she is not just conforming to another reality but is also changing it. Change is not adaptation—it has a creative element—and it is not housed in the student, but is an interactive process.

Bradley Rink introduces us to students' complex emotions attached to the idea of "Africa." He argues for fostering local knowledge as a way to break down fantasies and fears about the mystified continent. Like Rodriguez and Taïeb (and unlike Doerr and Kamagai), Rink advocates for a hierarchy of study abroad experiences; a successful experience, for Rink, is one in which the student does not remain only an observer of a landscape that is viewed, dominated, and objectified, but comes to engagement with the place he or she is in. Affect, being embodied, is a kind of engagement—through it we move from facile observers to engaged bodies.

Rink is also attentive to the fact that one of the motivations for study abroad participants can be the search for cultural capital. Nontraditional destinations allow students to see themselves as superior to other students whom they perceive as less adventurous. This motivation gives students a stake in finding "Africans" different.

In chapter 5, Hannah Davis Taïeb calls for the integration of the students into the critical reflection on the romance of study abroad and of the particular destination. This includes the exploration of *regards croisés*, the mutual gaze, the back-and-forth reciprocal romance associated with the Franco-American interactive moment. In the student contributions to this chapter, Kaitlin Rosenblum brings out the tension in study abroad discourse, between the desire for adventure and the desire for immersion in day-to-day mundane life. Emily Bihl evokes the specificity and individuality of romantic associations with the destination, as she dissects her own vision of a writer's Paris. Mai-Linh Bui shares the consequences of choosing to travel to the nonromanticized destination of the United States; in so doing, she gives us a glimpse of romantic views of difference as seen from Vietnam. Tara Kim brings out the unexpected consequences of study abroad, in that her travels to France elicited a new sense of belonging to the category "American."

Based on these student contributions, Taïeb argues that we can build a dialogue with our students, drawing on the mobilizing action of emotion and romance, while developing the ability to critique and question assumptions. For Taïeb, this involves an approach that looks not at a reified French culture but rather at the Franco-American mutual gaze; an interactive moment that can be elicited and discussed not only through readings, but also through engaging French students and professors in the classroom experience.

Neriko Musha Doerr shows how radically the emotional investment of the student shapes experience and subjectivities. The romance with Paris leads one student to seek out difference and cultural particularities constantly; although not emphasized, it is clear that orientation advice and health-and-safety preparation also bring out cultural differences and downplay similarities. The student who is in love with Paris focuses on trying to imitate Parisian ways, and dissociates from her fellow US students. Her emotional journey ends with a sense of disillusionment. In contrast, Doerr's second interviewee makes her way through her Spanish travels without much affective intensity, and notes cultural differences and similarities in a more matter-of-fact way, differentiating less between fellow students and others she meets.

Doerr points out the role of the discourse of immersion as a kind of lure, creating in the student a desire to become Parisian. At the same time, Doerr also argues against the establishment of a hierarchy defining failed and successful study abroad experiences. Instead, she argues for attentiveness to the specificity of each student's experience; each of the two students learned completely different lessons.

Yuri Kumagai, like Doerr, argues against the hierarchization of study abroad experiences and problematizes the discourse of immersion. The two contrasting students she interviews start with almost identical romantic notions of Japan. One student ends up disillusioned, and questions her own fantasies: after spending time in the mundane realities of her host family's life, and trying in various ways to fit in, she ends up with a painful sense of what exclusion can be like in Japan. The other student—with a lighter, more playful approach—finds herself in an easier contact with a wider variety of local people. Her host family makes hosting into a kind of culture work, shaping knowledge of their society (as host families are increasingly being asked to do).

But the first student, who denigrates her own experience, learns things from everyday life that she would not have learned at tea ceremonies; unlike the second student, she develops a visceral sense of the nature of exclusion. Furthermore, the second student does not only immerse herself in "traditional" Japanese practices, she also engages in transnational practices like salsa dancing. Apparently unexciting activities, moments of feeling rejected and excluded, transnational practices that are not romanticized—these are part of student learning; "failed" study abroad may involve long-term learning.

In Part III of this volume, Cori Jakubiak's chapter shows how marketing materials for English language voluntourism elaborate a romantic image of people of the Global South as exotic others who are at once "needy and compelling." Us/Them dichotomies create a false geography of inequality, turning attention from the realities of wealth in the Global South and poverty in the Global North. The emotional connections that can emerge between volunteers and local people are mobilized and their import is exaggerated in the idea that "one hug" can "make a difference"; Jakubiak argues that such practices serve to obscure long-term structural inequalities. Jakubiak links this to the emergence of "life politics"—an abandonment of grand political narratives, replaced by individual civic action involving consumption rather than collective action, all of this in the context of neoliberalism.

Jakubiak also considers the romantic desire for authenticity, for "real life," which can be interpreted as nostalgia for a nonalienated relationship to labor and community, or as a yearning for an alternative to commodification, predictability, and standardization. This brings out an internal tension in the voluntourism project: volunteers may be seeking values they see as traditional, yet they are embarked on a development project that is geared towards modernization. Furthermore, the authentic itself, paradoxically, is commodified.

The returned volunteers she interviews sometimes express a kind of renewed validation of American superiority. Few interviewees develop a critical perspective on their activities or reevaluate their starting beliefs. It is worth remarking that Jakubiak focuses purposefully on very short-term projects. One may still ask how research results might differ in long-term projects with more training and oriented towards critical reflexivity or a search for mutuality (Murphy, Tan and Allan 2009; Nenga 2011). Would a similar study in the context of social-justice-oriented community-engagement projects abroad have yielded similar results?

The chapter by Ruochen Richard Li begins to respond to this question, since he studied a long-term volunteer teaching project, World-

Teach, in the Marshall Islands. He uses two theoretical frameworks, that of modernization theory and that of anticolonial theory, to show different aspects of the volunteer project: according to modernization theory, volunteers are sharing inherently good practices; from an anticolonial perspective, volunteers are engaged in false generosity, and real change and learning can only come from the oppressed themselves taking on the educative project. Li notes that the volunteers in urban settings viewed their experience from an anticolonial perspective, and experienced the emotion of guilt; volunteers on the outer islands tended more to view their experience in terms of modernization theory. For urban volunteers, "their greater familiarity with modernization did not necessarily make them greater advocates of it."

Li's chapter further shows that in the encounter between the World-Teach volunteer and the Marshall Islander, romanticization takes place on both sides; the volunteer is imagining a pristine island life, while the Islander is admiring American ways. The volunteers are aware of this; overall, one gathers that the volunteers Li interviewed, unlike almost all of the short-term volunteers who spoke to Jakubiak, have a critical analytical perspective on what they are doing and feeling. They are aware of the tension between their own romanticization of Marshall island life and their desire to help modernize it and therefore transform it; and, the tension between wanting to be admired and share valued things from the West and not wanting to be exaggeratedly admired, leading to denigration of local culture. These conflicts are unresolved, and, Li suggests, unresolvable in the context of one-year stays—longer stints than many volunteer abroad programs, but still, perhaps, not long enough to force out the contradictions between feelings and actions that Li exposes.

Each of these chapters approaches the issue of affect from different angles, reflecting not only the author's research interests but also the specificity of the destination and the particular students or volunteers visiting. Nonetheless, they all address our overall theme of the mobilization and management of affect. Some chapters focused on the analysis of affect, in the context of study abroad discourses of immersion (Doerr, Kamagai) or in the context of a developed-developing binary (Jakubiak, Li); other chapters discuss how student affect is transcended and transformed in language learning (Rodriguez), or call for the management of students' affect for particular ends, such as ending prejudice about the destination (Rink), or suggest sharing critical reflection so that students take on and manage their own romantic notions in a creative and critical way or in dialogue with local students (Taïeb et al.).

Since our volume is geared towards both theory and practice, we now go on to discuss both theoretical and practical conclusions in the next two sections.

Contributions to the Anthropology of Affect

Anthropologists have investigated the ways affect has been mobilized and managed in changing political economies and sociocultural environments, shaping various subjects in due course, as discussed in Chapter 1. The encounter with the cultural Other in the context of relations of power, especially those of colonial and postcolonial contexts, has been discussed in terms of affect. This volume contributes to these discussions by examining affect in study abroad and volunteering abroad, little-studied areas in anthropology thus far, that involve encounter with the cultural Other in both explicit and implicit relations of power.

Chapters in this volume showed the range and breadth of the passions associated with study abroad and volunteering abroad, and a corresponding range in the ways that such passions can "work," can be mobilizing, can shape the experience of difference. Rodriguez and Rink have brought out the complex, contradictory, multifaceted passions that can be found, involving not just romanticization but fear, desire to incorporate the other or be incorporated, desire to lose oneself, to find oneself. Several of our authors also talked about the desire to help others, to repair the world, to find authenticity or community (Rink, Jakubiak, Li).

Anthropological studies discussed affect involving the cultural Other in relations of power, especially in colonial and postcolonial contexts. Chapters in this volume investigated the contours of affect in various relations of power—some explicit and others not—and how they influenced the ways the imagined border between the student and the cultural Other are constructed, perceived, and dismantled. They showed how our romantic notions, our desires, our emotional or motivational stances or points of departure can make us focus on difference or ignore it, can make us unaware of diversity within the destination or hyperaware of it, can give an entire continent a halo of meanings that occlude its diversity (Rink). They can make us unaware of poverty in some contexts and hyperaware of it in others (Jakubiak). The romanticized destination may create a stark distinction between people in the destination and people from home, resulting in distancing from one's fellow study abroad students in order to adapt to the destination (Doerr).

Relations of power not only influenced the type of affective investment students had but also bore a seed for transformation as administrators, teachers, and students themselves managed their affect. The legacy of colonial exoticism manifested in the study abroad students' desire as well as fear toward Africa could be transformed through their guided engagement with the particular realities of the city (Rink). Obvious relations of power in volunteer abroad contexts could be furthered through the mobilization of paternalistic affect that romanticizes helping and exoticizes those who receive it in English language voluntourism (Jakubiak) but also be challenged when the volunteers' romanticization of their own role as modernizers meets the local people's romanticization of the volunteers in the Marshall Islands (Li). Students also critically analyzed and managed their valorization and romanticization of European cities, especially Paris, through reflection on their ongoing production of subjectivities (Taïeb et al.) or on their interaction with the residents there (Doerr), which sometimes led to its transformation.

As discussed in Chapter 1 of this volume, using a Foucauldian concept of the subject, Fendler (1998) argues that having a particular kind of affect—desire for social justice, life-long learning, etc.—has become an important part of the current notion of the educated subject. Chapters in this volume provide concrete examples of the types of affect educated subjects (and also "helping subjects," volunteers) gain, sometimes unwittingly, in the process of studying abroad. These can include a complex entanglement of desire and fear toward the language and people of the destination, (Rodriguez, Rink), which may sometimes evoke a new kind of affect; navigated (Taïeb et al.) or unexpectedly unfolding (Doerr, Kamagai). Volunteers also come to feelings of romanticization and disillusionment; a sense of intimacy with others across geographical and class lines, which may nevertheless involve a profound acceptance that these lines can never be crossed (Jakubiak); an awareness, tinged with guilt, of the impossibility of simultaneously achieving pristine premodern life and transmitting modern values and opportunities (Li).

Paying close attention to the contextual nature of such affect and the subject positions of individuals involved, the chapters in this volume illustrate dynamics of diverse affect of the "educated subject" as well as the "helping subject" produced through study and volunteering abroad that perpetuated but also subverted relations of power.

Implications for Practice

Marketing vs. Educating: Analyzing the Mobilization of Affect

Love sells, passion motivates, desire leads people to reach for their wallets. Thus the marketing of study abroad mobilizes romantic images of place, of the study abroad adventure, of the achievement of cultural learning; the marketing of volunteering abroad mobilizes all these and also making a difference, achieving intimacy, finding community and authentic experience elsewhere than at home. The desire to belong to a global community and the (contradictory?) desire to experience difference and self-transformation—these emotions are all mobilized in the marketing of study and volunteering abroad.

Once romantic images have brought people to their dreamed-of destination, what is the study abroad professional to do? We are supposed to teach, to intervene to promote learning; what is our relationship with the student's romance with the destination? Are we expected to provide cultural difference, to mobilize local people not as partners or equals but as examples, demonstrating that difference? How is the educator to place him-/herself with regard to what is being sold? How can we respond to a commodification of the joys and passions of travel, of the encounter with the Other—a selling of the hero's quest? A commodification of cultural difference itself?

In the context of international volunteer projects, one may ask similar questions. Once we have recognized the sometimes-misleading marketing images, once we have recognized the sometimes-contradictory desires and motivations of volunteers as Jakubiak and Li pointed out, what responses can we have? Are we to provide the local partner, furnish community, artificially create a sense of making a difference? Or are there ways to work with volunteers and partners to create a process that takes into account and respects the emotions and motivations on all sides, and counters the distortions or confronts the contradictions?

We do not offer concrete answers here to fit all situations. As in the educational system as a whole, in study abroad there are tensions between the educative project and the economic framework in which it is integrated. What we suggest, however, is to take affect seriously throughout the process. That is, we encourage the analysis of how affect is mobilized in the marketing of programs, considering what is promised and pictured, and reflecting on how this corresponds or contradicts with program goals. For in some contexts, study abroad and volunteer abroad staff will be expected and encouraged to lead students towards a rethinking of their emotions. But in other contexts, staff may be expected to placate or calm emotion; or to respond to romantic images by providing "culture" and "community" or "authenticity" that lives up to the promise; or even to commodify their own emotion, by making their human warmth into a program selling point (cf. Hochschild 2003). By paying attention to affect, we can point out and balance such demands, taking a critical look at some of the legitimating discourses that frame our profession.

Managing Affect for Critical Engagement

Emotions can be managed with all kinds of goals: goals as disparate as creating long-term affective ties between US volunteers and members of Mexican NGOs, or improving productivity in a multinational corporation (Richard and Rudnyckyj 2009), as mentioned in Chapter 1. People manage their own emotions to free themselves from their power, or to manipulate or communicate with others, or to get what they want, or to get help, or to learn more about how they are experiencing what is around them. Professionals intervene to help people manage their emotions for particular ends: therapists do it, caregivers do it, and so do educators. Those who are not professionals, such as parents and friends, help others to manage emotion as well.

The question, then, is how to identify implicit or explicit goals in the management of affect. The theoretical lens we are developing in this volume is useful in that it gives us a vocabulary to distinguish between the goals of particular practices in the management of affect in study and volunteering abroad.

The prominent interculturalist Janet Bennett argues for working with affect like anxiety in order to combat prejudice: "[C]onsiderable research is reinforcing the notion that diminishing prejudice and stereotypes requires reduction of anxiety as our starting point. We live in an anxious world, fearful of the stranger. In the future, anxiety reduction will more clearly be viewed as the foundation for meeting cultural others" (Bennett 2015: xxvi). What are the ways of working with emotion that combat prejudice effectively? That work towards critical engagement? That promote critical thought and resistance? We have suggested interventions that diffuse the exotic thrill, normalize local environments, and promote egalitarian interaction with diverse kinds of people. Furthermore, such "critical interventions" can allow for a problematization of US-centered ideas and practices; a willingness to consider motives other than self-improvement, safety, survival, to maintain values such as solidarity; to raise political issues and questions of power rather than distracting from them (see Pagano and Roselle 2009). Such approaches engage with student affect, but not to ease adaptation and not to direct students towards a predetermined end established by an authority; rather, to allow students to pose problems, to bring up contradictions, to engage also affectively with others (Ceballos 2013; Vassallo 2013).

The "critical interventions" we advocate thus would take into account the breadth and diversity of student affective experience, each student having his or her own particular relationship to the particular destination (Doerr, Kamagai, Taïeb et al., Rodriguez). This is as opposed to standardizing our expectations through stage models of cultural development or an uncritical acceptance of goals like "intercultural competence" and "global citizenship"—which, as we have shown in Chapter 2, can be problematized and have various inflections. Instead, work with students and volunteers can be open-ended, as in recent practices that evoke the concept of mindfulness, or "self-witnessing," involving stillness and observation of emotion in order to allow for its transformation (as was explained by Tara Harvey, who is responsible for intercultural learning for CIEE, personal communication, see also Schaetti, Ramsey, and Watanabe 2008).

Catherine Menyhart, who also plays a major role in the development of training programs for CIEE, explains:

> I prefer to think of it as attending to emotion … like you're sidling up a friend on a park bench. "Hi sadness, what are you doing here? What can you teach me?" Which links to mindfulness. The thought of feeling sad is not something we're trying to escape from … we're noticing emotion … paying attention to it … These carry more of an exploratory and curious orientation rather than managing which is like "do something about it." (personal communication)

This mindful witnessing is more open-ended and less directive, and therefore liable to lead in more diverse and individualized directions.

At the same time, just as there are different meanings to terms like "intercultural competence," so there are different ways to be mindful; Purser and Loy (2013: 1) have pointed out clearly the distinction between standardized corporate mindfulness practice designed to calm employee discontent and increase productivity, and an ethical mindfulness. We can differentiate between ways of approaching student and volunteer affect that are designed to calm emotion and placate tensions, and those that allow for unexpected outcomes and could lead to action; those that reinstate predetermined notions of "difference," and those that are not only open-ended but also open towards the broader social context and towards ethical questions.

Attention to the particularities of each student goes along with attention to the particularities of each site, working towards local knowledge and the specificity of other units like cities (Rodriguez, Rink, this volume), resisting the tendency to encode and reify cultural difference, whether it be national, "Frenchness" or "Americanness," or continental "Africanness" and "Latin-Americanness" (Taïeb et al., Rink, Rodriguez, this volume; Ceballos 2013: 6).

"Critical interventions" can be activities in which students participate in cultural practices that provide heightened emotion, while simultaneously questioning and analyzing those practices. For example, Ray Casserly of CIEE's Belfast program leads students to participate in the St. Patrick's Day Parade in Dublin, but discusses as well the marketing and performing of "Irishness" and proposes to students an activity he calls "Spot the Paddy" to demonstrate the scarcity of Irish people in the parade (Casserly, personal communication). Thus along with sharing with students the thrill of difference, we can also share with them the thrill of understanding—in this case, critically understanding how difference is constructed in the context of relations of power.

Similarly, several of the authors in this book show how affective and cognitive processes work together. Rodriguez provides a deep analysis of the kinds of inner shifts that occur through respecting student engagement with Guanajato, its language and its particularities, an engagement that can lead to ongoing political commitment; Rink analyzes how his classes based on walking and observing brought students to an embodied relationship with the city in the present time, which shifted their fantasies about an archaic "Africa"; Taïeb et al. show how the sociological, anthropological, literary, and critical study abroad literature provided a vocabulary for students to rethink their romantic illusions.

Our contribution, then, to the debate about the best way for professionals to intervene in student experience, consists in the suggestion that we use the theoretical lens of the management of affect to distinguish between interventions in terms of their implicit and explicit goals (cf. Crawford, Ogden, and Lucas 2010). As we will continue to discuss below, we suggest a broader and more self-critical definition of what our goals can be—looking not only at student outcomes (the achievement of higher levels of cultural sensitivity as defined by an external authority figure) but also at the social and political sphere, the overall context in which we and our students are moving. We can distinguish between interventions that go too far, that micromanage and thus maintain students in the client role or confine them in solipsism; interventions that transmit reified shortcut notions of national cultures, obscuring diversity and contested notions "abroad"; interventions that serve to ease and placate rather than rouse and enliven. And we look for practices that aim to work against prejudice, critique power relations, and move towards critical engagement.

A Broad and Egalitarian Educative Community

In order to build this ethically shaped attention to affect, we suggest that it is important to develop a broad, egalitarian educative community. Such a community could include not only teachers and students, and volunteers and local partners, but also on-site staff and US-based staff.

Including on-site staff is important because they are often called upon to handle student or volunteer affect in myriad situations. Do on-site staff also respect and handle their own emotions? This would mean respect for oneself as a local person and as an intermediary—respecting one's own emotions, being willing to be attentive to them as well, to learn from them, to allow a "gut feeling" to take shape even if it does not fit with the dominant (US-based) discourses within study abroad. As short-term programs flourish, truncating encounters for students and multiplying brief visits, more and more work is done by the on-site professional, who is pushed to work more rapidly in a reinforced intermediary role, facilitating local contacts in fast motion. Ethical and egalitarian study abroad pedagogy and practice mean working to ensure respect for the local intermediary and insistence on employment conditions that allow education professionals the possibility, the time, to approach their own affect in a fruitful way and on their own terms.

With local partners, we can look for situations that allow for a creative and dialogic approach to affect. Several chapters in this volume suggest the importance of realizing that the pull of romanticization goes both ways—what Taïeb calls *regards croisés*, the mutual gaze. As discussed in Chapter 5, Americans studying abroad in France and French students about to study abroad in America have a common interest in discussing and "managing" their romantic visions. Similarly, while the volunteers in Li's study long for the "simple" island life, the Marshall Islanders they teach gaze longingly at the volunteers and emulate Lizzie McGuire; one could imagine a "critical intervention" that would bring volunteers and students together to deconstruct these passions.

Exchanges with local partners, involving a willingness to handle affect, can also bring up class differences, geopolitical realities, and questions of privilege, and can take shape in a way that is pertinent to the particular site in which it occurs. More and more, service-learning professionals both domestically and internationally are insisting on the importance of such critical reflections on privilege, structural inequality, and negative effects of volunteerism. They are then exploring making these reflections into dialogues that incorporate partners (Donahue and Mitchell 2010; Gilbert, Johnson, and Plaut 2009; Green 2003; Kiely 2004; Murphy, Tan and Allen 2009; Sin 2009; Strait and Lima 2009). Similar approaches can be used in study abroad.

With our students, study abroad professionals, like other educators, can develop an egalitarian learning community. Paulo Freire (1970) advocated the positioning of teacher and students not as the knower (teacher) filling the empty vessel (student) but as a teacher-student with knowledge in some areas learning together with student-teachers who also have knowledge in some areas based on their experience. In the context of study abroad, we can create a more egalitarian educative environment also by purposefully avoiding treating students as empty vessels to be filled, or standard types to be transformed in standard ways, or clients to be satisfied.

Their affect and development is key, but so are their interactions with each other and with the communities they are visiting. If their emotions are only to be manipulated through marketing images or catered to on site, then that leaves students stuck in the client role, which is ultimately isolating. If fear is responded to by adjusting the surroundings to soothe the fear, then we are in fact neglecting our responsibility to the student—in a sense, we are preventing the student from managing emotion, neglecting our role as educators and acting as service providers, arranging the scenery rather than opening up the environment (Engle and Engle 2003: 5–7), since the student's quest involves contact with and respect for others.

Thus, we have to learn to judge when "less is more," when to leave students the space and time to build their own "expanded itinerary" (Ceballos 2013), their own particular relationship to place and people; we have to know when and how to intervene, and when and how to delimit interventions to avoid a micromanagement of experience that takes away the nitty-gritty feel of everyday life with its problems. This means that, as educators, we are indeed intervening in their experience, but are doing so in a bounded way, with a consistent approach of respect for them—not as clients, but as full people—and also for ourselves, and for local partners.

Affect and Conceptual Tensions within Study Abroad and Volunteer Abroad

A critical approach to study and volunteer abroad involves teasing out and making visible the contradictions inherent in these activities. Attention to affect—that of students, volunteers, and in fact all participants in the process—can be a way to do so.

For study abroad, as we discussed in detail in Chapter 2, tensions have always been present in the legitimating discourses of the field: between the goal of spreading US ideals, and the goal of learning other ways; between the goal of building US leaders, and the goal of discovering new equal partners; between a decentering of the United States through a connection to "the global," and a global reach centered on the United States; between building world peace, and knowing one's enemies. Our work in this volume suggests that the study of affect can be a way to deepen our understanding of these contradictions and suggest ways to respond to them.

For example, studying students who expressed discontent and discouragement, both Doerr and Kumagai analyzed them not as indicating "failed" study abroad experiences but as evocative of contradictions in study abroad discourse and called for an acceptance of these varied student experiences as meaningful. Taïeb et al.'s chapter suggested that students themselves observe their own affect and manage it critically to expose tensions in discourse, as Rosenblum does, for example, when she points to the contradiction between the discourse of immersion and the discourse of adventure.

In volunteering abroad as well, there are tensions, as mentioned in Chapter 1: despite its altruism and good intentions, it can perpetuate hierarchical relationships between volunteers and those they come to serve, evade transforming structural inequality, impose what constitutes an ideal state of society, and merely benefit volunteers. We show that attention to affect illuminates these but also other tensions. For example, Jakubiak's work suggested that the search for authenticity and "real life" can be a misappropriation of other desires and drives to feel love and be helpful. She argued that we should be alert to the exaggeration of the effects of emotional exchange and the mobilization of love as a marketing ploy. Li pointed out the tension between the goal of development and the romantic image of the simple, authentic life. A critical intervention in such cases would aim not so much to ease volunteer experience but to raise critical consciousness, to point to the historical context, to raise issues about modernization.

We can find ways to reflect with our students on the origins of the romantic journeys by, for example, engaging them in critical views of tourism based on a Marxist approach—(e.g., MacCannell 1976). We can reflect on how to respect the strong emotions aroused on all sides during volunteering abroad, and yet resist their reduction to an emotional currency. What we suggest then is that along with creating practices designed for a "successful" volunteer experience for all concerned, we can also aim to provoke reflection and to deepen understanding of positioning in the historical context and in structures of power. If, as proposed above, local partners are included in the process, the ensuing reflection will be all the richer.

In this sense, we suggest once again broadening the contexts in which we take affect seriously as an object of analysis, and a source of knowledge, understanding, transformative or creative power. Affect can be a way to understand and transform "embodied feelings" of culture (M. Bennett and Castiglioni 2004), and it can also be an indicator of tensions, contradictions, power struggles, that are important to bring to light. By making visible the contrasting goals within study abroad and volunteer abroad, we can make informed choices about policy and pedagogy. And by accepting that some of these contradictions are irresolvable, that they are indicative of tensions and problems of our time, we make possible a more cogent and meaningful pedagogy "abroad."

Interdisciplinary Communication: Our Own Practice

Our own collaboration—a somewhat unusual partnership between an anthropologist working on the domain of study abroad, and a study abroad director with a PhD in anthropology—can be considered a rare kind of "interdisciplinary communication." As we worked together, we found ourselves reading and sharing two bodies of academic discourse—an anthropological corpus with invigorating critical approaches to education, the politics of difference, power relations, contemporary travel, and affect; and a corpus of works by international educators, involving research results aimed at critiquing and improving practice, at defining goals and assessing their achievement. We found our collaboration fruitful, however, not only due to the sharing of resources, but also because it led us to reflect on disciplinary and structural problems.

In the field of anthropology, the issue of knowledge production has been much discussed (Clifford 1986), as anthropologists take credit for the knowledge of informants who often remain anonymous. What has been talked about more marginally is anthropologists' relationships with those in other disciplines whose interests overlap with anthropologists but who engage in the issues from different angles. Those in such disciplines are often viewed as local experts, the implication being that they are likely to have less rigor in theoretical analyses, since they are allegedly trapped in their own system of knowledge and operation (Clifford 1986; Smith 1999). This also applies to applied anthropologists who often work with such local experts. For example, often devalued are educational anthropologists who seek to improve the educational achievement of marginalized groups of students without questioning the constructed nature of achievement, which more theoretically rigorous anthropologists would analyze.

In the field of international education, on the other hand, there is an openness to multidisciplinary perspectives (http://www.frontiersjournal.com/) including anthropology, psychology, communications, and other fields. However, there is an implicit understanding that research and writing should be geared towards improving practice, meaning there can be a certain intolerance for critical works about the field itself that analyze its workings without proposing suggestions for improvement.

We ended up feeling that we also crossed a border—or, through collaboration, broke through an unnecessary separation, a distancing between legitimated academic knowledge and the perhaps undervalued local knowledge and practice produced and put into play by the international educator; between theory for theory's sake, and research for action. Rather than accepting that theoretical works must be kept rigorously separate from practical considerations, we would argue that even highly critical theory can be useful to practitioners, and even brass-tacks discussions of practice can be useful to theorists; the pleasures and skills of the fields of education and research involve continually finding these uses, connecting reflection with action.

Producing an edited volume through collaboration—not only between the co-editors but also among contributors—allowed us to discuss similar issues from various viewpoints, to bring together perspectives that have been sequestered, revealing overlap in interest and intention and creating a fruitful conversation.

Directions for Future Research

We have argued for the importance of taking affect seriously, and considering in detail its role and its transformations. Building on this focus, we suggest four main directions for future research.

First, we can focus on the subjectivity of students. This could concern the question of belonging. As we discussed in Chapter 1, affect is a key element in the elaboration of new communities in that sentiments of belonging allow for links between people who have never met (such as members of a nation-state). In the context of the discourse of globalization, it makes sense to ask if study abroad and volunteer abroad programs have the goal of creating sentiments of belonging to an imagined global community. Is this goal present, explicitly or implicitly, in the way these programs are organized and in the discourses and practices surrounding them? Do the affective responses of students and volunteers reflect this kind of belonging? Or, do they reflect a reaffirmation of American particularities and a renewed sense of belonging to "Americanness" (Zemach-Berstin 2008: 34)? How might this sense of belonging to "America" have changed?

We can also focus on education and examine the educated subject (Fendler 1998, 2001) produced through study abroad programs. What kind of educated subject is expected to emerge from the process of study abroad (for such an attempt, see Doerr 2015a)? What is the specificity in the kind of affect he or she is supposed to have? How do border-crossing and its ideologies fit into the "technologies of developmentalism and interaction" that Fendler sees as educating today's "flexible souls"? What mechanisms in study abroad—advertisements, discourses such as that of immersion, program design—encourage specific affect for the study-abroad–educated subject? In detail, how is student affect managed, transformed in practice, in workshops and classes teaching leadership and cultural sensitivity? How do the types and contours as well as degree of students' affective investment shape the notion of the educated subject? What can we glean about subjectivities from the new forms of study abroad—involving shorter stints and often several sites, yet a focus on "culture learning"—rapid motion, and yet an instauration of mindfulness techniques and an attention to stillness? Does this foster a particular sort of educated subject—mindful yet in motion, adaptable and at ease with "culture" and "difference"? Can we look also at the contours of a "helping subject" emerging from the processes of volunteering abroad? And can we see a link between these abroad-educated subjects and neoliberalism or other economic and political structures of the early twenty-first century?

Second, we can broaden the kinds of border we investigate: What about the affect involved in crossing class boundaries? Or—for those working on prison education programs, like the innovative Inside-Out program (Atilya et al 2013, Davis and Roswell 2013) in which incarcerated and nonincarcerated people study together—what about the emotions incited by crossing the border between inside and outside the institution? How can a mixed classroom lead to a transformative approach to different emotional and motivational stances?

Furthermore, how do borders emerge? Does the notion of border crossing itself construct borders? Ray McDermott and Hervé Varenne (1995) argue that sociocultural environments push us to notice certain difference/borders over others (for example, we notice deaf persons only in an environment where few people use sign language). Then, what does having a border to cross tell us about our current sociocultural conditions? Doerr has argued elsewhere that talking about "learning" creates borders by suggesting the object of learning is novel to the student, thus different (Doerr 2016) and talking about certain acts of helping as "volunteering" creates a border between the person helping and the person being helped, given that, if you do the same act for your family member, it is usually not called "volunteering" (Doerr 2015b). What other ways are borders constructed through the very notion of "border crossing"?

Third, we can expand our object of study to more players involved in the processes of study and volunteer abroad. Almost all our authors did research or consulted only with students or volunteers. Research should include host families, international educators and other study abroad and volunteering abroad staff in the United States and throughout the world, teachers, university partners, nonprofit associations. The experiences and perspectives of host families and host communities are only occasionally included in research (see Doerr 2013 and Stephenson 1999 on host family perspectives; Crabtree 2013 and Sin 2009 on the perspectives of communities receiving volunteers), though they form an important part of the study and volunteering abroad experience.

Host families can work to produce a stereotypical image of the host society when portrayed in particular ways in study abroad marketing, but can also work to challenge such stereotypes in practice as students actually live with host families that defy such stereotypes. Researchers report diverse host family experiences that depend on the students' attitude—including their shyness (Kinginger 2008; Taguchi 2008; Yashima, Zenuk-Nishide, and Shimizu 2004), "colonial" attitude (Ogden 2007–2008), and willingness to spend time with and engage with the host family (Vande Berg 2009; Vande Berg, Connor-Linton, and Paige 2009). As to the host family, some act as informal teachers helping students adjust to the host society (Cohen et al 2005; Fobes 2005) or as advocates for students (Lindenberg 2015), but others may not be willing to engage with them (Kinginger 2008; Popadiuk 2009; Yashima, Zenuk-Nishide, and Shimizu 2004) or are only open to particular cultural differences (Doerr 2013). Therefore, the dynamics of interactions with host families are worth exploring.

Study abroad staff are also key actors in the processes we are looking at, since they operate between the US student and the local universities, families, and partners, setting up partnerships, arranging conversation exchange and cultural mentoring, finding host families, and working through conflicts in these areas. Volunteering abroad staff members are also in key intermediary roles, setting out to meet the needs of community organizations and also meet the need of incoming volunteers.

Yet another way to broaden the field is to go beyond the geographic focus of this volume: US study and volunteering abroad. Future research can compare American forms to other international educational systems. How do some of these same questions take shape in the European ERASMUS program? What are the forms and discourses of study abroad and volunteering abroad based in Canada, Japan, Denmark, Australia, China?

Fourth, we should investigate effects of the program practices. One area in which we see a field of research opening up is studying the marketing of study abroad and volunteering abroad, and the mobilization of romantic images therein (Doerr 2012; Zemach-Bersin 2009). Such research could be of interest not only to scholars of advertising, and in cultural studies, but would also be of interest to international educators and people working in marketing, as it raises questions about the nature of the outreach they are doing.

A related research direction would concern the commodification of cultural difference. Some researchers argue that globalizing processes standardized the criteria by which cultural difference around the world is measured (Wilk 1995), which then influenced the process of commodification of culture (Howes 1996). What kinds of ideas about culture are produced in the context of standardized study abroad programs? Who produces them? Are people learning to act out their own cultural forms in a commodified way (i.e., with the goal of receiving financial remuneration)? If so, how does this affect the nature of those cultural forms themselves? What is revealed and what is hidden by this process? Such research could also help professionals consider how to combat commodification and to find critical approaches to this question during the process.

Thus, we hope that future research will continue to explore pedagogies that are attentive to affect and its transformative movement, will continue to use affect as a theoretical lens to raise critical questions, will continue to bring together the preoccupations of the scholar and the practitioner. Research could focus on comparing programs and processes, including those that attempt to challenge the commodification of culture and experience, and look at the long-term qualitative effects of such actions, for students, volunteers, and all other parties concerned. Are there ways of working with affect that do work against prejudice, that do bring to light questions of politics and power rather than pushing them aside? What kinds of particular approaches and techniques lead to what kinds of long-term transformations for those involved?

Moving Forward

As the fields of study abroad and volunteering abroad have matured, competition for the student and volunteer markets has led to an intensification of various legacies that informed the emergence of study abroad, as we discussed in Chapter 2. The legacy of the Grand Tour regarding cultural development came to be highlighted as part of the product being proposed. We also can see the legacy of travel writing that reifies cultural difference, along with the reproduction of romantic images of Otherness. The legacy of the rite of passage highlights romantic images of the changes students and volunteers can make in themselves, and the legacy of the idealization of modernization romanticizes the changes volunteers can make in visited societies. The commercialization of study abroad and volunteer abroad, in the context of the commercialization of higher education as a whole (Bok 2004), threatens to further increase the commodification of experience in these contexts. At the same time, efforts have been made to bring back the focus on education, to develop critical engagement and partnership, and to work towards a more collegial, less rigid, decentered view of the world.

The ways that students will transform themselves, the ways they will influence those around them; these are as myriad and diverse as the students themselves, as specific and varied as those they will meet on their travels. As students and volunteers cross borders, to learn or to help, their emotions and romantic visions come into play. We have begun to explore here the many ways that affect works during study and volunteering abroad, including the ways that emotions and romantic images may be part of luring people into these programs, and ways that affect may be part of the process of learning and coming to engagement. It is our hope that this volume is a starting point to tackle this question of affect in study and volunteer abroad.

Dr. **Hannah Davis Taïeb** is an international educator, teacher, and writer who was the director of CIEE's Contemporary French Studies Program in Paris from 2003 to 2015. She has a Ph.D. in anthropology from New York University; her thesis, concerning unmarried women and changing conceptions of the self, was based on fieldwork in a middle-sized city in Morocco. After working with a research team in Lyon, Hannah settled permanently in France in 1992, where she first was the co-editor of a multilingual, multidisciplinary review, *Mediterraneans,* then taught intercultural and interpersonal communication at the American University of Paris, before entering the field of study abroad in the year 2000. While at CIEE, she ran Franco-American seminars, joint classes and study trips on subjects like disability, religious diversity and secularism, anti-Semitism and Islamophobia, chaplaincy and religion in prison, and special education. Independently, Hannah continues to teach about popular culture and *métissage,* religious diversity, and disability, co-teaches a Franco-American intercultural communication class, and runs volunteer and exchange activities with a Paris youth club.

Neriko Musha Doerr received a Ph.D. in cultural anthropology from Cornell University. Her research interests include politics of difference, language and power, and study abroad and alternative break experiences. Her publications include *Meaningful Inconsistencies: Bicultural Nationhood, Free Market, and Schooling in Aotearoa/New Zealand* (Berghahn Books), *The Native Speaker Concept* (Mouton de Gruyter), and *Constructing the Heritage Language Learner* (Mouton de Gruyter), and articles in *Anthropological Forum, Compare, Critical Discourse Studies, Discourse: Studies in the Cultural Politics of Education, Identities: Global Studies in Culture and Power*, and *Journal of Cultural Geography*. She currently teaches at Ramapo College in New Jersey, US.

Notes

We would like to thank Simone Weil Davis for her comments on an earlier version of this conclusion. Many thanks as well to Tara Harvey and Catherine Menyhart of CIEE for agreeing to be interviewed concerning their work on mindfulness, intercultural education, and leadership training. All errors are ours.

1. For simplicity, and to avoid the awkwardness of his/her s/he, we have alternated the use of feminine and masculine pronouns here.

References

Atilya, Shahad, Simone Davis, Keisha Green, Erin Howley, Shoshana Pollack, Barbara Sherr Roswell, Elle Turenne, Tyrone Werts, and Lucas Wilson. 2013. "From Safe Space to Brave Space: Strategies for the Anti-Oppression Classroom." In Simone Weil Davis and Barbara Sherr Roswell (eds), *Turning Teaching Inside Out: A Pedagogy of Transformation for Community-Based Education*. New York: Palgrave.

Bennett, Janet M. (ed.). 2015. *The Sage Encyclopedia of Intercultural Competence*. Thousand Oaks, CA: Sage.

Bennett, Milton J., and Ida Castiglioni. 2004. "Embodied Ethnocentrism and the Feeling of Culture: A Key to Training for Intercultural Competence." In Daniel Landis, Janet Bennett and Milton Bennett (eds), *Handbook of Intercultural Training*, 3rd ed. Thousand Oaks, CA: Sage, pp. 249–65.

Bok, Derek. 2004. *Universities in the Marketplace: The Commercialization of Higher Education*. Princeton, NJ: Princeton University Press.

Ceballos, Óscar. 2013. "Less Is More: The Ethics and Aesthetics of Expanded Itineraries in Education Abroad." Seville: Unpublished.

Clifford, James. 1986. "On Ethnographic Allegory." In James Clifford and George Marcus (eds), *Writing Culture: The Poetics and Politics of Ethnography*. Berkeley: University of California Press, pp. 98–121.

Crabtree, Robbin D. 2013. "The Intended and Unintended Consequences of International Service-Learning." *Journal of Higher Education Outreach and Engagement* 17(2): 43–66.

Cohen, Andrew D., R. Michael Paige, Rachel L. Shively, Holly A. Emert, and Joseph G. Hoff. 2005. *Maximizing Study Abroad Through Language and Cul-*

ture Strategies: Research on Students, Study Abroad Program Professionals, and Language Instructors. Minneapolis: Center for Advanced Research on Language Acquisition University of Minnesota.

Crawford, E., A. Ogden, and J. Lucas. 2010. "Empty Meeting Grounds: Situating Intercultural Learning in U.S. Education Abroad." Paper presented at the annual meeting of the 54th Annual Conference of the Comparative and International Education Society, Chicago. Retrieve 28 November 2014 from http://citation.allacademic.com/meta/p398690_index.html.

Davis, Simone Weil, and Barbara Sherr Roswell (eds). 2013. *Turning Teaching Inside Out: A Pedagogy of Transformation for Community-Based Education.* New York: Palgrave.

Doerr, Neriko. 2012. "Study Abroad as 'Adventure': Construction of Imaginings of Social Space and Subjectivities." *Critical Discourse Studies* 9: 257–68.

———. 2013. "Damp Rooms and Saying 'Please': Mimesis and Alterity in Host Family Space in Study-Abroad Experience." *Anthropological Forum* 23: 58–78.

———. 2015a. "Learner Subjects in Study Abroad: Discourse of Immersion, Hierarchy of Experience, and their Subversion through Situated Learning." *Discourse: Studies in the Cultural Politics of Education* 36(3): 369–382.

———. 2015b. "Volunteering as Othering: Understanding A Paradox of Social Distance, Obligation, and Reciprocity." *Partnerships: A Journal of Service-Learning and Civic Engagement* 6: 1–22.

———. 2016. "Learning as Othering: Narratives of Learning, Construction of Difference, and the Discourse of Immersion in Study Abroad." *Intercultural Education* 27(6).

Donahue, David M., and Tania D. Mitchell. 2010. "Critical Service Learning as a Tool for Identity Exploration." *Diversity & Democracy* 13(2).

Engle, Lilli, and John Engle. 2003. "Study Abroad Levels: Towards a Classification of Program Types." *Frontiers: The Interdisciplinary Journal of Study Abroad* 9: 1–20.

Fendler, Lynn. 1998. "What Is It Impossible to Think? A Genealogy of the Educated Subject." In Thomas S. Popkewitz and Marie Brennan (eds), *Foucault's Challenge: Discourse, Knowledge, and Power in Education.* New York: Teachers College Press, pp. 39–63.

———. 2001. "Educating Flexible Souls: The Construction of Subjectivity Through Developmentality and Interaction." In K. Hultqvist and G. Dahlberg (eds), *Governing the Child in the New Millennium.* New York: Routledge Falmer, pp. 119–42.

Fobes, Catherine. 2005. "Taking a Critical Pedagogical Look at Travel-Study Abroad: 'A Classroom with a View' in Cusco, Peru." *Teaching Sociology* 33(2): 181–194.

Freire, Paulo. 1970. *Pedagogy of the Oppressed.* New York: Continuum.

Gilbert, Melissa Kesler, Mathew Johnson, and Julie Plaut. 2009. "Cultivating Interdependent Partnerships for Community Change and Civic Education." In

Jean R. Strait and Marybeth Lima (eds), *The Future of Service-Learning: New Solutions for Sustaining and Improving Practice*. Sterling, VA: Stylus.

Green, Ann E. 2003. "Difficult Stories: Service-Learning, Race, Class, and Whiteness." *College Composition and Communication* 55(2): 276–301.

Hochschild, Arlie Russell. 2003. *The Managed Heart: Commercialization of Human Feelings*. Berkeley: University of California Press. First publication 1983.

Howes, David. 1996. "Introduction: Commodities and Cultural Borders." In David Howes (ed.), *Cross-Cultural Consumption: Global Markets Local Realities*. New York: Routledge, pp. 1–16.

Kiely, Richard. 2004. "A Chameleon with a Complex: Searching for Transformation in International Service-Learning." *Michigan Journal of Community Service Learning* 10(2).

Kinginger, Celeste. 2008. *Language Learning in Study Abroad: Case Studies of Americans in France. Modern Language Journal monograph vol 1*. Oxford: Blackwell.

Lindenberg, Lise. 2015. "International Student Programs in Ontario : An Examination of the Academic, Emotional, and Cultural Supports Offered to International Students in Ontario High Schools." A thesis submitted to the Faculty of Education in conformity with the requirements for the degree of Master of Education, Queen's University Kingston, Ontario, Canada.

MacCannell, Dean. 1976. *The Tourist: A New Theory of the Leisure Class*. University of California Press.

McDermott, Ray, and Hervé Varenne. 1995. "Culture as Disability." *Anthropology and Education Quarterly* 26: 324–48.

Murphy, Timothy, Jon Tan, and Christine Allan. 2009. "Service-Learning and the Development of Critical Reflexivity in Teacher Education in the United Kingdom and Republic of Ireland." In Jean R. Strait and Marybeth Lima (eds), *The Future of Service-Learning: New Solutions for Sustaining and Improving Practice*. Sterling, VA: Stylus.

Nenga, Sandi Kawecka. 2011. "Volunteering to Give Up Privilege? How Affluent Youth Volunteers Respond to Class Privilege." *Journal of Contemporary Ethnography* 40: 263–89.

Ogden, Anthony. 2007-08. "The View from the Veranda: Understanding Today's Colonial Student." *Frontiers: The Interdisciplinary Journal of Study Abroad* XV winter

Pagano, Monica, and Laura Roselle. 20009. "Beyond Reflection Through an Academic Lens: Refraction and International Experiential Education." *Frontiers* 18(Fall).

Popadiuk, Natalee. 2009. "Unaccompanied Asian Secondary Students Studying in Canada." *International Journal of Advanced Counseling* 31: 229–243.

Purser, Ron, and David Loy. 2013. "Beyond McMindfulness." *Huffington Post*, 1 July.

Richard, Analiese. and Daromir Rudnyckyj. 2009. "Economies of Affect." *Journal of the Royal Anthropological Institute* 15(2): 57–77.

Schaetti, Barbara F., Sheila J. Ramsey, and Gordon C. Watanabe. 2008. *Making a World of Difference: Personal Leadership: A Methodology of Two Principles and Six Practices*. Seattle: Flying Kite.

Sin, Harng Luh. 2009. "Who Are We Responsible to? Locals' Tales of Volunteer Tourism." *Geoforum* 41: 983–92.

Smith, Linda Tuhiwai. 1999. *Decolonizing Methodologies: Research and Indigenous Peoples*. London: Zed Books.

Stephenson, Skye. 1999. "Study Abroad As a Transformational Experience and Its Effect upon Study Abroad Students and Host Nationals in Santiago, Chile." *Frontiers* 5.

Strait, Jean R., and Marybeth Lima (eds). 2009. *The Future of Service-Learning: New Solutions for Sustaining and Improving Practice*. Sterling, VA: Stylus.

Taguchi, Naoko. 2008. "Cognition, Language Contact, and the Development of Pragmatic Comprehension in a Study-Abroad Context." *Language Learning* 58(1): 33–71.

Ting-Toomey, Stella, and Tenzin Dorjee. 2014. "Language, Identity, and Culture: Multiple Identity-Based Perspectives." In Thomas M. Holtgraves (ed.), *The Oxford Handbook of Language and Social Psychology*. Oxford Handbooks online.

Vande Berg, Michael. 2009. "Intervening in Student Learning Abroad: A Research-Based Inquiry." *Intercultural Education* 20(1–2): 15–27.

Vande Berg, Michael., Jeffrey Connor-Linton, and R. Michael Paige. 2009. "The Georgetown Consortium Project: Interventions for Student Learning Abroad." *Frontiers: The Interdisciplinary Journal of Study Abroad* XVIII.

Vande Berg, Michael, R. Michael Paige, and Kris Hemming Lou. 2012. *Student Learning Abroad: What Our Students Are Learning, What They're Not, and What We Can Do About It*. Sterling, VA: Stylus.

Vassallo, Stephen. 2013. "Critical Pedagogy and Neoliberalism: Concerns with Teaching Self-Regulated Learning." *Studies in Philosophy and Education* 32(6): 563–80.

Wilk, Richard. 1995. "Learning to Be Local in Belize: Global Systems of Common Difference." In Daniel Miller (ed.), *Worlds Apart: Modernity through Prism of the Local*. London: Routledge, pp. 110–33.

Yashima, Tomoko., Lori Zenuk-Nishide., and Kazuaki Shimizu. 2004. "The Influence of Attitudes and Affect on Willingness to Communicate and Second Language Communication." *Language Learning* 54(1): 119–152.

Zemach-Bersin, Talya. 2008. "American Students Abroad Can't Be Global Citizens." *Chronicle of Higher Education* (7 March).

———. 2009. "Selling the World: Study Abroad Marketing and the Privatization of Global Citizenship." In Ross Lewin (ed.), *The Handbook of Practice and Research in Study Abroad: Higher Education and the Quest for Global Citizenship*. New York: Routledge, pp. 282–302.

Villa Jovis, Capri, March 2011

When we started looking for a good cover image for our book, we thought about how fitting it would be to have contributions from students and volunteers, emerging from their own experiences. So, we sent around a prompt as widely as we could, asking those who have studied or volunteered abroad for images and short texts expressing their own individual takes on the romance and affect connected to these activities. We were very pleased to have so many good submissions and we thank all who contributed and our colleagues who passed the word. The image above, taken by Carla Villacís, was selected by the publisher for the cover of this book. So many other images and texts were interesting that we decided to include this photo essay here. What follows is a selection of student and volunteer images and texts, reflecting many particular views of the romance of crossing borders.

— Hannah Davis Taïeb and Neriko Musha Doerr

This photo itself was partially accidental, the boy in the picture happened to step into the light as I took the shot; I originally intended to capture only the light coming through the doors decorated with such incredible Moroccan architecture. This in itself embodies my experience, as fate and serendipity step in and become a part of the study abroad experience, some of the greatest memories, moments, and lessons are novelty and accident. I know this was not only my experience but true for many if not all student travelers.

Rabat, Morocco, 2016

We travel as students looking to discover new things and challenge ourselves. But when we look to achieve these goals, they don't happen as we plan, there is always confusion and surprise, always an unexpected element, so often for the better. There is also the physical act of the boy embodying this experience. He is looking out into the bright light of the unknown, something to symbolize the discovery and the surprises that await those of us who take on the challenge and adventure of studying abroad.

— Morgan Greer

It was my second trip to Costa Rica, this time as a trip leader. This was the breath taking horizon at a small pueblo on the way back home from Monteverde. It was tranquil and relaxing after a long day of zip lining and hiking. *"Pura Vida"* is a simple phrase constant in Costa Rica, and this picture, to me, encapsulates those exact sentiments.

It was our first solo adventure during our Study Abroad Program in Spain. We chose to go to *la corrida de toros* to further experience Spain's traditions. This was the only picture my friend managed to take in the midst of all the *toro* madness.

Puppy, perhaps the most famous and saccharine of monuments in Bilbao, Spain, was always a good landmark to let my friends and I know we're close to home when we get lost.

— Richard Suarez

Studying abroad provided me with unforgettable experiences. My feelings varied depending on the occasion. At times I felt lonely and sought out comfort in the landscapes that surrounded me, at others I felt deeply connected to strangers around me.

Lago de Como, Lombardia, 2013

I felt empowered by the opportunity to explore and challenge myself, yet I also felt small in the presence of nature and all the things I failed to understand. I was fortunate to spend time in Italy twice, during and after college. I am grateful for the moments that contributed to my growth at two very different stages in my life.

Capri, March 2011

Agrigento, Sicily, May 2011

From memories to friends to pictures, Italy continues to grant me special opportunities for contemplation and wonder

— Carla Villacís

This photo was taken at Blue Waters near Mysore India. The water, though beautiful is the result of a dam which displaced local villagers. When I first looked out at the vast blue I admired its beauty, once I was told about the lives that was changed as a result of the dam, my heart sunk.

The Mandela represent the togetherness of the group that I traveled with. Every flower petal was put in place by one of my peers. The beauty, though grand is only temporary, this moment taught me to celebrate temporary things.

— Lee-Anna John

Index